United Nations peacekeeping operations

United Nations peacekeeping operations: Ad hoc missions, permanent engagement

Edited by Ramesh Thakur and Albrecht Schnabel

**United Nations
University Press**

TOKYO · NEW YORK · PARIS

United Nations University Press
The United Nations University, 53-70, Jingumae 5-chome, Shibuya-ku, Tokyo, 150-8925, Japan
Tel: +81-3-3499-2811   Fax: +81-3-3406-7345
E-mail: sales@hq.unu.edu
http://www.unu.edu

United Nations University Office in North America
Room DC2-2050–2058, New York, NY 10016, USA
Tel: +1-212-963-6387   Fax: +1-212-371-9454
E-mail: unuona@igc.apc.org

United Nations University Press is the publishing division of the United Nations University.

Cover design by Joyce C. Weston
Cover photograph by UN/DPI

Printed in Hong Kong

UNUP-1067
ISBN 92-808-1067-7

Library of Congress Cataloging-in-Publication Data

United Nations peacekeeping operations : ad hoc missions, permanent engagement / edited by Ramesh Thakur and Albrecht Schnabel.
    p.   cm.
Includes bibliographical references and index.
ISBN 9280810677 (pbk.)
1. United Nations – Peacekeeping forces. I. Thakur, Ramesh Chandra, 1948–
II. Schnabel, Albrecht.
JZ6374 .U555 2001
341.5′84—dc21   2001004564

Contents

For the peacekeepers who died in the line of duty
They gave their lives for peace

Acknowledgements

The idea for this book was triggered by the United Nations University's October 1999 UN Day Symposium on Peacekeeping, in which some of the book contributors participated. The positive response to the symposium encouraged us to invite our speakers, along with other selected contributors, to join in an examination of the lessons that should be learned from past peacekeeping practices for future peacekeeping operations. The contribution of our book to the ongoing debate on the nature, legality, and practicality of peacekeeping lies in the unique composition of the chapter contributors – half of them are academic "observers" of peacekeeping, while the other half are practitioners who have been intimately involved, in the field and at UN Headquarters, in the planning and execution of some of the most crucial peacekeeping operations of the past 10 years. We hope that the combined insights of these contributions will prove useful to scholars, practitioners, and students of UN peacekeeping.

We are indebted to Yoshie Sawada, our administrative assistant, and Chifumi Mizutani, the programme's secretary, for their tireless support in the many administrative aspects of this project.

The publication of this book benefited greatly from the support we received from UNU Press and its Head, Janet Boileau. We greatly appreciate the careful copyediting work by Cherry Ekins, and the very helpful comments provided by the anonymous peer reviewers of the draft manuscript. Finally, we are indebted to our families who have again endured the many hours we spent on this, our second, co-edited book project.

As the UN's peace and humanitarian assistance activities creep into increasingly dangerous conflict zones, the risks associated for those working for the United Nations, regional organizations, or NGOs become ever greater. We dedicate the book to those who have lost their lives as peacekeepers in the service of a more peaceful and just world.

Ramesh Thakur
Albrecht Schnabel
Tokyo, May 2001

List of acronyms

ACABQ	UN Advisory Committee for Administrative and Budgetary Questions
ACRF	African Crisis Response Force
ACRI	US African Crisis Response Initiative
AFP	Australian Federal Police
AIDS	acquired immune deficiency syndrome
ASEAN	Association of South-East Asian Nations
BRIMOB	Brigade Mobil (Indonesian police mobile brigade)
C3I	command, control, communications, and intelligence
CAR	Central African Republic
CIA	US Central Intelligence Agency
CIMIC	civil/military cooperation
CIS	Commonwealth of Independent States
CISPKF	CIS Peacekeeping Force
CNRT	Council for the National Resistance of Timor
CSCE	Conference for Security and Cooperation in Europe
DAM	UN Department of Administration and Management
DFAT	Department of Foreign Affairs and Trade (Australia)
DPA	UN Department of Political Affairs
DPKO	UN Department of Peacekeeping Operations
DPMC	Department of the Prime Minister and Cabinet (Australia)
ECOMOG	ECOWAS Monitoring Group (Liberia and Sierra Leone)
ECOWAS	Economic Community of West African States
ECPS	UN Executive Committe on Peace and Security
EISAS	UN ECPS Information and Strategic Analysis Secretariat

EU	European Union
FOD	UN Field Operations Division
FUNCINPEC	National United Front for an Independent, Neutral, Peaceful, and Cooperative Cambodia
ICISS	International Commission on Intervention and State Sovereignty
ICRC	International Committee of the Red Cross
IDP	internally displaced person
IFOR	NATO Implementation Force (former Yugoslavia)
IGO	intergovernmental organization
IMTF	integrated mission task force
IMU	Islamic Movement of Uzbekistan
INTERFET	International Force in East Timor
IPKF	Indian Peacekeeping Force (Sri Lanka)
ISDSC	Inter-State Defence and Security Committee (Southern Africa)
JCC	Joint Control Commission (Moldova/South Ossetia)
JMC	Joint Military Commission
KFOR	Kosovo Force
KPNLF	Khmer People's National Liberation Front (Cambodia)
MFO	Multinational Force and Observer Group (Sinai)
MINURCA	UN Mission in the Central African Republic
MISAB	Inter-African Mission in Monitor the Implementation of the Bangui Agreements
MLO	military liaison officer
MNF	Multinational Force (Lebanon)
MOG	military observer group
MONUC	UN Organization Mission in the Democratic Republic of Congo
MRD	motor rifle division
MVD	Ministry of International Affairs (Russia)
NATO	North Atlantic Treaty Organization
NGO	non-governmental organization
OAS	Organization of American States
OAU	Organization of African Unity
OCHA	UN Office for the Coordination of Humanitarian Assistance
ONUC	UN Operation in Congo
OSCE	Organization for Security and Cooperation in Europe
PKO	peacekeeping operation
PolRI	Indonesian police force
PPS	parent police service
PSO	peace support operation
RECAMP	Renforcement du Capabilité African pour Maintien la Paix (Reinforcement of African Military Peacekeeping Capacity)
RPTC	SADC Regional Peacekeeping Training Centre
RUF	Revolutionary United Front (Sierra Leone)
SADC	Southern African Development Community
SFOR	Stabilization Force (former Yugoslavia)

SNC	Supreme National Council (Cambodia)
SOFA	status of forces agreement
SOP	standard operating procedure
SPA	UN Office for Special Political Affairs
SRSG	special representative of the Secretary-General
TNI	Tentara National Indonesia
UNAMET	UN Assistance Mission in East Timor
UNAMIC	UN Advance Mission in Cambodia
UNAMIR	UN Assistance Mission for Rwanda
UNAMSIL	UN Assistance Mission to Sierra Leone
UNAVEM III	UN Angola Verification Mission III
UNDP	UN Development Programme
UNEF I	First UN Emergency Force
UNFICYP	UN Force in Cyprus
UNHCR	Office of the UN High Commissioner for Refugees
UNIDIR	UN Institute for Disarmament Research
UNIFIL	UN Interim Force in Lebanon
UNIKOM	UN Iraq-Kuwait Observer Mission
UNITAF	Unified Task Force (Somalia)
UNMIH	UN Mission in Haiti
UNMIK	UN Interim Administration Mission in Kosovo
UNMOGIP	UN Military Observer Group in India and Pakistan
UNMOT	UN Mission of Observers in Tajikistan
UNOMIG	UN Observer Mission in Georgia
UNOMSIL	UN Observer Mission to Sierra Leone
UNOSOM	UN Operation in Somalia
UNOSOM II	Second UN Operation in Somalia
UNPA	UN Protected Area
UNPREDEP	UN Preventive Deployment (Macedonia)
UNPROFOR	UN Protection Force (former Yugoslavia)
UNSAS	UN Standby Arrangements System
UNTAC	UN Transitional Authority in Cambodia
UNTAET	UN Transitional Administration in East Timor
UNTEA	UN Temporary Executive Authority (West Irian)
UNTSO	UN Truce Supervision Organization
UTO	United Tajik Opposition
WEU	Western European Union

Part I

Challenges of post-Cold War peacekeeping

1

Cascading generations of peacekeeping: Across the Mogadishu line to Kosovo and Timor

Ramesh Thakur and Albrecht Schnabel[1]

As we step over the threshold from one century to the next, the United Nations is faced with growing demands for collective intervention alongside declining confidence in its effectiveness and efficiency, diminishing financial support for its activities by some leading industrialized countries, and gathering storm clouds in the direction in which it seems to be headed, propelled by the challenge of humanitarian intervention.[2] Serious doubts have been expressed about the institutional capacity of the UN system to cope with the multitude of challenges confronting it in the new millennium. In the meantime, the challenge of peacekeeping shows no sign of abating. Since UN peacekeeping was launched over 50 years ago in the Middle East, more than 50 operations have been deployed. Many have played critical roles in ending or managing conflicts in Africa, Asia, Central America, and Europe.

During the Cold War, UN peacekeeping forces were interposed between warring parties and used to forestall major power confrontations across global faultlines. The number of peacekeeping operations increased dramatically after the end of the Cold War as the UN was placed centre stage in efforts to resolve outstanding conflicts. However, the multiplication of missions was not always accompanied by coherent policy or integrated military and political responses. When the missions encountered problems, the "crisis of expectations"[3] of the late 1980s and early 1990s in turn gave way to a crisis of confidence-cum-credibility in

3

UN peacekeeping in the late 1990s, and member states began to limit their military, political, and financial exposure.

Yet the need for UN peacekeeping remains and will continue. The causes of conflict are many, but the fact of conflict remains a constant feature of international affairs. More and more conflicts break out within borders, not between countries. They still pose major challenges to regional stability. UN peacekeeping may not necessarily be the best instrument for the task at hand in every instance. When should the international community mandate peacekeeping tasks to the UN? What makes for their success and failure? When should the UN act in partnership with regional institutions? What is the relationship between military troops, political negotiations, and organizational requirements at the UN Secretariat? How, in the end, can we reconcile "the temporary nature of specific operations with the evident permanence of peacekeeping and other peace operation activities as core functions of the United Nations"?[4]

This volume explores the evolution of peacekeeping, particularly since the early 1990s, a period that was characterized by much initial enthusiasm and hopes for a United Nations that would find a more agreeable international environment for more effective and sustained operations to secure peace where it existed, and to provide peace where it did not. The end of the Cold War unleashed new possibilities in international cooperation – both between the former superpower antagonists and within the UN's premier organ responsible for the provision of international peace and security, the Security Council. Secretary-General Boutros-Ghali hoped to unleash and instil a new sense of international responsibility, one which would allow the world organization to address the many new security challenges, foremost internal conflicts, emerging from the long peace of the Cold War era. Peacekeeping has always been one of the most visible symbols of the UN role in international peace and security. And it was the world's disappointment with the performance of UN peacekeeping operations over the years that followed which became so symbolic of the UN's failure to emerge from the ashes of the Cold War as a rejuvenated key player in international and, increasingly, internal peace and security. This book reflects some of the thinking, some of the experiences in the UN and in the field, some of the frustrations, and some of the hopes of this past decade. It combines academic analysis, field experience, and reflection with forward-looking proposals (including the suggestions of, and responses to, the recent Brahimi Report) for more effective peace operations designed and deployed by the UN in partnership with regional, subregional, and local actors. The various chapters in this book confirm, among others things, the reality of differences among academics, international civil servants, and generals in their respective cultures of reflection, introspection, and analysis.

The contributions to this volume are grouped in four parts. The first part outlines the challenges of post-Cold War peacekeeping; the second part sheds light on regional experiences of peacekeeping missions, with an emphasis on the post-Soviet region and Africa. In the third part practitioners with extensive field experience in peacekeeping share their specific experiences in Cambodia, former Yugoslavia, and East Timor. Finally, the fourth part takes stock of the recent record of UN peacekeeping, and of the UN's own attempt to analyse, evaluate, and reform its performance in peace operations.

This introductory chapter is designed to provide the basic background for the chapters to follow. It does this by first outlining the succeeding generations of peacekeeping operations that have been established since the early years of the United Nations after the Second World War. It then analyses some of the critical issues that have arisen for international peacekeeping missions in the types of inter-group fighting that comprise today's "normal" conflict.

In Chapter 2, Roger Mac Ginty and Gillian Robinson examine the intricacies of ethnic conflict, and the challenges they pose for UN peace operations. They argue that in these situations traditional peacekeeping is ill-placed, and peace enforcement is often neither doable nor desirable. Instead, smaller-scale interventions, mostly of a preventive nature and in close collaboration with local actors, hold greater promise to be effective in the long run (see also the concluding chapter by Schnabel and Thakur).

Hisako Shimura, a former UN official working for the Department of Peacekeeping Operations (DPKO) and recently a member of the Brahimi Panel, examines the role of the UN Secretariat in organizing peacekeeping in Chapter 3. She shows that the Secretary-General and the UN Secretariat at large have played unusually dominant roles in the organization and management of peacekeeping operations. While she does not criticize this prominence, she points to the fact that it is those powerful actors who need to be placed in a better position to recognize potential problems at an early stage and to respond swiftly and competently. They must do so with the professionalism that would be expected from the United Nations, and in particular from the DPKO, but is not forthcoming in the face of inadequate resources and personnel to meet these ever-increasing challenges.

In Chapter 4, Michael O'Connor looks at effectiveness in peacekeeping from a different perspective – that of the mission on the ground. He argues that peace agreements have to be policed actively and forcefully. This is only possible if peacekeeping missions can rely on well-trained military personnel on the ground and on sound military advice from UN Headquarters.

In Chapter 5, Neil MacFarlane examines the virtue and utility of subcontracting peacekeeping tasks to regional organizations. While sub-contracting – usually to regional and subregional organizations in the South – takes the pressure off the North to become involved in conflicts throughout the developing world, there are also clear advantages for the South; those regions that would not normally see external involvement must improve their own capacity to address war and suffering. Indeed, regional approaches may be the ticket to long-term sustainability of peace operations in protracted conflicts. MacFarlane examines regional peacekeeping in the context of the Commonwealth of Independent States. While CIS- and Russian-dominated peacekeeping has been less than ideal, in the absence of any other takers (including the United Nations), growing signs of more conflict throughout the region, and less willingness by Russia to bear the cost of regional security provision, we may soon "look back with slight nostalgia on the days when Russia could and would police the region".

In Chapter 6, Mark Malan studies the peacekeeping capacity of African countries, both as participants in UN peacekeeping missions abroad and in organizing their own missions on the continent. Focusing on the recent UN mission in Sierra Leone, Malan questions the application of "lean peacekeeping" as a way to offer African solutions to African problems. UNAMSIL in Sierra Leone was a very public failure in peacekeeping on a continent where few lessons have been learned from past failures, and where no military doctrine for peacekeeping and, more so today, peace enforcement has developed. Malan presents the concept of "conflict termination operations" through an indigenous but externally funded "African Legion", a force which could quickly bring conflicts to a halt, allowing traditional peacekeepers to deploy in situations in which there actually is a peace to be kept. Only such an élite legion, or so argues Malan, would be capable of preventing another Rwanda from happening.

In Chapter 7, Vere Hayes argues that more peacekeepers on the ground or tougher mandates will not bring much improvement to weak and in-efficient peace operations unless arms, training, and command and control are also upgraded. Unless forces have credible combat power, supported both by the political will to employ such power and the professional skills of the individual soldier to use it, peace support missions will become pawns in the hands of conflicting parties, and not the guardians of peace and stability they are supposed to be. Drawing on the African context, Hayes argues that peacekeepers must be well trained as combat soldiers, and that the political will has to exist to use peacekeepers in robust defence of a mission's mandate against spoilers. Hayes proposes regionwide training exercises that would produce a large pool of adequately trained peacekeepers across all ranks who could and should participate in collaborative regional missions.

Many of the issues so far discussed are then fleshed out in the context of very specific first-hand experiences of peacekeepers in Cambodia, former Yugoslavia, and East Timor. In Chapter 8, Yasushi Akashi discusses the politics of UN peacekeeping from Cambodia to Yugoslavia. Drawing on his experience as special representative of the Secretary-General in both theatres, Akashi comments on the role of the Security Council, the relations between the field and UN Headquarters, the necessity for post-conflict peace-building commitments, the lack of unity of the permanent five in the Security Council, and the absolute requirement of sustained diplomatic effort, without which mission creep and fatigue are unavoidable. Akashi supports recent efforts to take a pragmatic approach to peacekeeping – one that allows the international community to be more assertive as long as a mission is well funded, well organized, and required to avert humanitarian disasters.

In Chapter 9, John Sanderson reflects on his experience in Cambodia, and on developments there since UNTAC was concluded in 1993. He expresses his frustration over what has been a slow and shaky recovery process after the war. He attributes the failure to win the peace on the UN's inexperience with post-conflict peace-building, and its failure to "rapidly deploy forces to field high-quality administrators in sufficient numbers to provide effective supervision and governance in disrupted states". While more field experience exists today to avoid such problems, the capacity is still lacking to occupy and run countries emerging from war. Sanderson argues that only such a capacity will allow the United Nations to generate lasting improvement.

Satish Nambiar, in his contribution in Chapter 10, reminds us that there is an important difference between non-coercive peacekeeping and punitive peace enforcement. In contrast to other contributors to this volume, General Nambiar maintains that force must be used only if it is well conceived and the consequences are well understood. Above all, the pursuit of political solutions and concurrent peace-building activities have to exploit the space created by peace enforcement and peacekeeping operations – the failure to do so leads only to further disarray, and it is the peacekeepers who tend to be blamed. Nambiar draws on his experience in former Yugoslavia and reflects on the damage done to the United Nations through its failure to address Kosovo's problem at an early stage and through NATO bypassing the Security Council to launch its air war over Kosovo. While humanitarian law may well deserve to be enforced with military might, this might must come from the United Nations, and not some dominant country or regional alliance.

John McFarlane and Willliam Maley round off this section with a discussion of civilian police in UN peace operations in Chapter 11. Fragmented war-torn states with a serious inability to perform the normal functions of a sovereign state, delegitimized over years of war and chaos, disorder, and lawlessness on the streets, have little capacity to deal with further fragmentation and subsequent violence. In such a context indigenous police and military forces are often more destructive than constructive. It is the external military and police forces that need to step into this power vacuum and facilitate the creation of a minimum acceptable security environment. McFarlane and Maley note that the role of the civilian police is frequently undervalued in comparison to the role of military forces. It is the police officer who often gains the respect of the local population, contributes most directly to the reconstitution of local security and order, and, after military peacekeepers have withdrawn, continues to assist the population to recreate a semblance of orderly and stable social life. Drawing on the experience of the Australian Federal Police component of UNTAET in East Timor, McFarlane and Maley assess the gap that still exists between the crucial role played by civilian police in peacekeeping and peace-building missions (which are, after all, not merely military operations) and the little recognition they receive from the United Nations and other key players in the organization and implementation of peace operations.

The final section of the volume begins with Margaret Karns and Karen Mingst's discussion of four dilemmas confronting peacekeeping amid the changing role of the United Nations in Chapter 12. They argue that UN peace operations are plagued basically by four main problems: the shift from interstate to intrastate conflict and the related challenges of when, how, and by whom intervention in civil conflict may be justified; the changing international expectations and interpretations of the international community's responsibility to respond to gross humanitarian violations; the changing, rising number, and diversity of non-state, interstate, and suprastate actors involved in peace operations; and the question of leadership in future peace operations within and outside the United Nations. In the years to come the United Nations will likely be torn and constrained by the contest between new and old norms of sovereignty and intervention; the emerging role of regional organizations and ad hoc coalitions of states, some of which will not seek UN approval for missions that they find desirable and necessary; and the role and demeanour of the USA. It will not be easy for the United Nations to carve out a role that allows for leadership, legitimacy, and the record to go with it.

Finally, in Chapter 13, Albrecht Schnabel and Ramesh Thakur discuss the recently published Brahimi Report, commissioned by the Secretary-General to seek creative solutions to the chronic peacekeeping failures of the 1990s. They argue that, despite the fact that the Brahimi Report makes far-reaching demands on the United Nations and its member states, it nevertheless constitutes only the minimum required reform agenda that would need to be followed and implemented to bring lasting legitimacy to UN peace operations. The chapter further assesses a neglected yet important part of the Brahimi Report – the importance of both effective and early prevention of violence, as well as the need for unqualified, effective, and concerted intervention when human rights are violated on a mass scale. The discussion emanating from the Brahimi Report and the consistency with which its main findings and recommendations have echoed through the writings of practitioners and academics alike (in this volume as well as in other contributions to this ongoing debate) are testimony to the commonsensical nature of most of its suggestions.

The six generations of peacekeeping

Terms like "peacekeeping", "peace support operations", and "peace operations" are used generically to refer to missions and operations that fall short of military combat between clearly recognizable enemies. Different analysts use different typologies to classify the many operations that have been mounted in five decades of UN experience. The early distinctions were between observer and peacekeeping missions. But the latter developed too many variations for the one term to retain conceptual clarity. It is possible, for example, to classify them by type of actor. Thus Henry Wiseman divides peacekeeping operations firstly into UN, regional, and independent ad hoc missions. Alternatively, they may be grouped chronologically. Thus Wiseman divides UN operations into the nascent period (1946–1956), the assertive period (1956–1967), the dormant period (1967–1973), and the resurgent period (1973–1978).[5] The last period's nomenclature was clearly premature: the real resurgence came after the end of the Cold War. Or they may be classified by functions and tasks, as done by Paul Diehl, Daniel Druckman, and James Wall – observation, election supervision, humanitarian assistance, preventive deployment, interposition, pacification, collective enforcement, etc.[6] The trouble with this is that many different functions can be carried out by any one operation, and functions of the same operation can change over time. The present authors prefer to classify in a way which allows one to distinguish between peacekeeping missions overall.

First generation: Traditional peacekeeping – pending peace

Article 1(1) of the UN Charter declares the primary purpose of the organization to be the maintenance of international peace and security. The world failed to realize a collective security system centred on the United Nations during the Cold War, and appears no nearer to the goal today.

With a reliable system of collective security proving unattainable, states moved to guarantee national security by means of collective defence – that is, alliances such as the North Atlantic Treaty Organization (NATO) and the Warsaw Pact – and the international community groped towards damage-limitation techniques to avoid and contain conflicts. Peacekeeping evolved in the grey zone between pacific settlement (Chapter VI of the UN Charter) and military enforcement (Chapter VII). Its primary purpose was to supervise and monitor a cease-fire. Peacekeeping operations had no military objectives, were barred from active combat, were located between rather than in opposition to hostile elements, and were required to negotiate rather than fight.

The cardinal distinction between collective security and first-generation peacekeeping lay in their reliance upon force and consent respectively. Traditional peacekeeping had several distinguishing characteristics:

- consent and cooperation of parties to the conflict;
- international backing, especially in the UN Security Council;
- UN command and control;
- multinational composition;
- no use of force;
- military neutrality between the rival armies;
- political impartiality between the rival countries.

Second generation: Non-UN peacekeeping

Traditional peacekeeping was thus under UN auspices and command and control. There was a reaction against UN peacekeeping because of widespread, although not always accurate, perceptions that UN operations led to diplomatic ennui and could not be freed of the Cold War rivalry and other highly politicized antagonisms that had infected large parts of the UN system. The term "second generation" was appropriated in the 1990s by analysts who came late to the study of this novel institution, not by those who had devoted themselves to the subject during the years when peacekeeping was less fashionable.[7]

It makes more sense to use the term to refer to a spate of peacekeeping operations that were mounted either unilaterally or multilaterally, but in any case outside the UN system. These include the Commonwealth peacekeeping operation for overseeing the conversion of Rhodesia into Zimbabwe,[8] the Multinational Force and Observers (MFO) Group in the Sinai,[9] the Multinational Force (MNF) in Beirut,[10] and the Indian Peacekeeping Force (IPKF) in Sri Lanka. The precursor to this sort of extra-UN peacekeeping operations might well be said to have been the international control commissions in Indochina set up pursuant to the Geneva Agreements of 1954.[11]

Some of these efforts were successful, including the Commonwealth operation in Zimbabwe and the MFO in Sinai. Others were largely failures, for example the MNF in Beirut and the IPKF in Sri Lanka. The reason why it makes sense to identify this phase of peacekeeping as second generation is the intergenerational structural continuity implied by the metaphor. There is a direct lineage from traditional UN peacekeeping to the expanded peacekeeping of the third generation onwards in the 1990s. On the one hand, the non-UN operations adopted most of the principles of third-party military interposition and buffering from traditional UN peacekeeping. The MFO, for example, is virtually the classic UN model of a peacekeeping force, and has often had force commanders with direct UN experience. On the other hand, they expanded the range of tasks and functions that were required beyond just military interposition, as in Indochina in the 1950s and Zimbabwe in the 1970s. Both the MNF in Beirut and the IPKF in Sri Lanka in the 1980s foreshadowed the conceptual and operational challenges that were to confront and destroy the UN Operation in Somalia (UNOSOM) in the 1990s when enforcement was forced into a shotgun marriage with peacekeeping.

Third generation: Expanded peacekeeping – peace reinforcement

Traditional peacekeeping therefore aimed to contain and stabilize volatile regions and interstate conflicts until such time as negotiations produced lasting peace agreements. By contrast, the third generation of peacekeeping saw missions being mounted as part of package deals of peace agreements, for example in Namibia and Cambodia. The peacekeeping mission was an integral component of the peace agreement and was meant to complete the peace settlement by providing third-party international military reinforcement for the peace process.

The pace of peacekeeping accelerated under the impact of the end of the Cold War. In the early 1990s, Cold War acrimony between the superpowers gave way to a new world order harmony. With unprecedented cooperation among the five permanent members, the UN Security Council was relieved of the disability of great-power disagreement. The proliferation of peacekeeping missions in the early 1990s was testimony to the enhanced expectations of the United Nations in the new order. When the Nobel Peace Prize was awarded to UN peacekeeping in 1988, just over 10,000 persons from 35 countries were serving with seven operations, at an annual cost of US$230m. At their peak around mid-1994, there were 17 UN peacekeeping operations at an annual cost of almost US$4bn employing a total of more than 87,000 troops, police, and civilian officers.

Reflecting the changing nature of modern armed conflict, UN operations expanded not just in numbers but also in the nature and scope of their missions. The "simple emergencies" of yesteryear required the United Nations to cope with organized violence between states fighting across an international border. By contrast, "complex emergencies" produce multiple crises all at once:[12] collapsed state structures; humanitarian tragedies caused by starvation, disease, or genocide; large-scale fighting and slaughter between rival ethnic or bandit groups; horrific human rights atrocities; and the intermingling of criminal elements and child soldiers with irregular forces. Reflecting this, third-generation operations – of which Cambodia, in which both Yasushi Akashi and John Sanderson were involved, was a particularly good example[13] – had to undertake the following types of tasks:

• military disengagement, demobilization, and cantonment;
• policing;
• human rights monitoring and enforcement;
• information dissemination;
• observation, organization, and conduct of elections;
• rehabilitation;
• repatriation;
• administration;
• working with or overseeing the operations of regional or non-UN peacekeeping operations.

Fourth generation: Peace enforcement

The efforts of the United Nations and member states did not always meet demand. On the basis of its actions and inaction in Somalia, Bosnia, and Rwanda, wrote a critic, "the UN has become not a friend of world stability but a menace. Wherever it intervenes, peace is neither made nor kept but postponed."[14] The UN's credibility was seen to have been lost, in particular, in the tide of refugees swarming on the highways and byways of former Yugoslavia: a veritable symbol of human misery. A columnist with *The Economist* mentioned the following as Bosnia's contribution to doublespeak: "safe area" means a deadly dangerous place; a "rapid reaction" will occur next month, maybe; and a "protection force" is one that offers neither.[15] While the cynics might conclude that Bosnia was the UN's Viet Nam, the romantics might respond that it is better explained as the UN's Munich: a failure of collective nerve and will. A peacekeeping operation in a theatre where there was no peace to keep, the UN Protection Force (UNPROFOR) in former Yugoslavia offered neither safety to the local people, solace to the displaced and dispossessed, nor even the consolation to the international community of having done the job to the best of their ability. Its failure to prevent the horrors of Srebrenica in 1995 remains a stain on the world conscience for passivity in the face of the calculated return of "evil" to Europe and a tragedy that, in the words of the official UN report, "will haunt our history forever".[16]

The pace of developments raced ahead even of third-generation operations. In Somalia and elsewhere the United Nations attempted "peace enforcement", with results that were anything but encouraging[17] – hence General Sir Michael Rose's metaphor, used in the title of this chapter, of "the Mogadishu line" that peacekeeping forces dare cross only at their peril.[18] While the conceptual issues associated with peace enforcement will be discussed below, Somalia most clearly represented the birth (and death) of the fourth generation of UN peacekeeping.

Fifth generation: Peace restoration by partnership

Partly as a consequence of the disastrous venture into peace enforcement, in Bosnia and Haiti UN peacekeeping underwent a further metamorphosis into the fifth generation of enforcement operations – authorized by the UN Security Council, but undertaken by a single power or ad hoc multilateral coalitions. The United Nations itself took back responsibility for a traditional-type consensual peacekeeping once the situation had stabilized,[19] but with the tasks of third-generation expanded peacekeeping. (Although UNOSOM had been preceded by the US-led Unified Task Force, UNITAF, the latter did not engage in enforcement.) Modifying the Gulf War precedent somewhat, this was the pattern that emerged of UN-authorized military action by the USA in Haiti, France in Rwanda, Russia in Georgia, and NATO in Bosnia. Neil MacFarlane in Chapter 5 and Mark Malan in Chapter 6 note the many challenges of regional peacekeeping in the CIS and Africa, respectively. The danger is real, nevertheless, that major powers take military action only when and where their national interests are engaged. The United Nations by contrast is the political embodiment of the international community and the custodian of the international interest.

Sixth generation: Multinational peace restoration, UN state creation

East Timor represents the evolution into the most recent, sixth generation of peacekeeping. A UN-authorized multinational force is prepared for combat action if necessary, and is given the mandate, troops, equipment, and robust rules of engagement that are required for such a mission. However, the military operation is but the prelude to a *de facto* UN administration that engages in state-making for a transitional period. That is, a "nation" is granted independence as a result of UN-organized elections. But the nation concerned has no structures of "state" to speak of. It is not even, like Somalia, a case of a failed state; in East Timor a state has had to be created from scratch. The United Nations has finally confronted and addressed, in East Timor, the dilemma that haunted it in the Congo in the 1960s and Somalia in the 1990s, namely that peace restoration is not possible without the establishment of law and order. But in a country where the writ of government has either collapsed or is non-existent, the law that is made and enforced so as to provide order can only be that of the United Nations or of another foreign power (or coalition).

Crossing the Mogadishu line

A significant cost of the cascade of generations of peacekeeping within a highly compressed time-frame is that most of the major operations today have little real precedent to go by; each has to make and learn from its own mistakes. The lessons-learned unit of the UN Department of Peacekeeping Operations must feel like Alice in Wonderland: running harder and harder just to stay in one place. There are three sets of reasons for the cascade of many generations of peacekeeping under the accelerated pace of developments over the last decade or so. The first concerns the difficulty of reconciling the tension between the primary unit of formal world order and UN membership being the sovereign state, on the one hand, and the declining salience of interstate violence on the other hand. The second concerns the difficult and painful learning curve with regard to the proper balance between consensual and muscular operations in contemporary armed conflicts within the borders of UN member states. The "Mogadishu line" is a shorthand metaphor for capturing both sets of problems. The third and final set concerns the shifting relative balance away from state rights to human rights in contemporary world affairs, and the resulting pressures on the international community to countenance armed intervention for humanitarian reasons.

Peacekeeping in civil wars

East Timor represents one type of intrastate conflict that was fought over the formation of a new state. Another type of internal conflict concerns cases where there is no challenge to the territorial *status quo*, only to the political: that is, different factions compete and fight to be recognized as the sole legitimate government of a country whose territorial boundaries remain uncontested. Cambodia was one such example. Others include Afghanistan and Angola, "orphans of the Cold War" in Dame Margaret Anstee's evocative metaphor.[20] The end of the Cold War did not mean an end of history, nor even the end of all war.

The United Nations was designed to keep world peace, if necessary by going to war against aggressors. The transient Cold War hostility and the more enduring structural realities of diverging major power interests put paid to the rhetoric of indivisible peace. As the system of collective security proved elusive but conflicts did not abate, creative solutions were found to inject a stabilizing UN presence through unarmed and impartial UN peacekeepers who conducted holding rather than military operations. Internal ethno-national conflicts, discussed by Roger Mac Ginty and Gillian Robinson in Chapter 2, reflect weaknesses in state capacity. Complex humanitarian operations are at the cutting edge of the UN's core function in the new world disorder. Their well-publicized failures in the Balkans, Somalia, Rwanda, Angola, and Sierra Leone have damaged the core credibility of the organization.

UN intervention in internal conflicts raises the impossible political question of how the world body, committed to maintaining the territorial integrity of member states, will decide when to support and when to oppose the "legitimate" government against attempts at secession. The refusal to talk to one party in a civil war, because it is considered to be "illegitimate", reduces the chances of ending it. To be effective, the United Nations must negotiate with all significant sectarian leaders. But in doing so, the United Nations endows them with a degree of legitimacy. In return, however, leaders of ill-disciplined and uncoordinated guerrilla groups may be unable or unwilling to honour the agreements made with the United Nations. Does the writ of the rebels and secessionists run deep and wide enough for the leaders who have signed the agreements to be able to deliver a cease-fire that will hold? The safety measure for guerrilla groups is that they do not have strict chains of command; they exist in isolation, operating from self-contained cells. Units at the end of such a loose chain of command may not receive or accept directives from above.

If there is no effective government in power, then attempts by the United Nations to impose its own law and order can provoke fierce backlash from armed bandit groups. This is what happened to the humanitarian peacekeeping mission in Somalia. There was a blurring of the line between combatants and civilians because irregular forces merged, like fish in the ocean, with the local population.

Civil wars scatter UN troops thinly over a wide geographical area under a tenuous cease-fire. These troops are more vulnerable to attacks when not deployed at fixed positions in a neutral area. The result can be that the United Nations has to devote more time, resources, and personnel to protecting its mission than to accomplishing its goals – or risk having its soldiers taken hostage.

Robust peacekeeping

Should the United Nations use force against those who would challenge its authority, as in Bosnia, Somalia, and Sierra Leone? The crisis that confronted the UN peacekeeping operation in Sierra Leone in May 2000 was a sad commentary on lessons learnt, not learnt, and forgotten over five decades of peacekeeping. Dag Hammarskjöd created the first UN peacekeeping force in 1956 in the Suez. He restricted the use of force to self-defence, defined as the protection of the lives of UN soldiers and of the positions held by them under a UN mandate. In *An Agenda for Peace*, the new Secretary-General Boutros Boutros-Ghali implied that future peacekeeping operations could be organized without the consent of all the parties.[21] This did not happen.

In late 1999, the United Nations issued a remarkably frank, self-critical report on its role in events leading to the death of thousands of civilians under its protection in Srebrenica in 1995. The grim yet poignant text chronicled a tragedy of mostly avoidable errors. Secretary-General Kofi Annan assumed full responsibility for these mistakes by the United Nations, which had occurred during his watch as Under-Secretary-General for Peacekeeping. A month after the Srebrenica report, an international panel convened by Annan tabled a similarly sobering report on the UN's failure to prevent the genocide of half a million Rwandans in 1994.[22] Another panel, convened by the Organization of African Unity (OAU), was not shy in pointing the finger of almost criminal blame at some of the permanent members of the UN Security Council as well as UN staff:

As to the UN Secretariat, a directive was sent from headquarters in New York to General Dallaire indicating that the UN forces could, if absolutely necessary, exceed their mandate in one solitary circumstance: the evacuation of foreign nationals. We, the panel, viewed the directive with incredulity. It was a shocking double standard. No such directive was ever issued on behalf of the rescue of Rwandans.[23]

In all these cases, the predicament of peacekeeping soldiers on the ground was that they were unable to move forward into an unwinnable battle, unable to stay put taking casualties for no purpose, and unable to withdraw without damaging national and UN credibility.

Turning a peacekeeping mission into a fighting force creates two problems. First, it calls for a long commitment. Foreign armies, including those fighting under the UN blue flag, cannot impose peace on civil wars without also imposing foreign rule: this was the logic of colonialism. Second, they cannot join the fray without taking sides in the civil war. But to take sides is to become aligned to one and therefore the enemy of the other. If the faction against which the United Nations takes up arms were genteel and law-abiding, then the United Nations would not need to resort to such action in the first place. Yet when UN personnel come under attack, the organization does not have the means to defend them. If it calls on mainly Western armies for protection, it will be seen even more as a tool of the West.

In other words, ground realities since the end of the Cold War have highlighted the large gap between the two familiar poles of traditional peacekeeping and Chapter VII enforcement. There is a need for a conceptual and policy bridge for a transition from Chapter VI to Chapter VII. At present there is no continuum from consensual peacekeeping to collective enforcement. Because the mechanism for setting up a collective security force under Chapter VII does not exist, the United Nations has resorted to subcontracting enforcement operations. Yet the belief persists in many modern military forces that peacekeeping is for wimps, not for real soldiers, even though the most common form of insecurity today – wars within state borders – calls for complex peacekeeping operations as the tool of choice by the international community. Those with the military capacity lack the political will to take part in robust UN peacekeeping; those with the will lack the means.

"Humanitarian" intervention

Reading the UN Charter, there is little doubt that a basic premise underpinning the organization is the notion of inalienable human rights that are universally valid. Many governments argue in favour of a relativist interpretation of human rights. Yet there is no society in which individuals do not want adequate food and shelter, the ability to be able to speak freely, to practise their own religion, and to avoid torture and imprisonment by the state without first being charged and subjected to a fair trial. None of this is culture-specific.

A steady loss of government control over transborder exchanges has been accompanied by increased demands and expectations of the United Nations from the peoples of the world. In the case of human rights, this takes the form of people seeking the protection of the international organization from abuses by their own governments. Governments, however, continue to be suspicious of claims by international bodies of a qualified right to intervene.

In practice, the legitimacy of intervention turns upon the answer to questions about the four main elements involved in any act of intervention: actor, act, target, and purpose. The most immediately acceptable justification for intervention is the collectivist principle: not *why* intervention was undertaken, but *who* took the decision to intervene. Since 1945, the most widely accepted legitimator of international action has been the United Nations. The International Bill of Rights after all comprises three seminal UN accomplishments: the Universal Declaration of Human Rights of 1948, and the two covenants on civil-political and socio-economic-cultural rights of 1966. The Universal Declaration is the embodiment and proclamation of the human rights norm. The covenants added force and specificity, affirming both civil-political and social-economic-cultural rights, without privileging either set. Together they embody the moral code, political consensus, and legal synthesis of human rights.[24]

The international community has been confronted with the dilemma of the tension between respect for national sovereignty and the concomitant principle of non-interference, and the rising chorus of international concern at gross human rights atrocities. The United Nations faced fresh charges of dereliction of duty after the referendum on autonomy or independence held in East Timor in 1999. On the one hand, some argued that the United Nations had fulfilled its part of the bargain brilliantly, with a 98 per cent voter turnout and a decisive electoral verdict. The Indonesian military had failed to live up to their side of the bargain in ensuring adequate security. On the other hand, however, others argued that the Indonesian military's failure was predictable and should have been anticipated. The United Nations therefore had a responsibility to ensure the safety and security of the people who had reposed their trust in the international community but were betrayed – the very point that General Sanderson makes about Cambodia.

The search for standby arrangements that will provide rapid reaction capability to the United Nations when confronted with humanitarian crises of horrific proportions is an effort to lessen the reliance on major powers whose national interests may diverge in important ways from the international interest vested in the world organization. Conversely, if the national interests of the major powers are not at stake, then it is correspondingly more difficult to secure their substantial involvement on purely humanitarian considerations.

Complex emergencies may require comprehensive and integrated responses from several actors. There is scope for a partnership between UN peacekeeping, peace-restoring and peacemaking operations; and between UN operations and the activities of regional and non-governmental organizations (NGOs). We are already witnessing divisions of labour between the various regional and international actors based on their comparative advantages. We should, however, be sensitive to the dangers of the tribalization of peacekeeping if regional bodies begin to claim ownership of conflicts within their areas of geographic coverage. Wider international participation is necessary for reasons of legitimacy, solidarity, and capacity.[25]

Another note of caution is that a peacekeeping mission can be largely successful, yet the eventual outcome may not be fully satisfactory. Quick-fix solutions and instant democracy are insufficient unto themselves. Peacekeeping is but a point on the continuum from pre-conflict peace-building to post-conflict peace reconstruction. It must be integrated with the search for a political solution. A peace agreement is no solution if it does not last the distance. Sometimes the desire to bring an interminable conflict to a quick end, and the use of peacekeeping troops for this purpose, can override the need to ensure that the terms of the settlement are honourable, just, and likely to endure. The requirements for sustainable peace are different from those of Band-Aid or fire-fighting responses.

This is shown up only too starkly in Cambodia. General Sanderson notes in Chapter 9 that his heart weeps for the Cambodian people. The UN Transitional Authority in Cambodia (UNTAC) was a success, in that it fulfilled its mandate in time and under budget. But, reflecting deficiencies and shortcomings of the UN system as a whole rather than of the peace-keeping operation *per se*, UNTAC lost focus on the principal objective of its mandate, which was to leave Cambodia with effective democratic government. Instead, it acquiesced in decisions that paved the way for a political system of underlying criminality.

Review and reform of UN peacekeeping

Kofi Annan appointed a high-level international panel, led by Lakhdar Brahimi, a former special representative of the Secretary-General, and including Hisako Shimura, who writes of the Secretariat perspective on peacekeeping in Chapter 3, to make recommendations for changes in UN peacekeeping. It reported its findings in August 2000.[26] The general thrust of its recommendations is that the United Nations should define the peacekeeping mission, bring the force needed for the purpose, and do what is required to get the job done.

Peacekeeping shortcomings and reforms can be addressed at three levels: policy, managerial, and operational.[27]

Policy responsibility vests mainly in the member states, in particular those who are on the UN Security Council and especially the five permanent members (P5). The Brahimi Report reaffirms the need for the United Nations to get serious about conflict prevention. Annan's efforts to address the root causes of conflict in many regions and countries – including abusive governments, the absence of democracy, gross violations of human rights, predatory economic policies, and the still-booming international sale of weaponry – deserve more support from member states. The Security Council must move beyond its current pattern of reaction and address potential crises holistically and at root before violence breaks out. As necessary and logical this may seem, however, taking effective preventive action remains a daunting task, as Albrecht Schnabel and Ramesh Thakur note in Chapter 13.

The need for clear mandates and goals, matching military and financial resources, performance benchmarks, etc., has long been recognized but rarely followed. Disagreement among Security Council members is papered over by ambiguous language, the price for which is paid by peacekeepers in the field. Another well-known lesson is that peacekeepers cannot function where there is no peace to keep. Missions keep being mounted in the Micawberesque belief that everything that can go right will go right. The Brahimi panel comments on the UN tendency to base decisions on best-case planning assumptions in situations with a history of worst-case behaviour. Yet a third lesson, learnt at great cost and human suffering in the 1990s, is that the need for impartial peacekeeping should not automatically translate into moral equivalence among the conflict parties on the ground.

The Brahimi Report criticizes the Security Council's record of decisions unsupported by the necessary resources to implement them. It recommends that no Council decision be taken to create a peacekeeping operation (or substantially change its mandate) until the Secretary-General can certify that the necessary personnel and equipment have been offered. This recommendation, if adopted, should cut down on the number of unrealistic resolutions that have been debasing the Council's currency in recent years.

More open and democratic decision-making procedures by the Security Council would also help to promote a culture of accountability: member states should be held responsible for disasters flowing from flawed policy.

So should UN officials. Policy failures are compounded by managerial mistakes made by the Secretariat. As US Permanent Representative Richard Holbrooke and others have noted, the DPKO is effectively the UN's ministry of defence, except that it is on a more or less permanent war footing. Its human, technical, logistical, and financial capacity to engage in this mammoth, worldwide, round-the-clock task is underwhelming. Many former force commanders, including Generals John Sanderson and Satish Nambiar, have commented on the strategic disconnect between their needs in the field and the calibre and professionalism of military advice available to the Secretary-General in New York. In Chapter 4 Michael O'Connor considers a revised Military Staff Council and solid military expertise in the DPKO as one of the most crucial, but hitherto neglected, components of successful peace operations.

The United Nations needs to develop the professional civil service culture of providing advice that is sound, based on a thorough assessment of options, independent of what might be politically popular or fit the preconceptions of the decision-makers, and free from fear of consequences for politically neutral officials. Where clearly unimplementable missions have been approved because of confused, unclear, or severely under-resourced mandates, the United Nations has to learn to say "No". The Brahimi panel advised the United Nations to reject contributions if they do not measure up with respect to the training and equipment needed for the job. The Secretariat is advised to tell the Security Council what it needs to hear, not what it wants to hear. This recommendation seems to target the cosy relationship that has grown up between the Secretariat and the P5, which often get to vet the Secretariat's advice before it is proffered to the full Council. The practice has been much criticized, for it has resulted in bad recommendations from successive Secretaries-General to the Council shaped by the P5 on the basis of what their governments were prepared to support rather than on what the situation required.

Timidity masquerading as political neutrality has also led to the operational failure to confront openly those who challenge peacekeeping missions in the field. The United Nations, while striving to remain impartial, should suspend its long-standing attachment to neutrality between belligerents if one or several pursue morally reprehensible goals in repugnant ways. That is, the United Nations should no longer extend, directly or indirectly, a seal of moral equivalency in its relations with combatants. Impartiality should not translate into complicity with evil. The UN Charter sets out the principles that the organization must defend and the values that it must uphold. The reluctance to distinguish victim from aggressor implies a degree of moral equivalency between the two and damages the institution of UN peacekeeping.

In order to arrest and reverse the sense of drift, UN approaches to peacekeeping need to reflect the multifaceted nature of UN action in countries afflicted by mostly civil wars. This means promoting the rule of law and economic recovery by integrating the military, policing, institution-building, reconstruction, and civil administration functions of peace-keeping operations to a much greater degree than in the past. This is particularly true where the United Nations substitutes for collapsed local governments, as in Kosovo and East Timor. Experience has shown that reconstructing state institutions responsible for establishing the rule of law is considerably more challenging than merely keeping the peace. The United Nations is encouraged by the Brahimi panel to develop a generic legal framework generally applicable where state institutions collapse (as in Kosovo and East Timor). International legal personnel (judges, prosecutors, investigators) could then operate, albeit with sensitivity to local traditions, to restore law and order in the absence of local political authority.

Countries with large financial and military resources are reluctant to deploy either to address African conflicts.[28] This also will have to change if UN credibility on peacekeeping is to be restored. In order to reoccupy its niche as a major actor in international security, the United Nations requires consistency of purpose, the resources to give it substance, and a convincing attention span. The importance of credibility for regional peacekeeping in Africa is further underlined by Brigadier Hayes in Chapter 7.

Conclusion

International organizations touch our daily lives in myriad ways. They are an important means of arranging the functioning of the state-based international system more satisfactorily than had proven to be the case in conditions of international anarchy. The United Nations lies at their legislative and normative centre. If it did not exist, we would surely have to invent it. Considering the ill-fated history of the League of Nations, the UN founders would have felt pride and satisfaction that their creation is still intact at the dawn of the new millennium, embracing virtually the entire international community. Yet their vision of a world community equal in rights and united in action is still to be realized.

Like the League of Nations in the inter-war period, the United Nations embodies the idea that aggressive war is a crime against humanity, with every state having the interest, right, and duty to collaborate in preventing it. The innovation of peacekeeping notwithstanding, the United Nations has not lived up to expectations in securing a disarmed and peaceful world. For the United Nations to succeed, the world community must match the demands made on the organization by the means given to it. The UN's financial difficulties are compounded by perceptions, not always justified, of bureaucratic inefficiency. Based on human solidarity and transcending national perspectives, the United Nations provides and manages the framework for bringing together the world's leaders to tackle the pressing problems of the day for the survival, development, and welfare of all human beings everywhere.

Peacekeeping evolved as partial compensation for the gap between the Charter rhetoric and the Cold War reality of collective security. As Yasushi Akashi notes in Chapter 8, many of the lessons learnt are restatements of long-held convictions by the peacekeeping community: the lack of unity among the major powers; the imprecision, ambiguity, proliferation, and inconsistencies of the mandates approved by the UN Security Council; the lack of coordination between the legislative bodies at UN Headquarters in New York and the peacekeeping operations in the field; the unwillingness of the parties to the conflict to trust UN diplomacy rather than their own arms; and the incongruence between the mandate and resources given to the peacekeeping missions.

In the past, the United Nations has emphasized abortion to the neglect of prophylaxis. It needs to sharpen its skills at identifying potential conflicts before the fact so that parties to disputes can be brought together during the period of infancy. The United Nations also needs to become involved in post-conflict peace-building by identifying, supporting, and deepening the structures that will consolidate peace and enhance people's sense of confidence and well-being.[29] Peacekeeping is a circuit breaker in a spiralling cycle of violence. The problem with traditional peacekeeping was that it could at best localize the impact of conflicts and then freeze them. Rarely did the United Nations prevent conflicts from breaking out or resolve them after they did. The sixth-generation model for East Timor has finally come to terms with this requirement. It remains to be seen how successful it will be, and whether it can be replicated elsewhere.

In the midst of the swirling tides of change, the United Nations must strive for a balance between the desirable and the possible. Its dilemma is that it must avoid deploying forces into situations where the risk of failure is high, but not be so timid as to transform every difficulty into an alibi for inaction. The Charter was a triumph of hope and idealism over the experience of two world wars. The flame flickered in the chill winds of the Cold War, but has not yet died out. The organization's greatest strength as the only universal forum for cooperation and management is its mobilizing and convening potential. The global public goods of peace, prosperity, sustainable development, and good governance cannot be achieved by any country acting on its own. The United Nations is still the symbol of our hopes and dreams for a better world, where weakness can be compensated by justice and fairness, and the law of the jungle replaced by the rule of law.

The United Nations has to strike a balance between realism and idealism. It will be incapacitated if it alienates its most important members, in particular the USA. Its decisions must reflect current realities of military and economic power. Margaret Karns and Karen Mingst note in Chapter 12 that the United Nations faces the dilemma of reducing dependence on the USA, yet creating and sustaining US diplomatic, material, and financial support in order to meet the demands and expectations from different pockets of crises around the world for peacekeeping operations in the future. But the United Nations will also lose credibility if it compromises core values. It is the repository of international idealism, and utopia is fundamental to its identity. Even the sense of disenchantment and disillusionment on the part of some cannot be understood other than in this context.

Notes

1. The views expressed in this chapter are the personal opinion of the authors. They do not necessarily reflect the views of the United Nations University.
2. See Kofi Annan, *Facing the Humanitarian Challenge: Towards a Culture of Prevention*, New York: UN Department of Public Information, 1999.
3. The phrase is taken from Ramesh Thakur and Carlyle A. Thayer (eds), *A Crisis of Expectations: UN Peacekeeping in the 1990s*, Boulder: Westview, 1995.
4. *Report of the Panel on United Nations Peace Operations*, A/55/305-S/2000/809, New York: UN General Assembly/Security Council, 21 August 2000, p. xiii.
5. Henry Wiseman, "The United Nations and international peacekeeping: A comparative analysis", in UN Institute for Training and Research, *The United Nations and the Maintenance of International Peace and Security*, Dordrecht: Martinus Nijhoff, 1987, pp. 263–333.
6. Paul F. Diehl, Daniel Druckman, and James Wall, "International peacekeeping and conflict resolution: A taxonomic analysis with implications", *Journal of Conflict Resolution*, Vol. 42, No. 1, February 1998, pp. 33–55.
7. The two most prominent analysts, at least in English, were Professor Alan James and veteran UN peacekeeper Major-General Indar Jit Rikhye. General Rikhye was also the founding president of the International Peace Academy in New York. See in particular Alan James, *The Politics of Peacekeeping*, New York: Praeger, 1969; Alan James, *Peacekeeping in International Politics*, New York: St Martin's Press, 1990; Indar Jit Rikhye, Michael Harbottle and Bjørn Egge, *The Thin Blue Line: International Peacekeeping and Its Future*, New Haven: Yale University Press, 1974; and Indar Jit Rikhye, *The Theory and Practice of Peacekeeping*, London: C. Hurst, 1984. See also Paul F. Diehl, *International Peacekeeping*, Baltimore: Johns Hopkins University Press, 1993; and Henry Wiseman (ed.), *Peacekeeping: Appraisals and Proposals*, New York: Pergamon, 1983. Representative works from more recent times include William J. Durch, *The Evolution of UN Peacekeeping: Case Studies and Comparative Analysis*, New York: St Martin's Press, 1993; John Mackinlay and Jarat Chopra, "Second-generation multinational operations", *Washington Quarterly*, Vol. 15, 1992, pp. 113–134; and Steven R. Ratner, *The New UN Peacekeeping: Building Peace in Lands of Conflict after the Cold War*, New York: St Martin's Press, 1996. The United Nations itself has published straightforward and authoritative accounts in *The Blue Helmets: A Review of United Nations Peacekeeping*, 3rd edn, New York: UN Department of Public Information, 1996.
8. See Henry Wiseman and Alastair Taylor, *From Rhodesia to Zimbabwe*, New York: Pergamon Press for the International Peace Academy, 1981.
9. See Mala Tabory, *The Multinational Force and Observers in the Sinai*, Boulder: Westview, 1986.
10. See Ramesh Thakur, *International Peacekeeping in Lebanon: United Nations Authority and Multinational Force*, Boulder: Westview, 1987.
11. See Ramesh Thakur, *Peacekeeping in Vietnam: Canada, India, Poland and the International Commission*, Edmonton: University of Alberta Press, 1984.
12. The Congo crisis of the 1960s, and the UN operation there from 1960 to 1964, could be said to have been precursors to the complex emergencies and third-generation missions.
13. See Michael W. Doyle, *UN Peacekeeping in Cambodia: UNTAC's Civil Mandate*, Boulder: Lynne Rienner, 1995; Trevor Findlay, *Cambodia: The Legacy and Lessons of UNTAC*, Stockholm: Stockholm International Peace Research Institute, 1995.
14. Simon Jenkins, "Fanning the flames of war", *The Times* (London), 9 November 1994.
15. Johnson, "The injuries of war", *The Economist* (London), 29 July 1995, p. 72.

16. *Report of the Secretary-General Pursuant to General Assembly Resolution 53/35 (1998)*, New York: UN Secretariat, November 1999, paragraph 503.

17. See Samuel M. Makinda, *Seeking Peace from Chaos: Humanitarian Intervention in Somalia*, New York: Lynne Rienner for the International Peace Academy, 1993; and Ramesh Thakur, "From peacekeeping to peace enforcement: The UN Operation in Somalia", *Journal of Modern African Studies*, Vol. 32, September 1994, pp. 387–410.

18. Michael Rose, "The Bosnia experience", in Ramesh Thakur (ed.), *Past Imperfect, Future UNcertain: The United Nations at Fifty*, London/New York: Macmillan/St Martin's Press, 1998, p. 139.

19. For an excellent analysis of the issues surrounding such a division of labour, see David Malone, *Decision-Making in the UN Security Council: The Case of Haiti, 1990–1997*, Oxford: Clarendon, 1998.

20. Margaret Joan Anstee, *Orphan of the Cold War: The Inside Story of the Collapse of the Angolan Peace Process, 1992–93*, New York: St Martin's Press, 1996. On Afghanistan see William Maley (ed.), *Fundamentalism Reborn? Afghanistan and the Taliban*, New York: New York University Press, 1998.

21. Boutros Boutros-Ghali, *An Agenda for Peace: Preventive Diplomacy, Peacemaking and Peacekeeping*, New York: UN Department of Public Information, 1992, paragraph 20.

22. *Report of the Independent Inquiry into the Actions of the United Nations During the 1994 Genocide in Rwanda*, S/1999/1257, New York: United Nations, 15 December 1999.

23. Stephen Lewis, "After Rwanda, the world doesn't look the same", *International Herald Tribune*, 10 July 2000. Lewis was one of the members of the OAU panel. General Romero Dallaire was commander of the UN force in Rwanda at the time of the genocide.

24. Ramesh Thakur, "Teaming up to make human rights a universal fact", *International Herald Tribune*, 10 December 1998.

25. Olara A. Otunnu, "Promoting peacemaking and peacekeeping: The role and perspective of the International Peace Academy", in Thakur, note 18, pp. 213–214.

26. *Report of the Panel on United Nations Peace Operations*, note 4.

27. This section is drawn mainly from David M. Malone and Ramesh Thakur, "UN peacekeeping: Lessons learned?" *Global Governance*, Vol. 7, No. 1, January–March 2001, pp. 11–17.

28. For a recent collection of essays examining the peacekeeping requirements for Africa, see Jakkie Cilliers and Greg Mills (eds), *From Peacekeeping to Complex Emergencies: Peace Support Missions in Africa*, Johannesburg and Pretoria: South African Institute of International Affairs and Institute for Security Studies, 1999.

29. This was recognised by Boutros-Ghali in *An Agenda for Peace*, note 21, paragraphs 55–59.

2

Peacekeeping and the violence in ethnic conflict

Roger Mac Ginty and Gillian Robinson

There is an immense literature on peacekeeping, much of it concentrating on reconceptualisations of peacekeeping after the end of the Cold War, the need for structural reform of the UN system, and case studies of particular peacekeeping operations. On the whole, however, the literature fails to give due attention to the nature of the conflict and violence to which peacekeeping and its successor types of intervention have been applied. To be effective, techniques used to manage and ameliorate the effects of ethnic conflict require a sophisticated understanding of the nature of the conflict and violence involved. This chapter will explore the nature of ethnic conflict and the violence often associated with it, and will also examine some of the main problems which ethnic conflict presents to peacekeeping. It is argued that peacekeeping, in its traditional form, is often an inappropriate form of intervention in cases of ethnic conflict. This is not necessarily an argument in favour of second- or third-generation UN peace operations. Instead, it is developed into an argument that smaller-scale, often multiple, interventions, such as human rights monitoring and the introduction of confidence-building measures, hold a greater possibility for success. The United Nations has an enormous capacity to contribute to these forms of intervention.

Given the increased prominence of ethnic conflict in recent years, it is reasonable to expect that the international organization charged with the maintenance of international peace and security, the United Nations, would intervene to facilitate the settlement and resolution of conflicts.

This is particularly the case because of the capacity of many ethnic conflicts to spill over beyond state boundaries and become an international threat. However, the United Nations is faced with an immediate problem. It is an organization of nation-states and rests, even in the post-Cold War era, on strictly defined notions of state sovereignty. Many ethnic groups, however, hold an entirely different view, and their very *raison d'être* is often one of secession; to break away from an established state. Although the UN's attitude towards self-determination has become more relaxed, the organization retains an emphasis on state sovereignty.[1] The United Nations can find itself in an invidious position, attempting to deal with the conflicting claims of those supportive of a state's boundaries and institutions and those who oppose them. Yet the organization operates at the state level, and has few formal channels for communication with non-state groups. Another fundamental problem stems from the tendency of member states to withhold their consent for UN intervention in matters they deem to be within their domestic jurisdiction.[2] The 1995 *Report of the Independent Working Group on the Future of the United Nations* stresses that traditional peacekeeping methods are inappropriate for those occasions in which armed conflict occurs within a state, civil authority is challenged or collapses entirely, and factional struggles for dominance are under way.[3] It goes on to urge consistent and principled guidelines to deal with this recurrent problem. Using this as a starting point, it is useful to examine the nature of ethnic conflict in more detail.

The peculiarities of ethnic conflict

It is important to be clear about what is meant by the term "ethnic conflict". In fact the term is confusing and suggests that ethnicity is the root cause of conflict. For the purposes of this chapter, a more generic meaning is attached to ethnic conflict: intergroup as opposed to interstate conflict. Other terms such as civil conflict, civil war, internal wars, or intrastate wars approximate to the same matter. The authors contend that ethnicity *per se* is not the cause of conflict. Although ethnicity may not be the initial trigger, conflicts can become "ethnicized", or adopt features that suggest that the conflict revolves around ethnicity or identity. In fact, more prosaic factors normally lie behind the origin of "ethnic conflicts". Usually these are access to political, economic, social, or cultural resources. Protagonists may articulate their cause in terms of ethnicity or identity, and may be mindful of the powerful mobilizing potential of identity claims, but the essential origins of the conflict are usually more mundane.

Part of the problem is that ethnic conflict has become a useful shorthand for the complex range of post-Cold War conflicts that dominated headlines during the 1990s. With the term comes a perceptual baggage that ethnic conflict is somehow primordial and irrational. This is illustrated by a 1995 journalistic account from the former Yugoslavia: "Bosnia is a formidable, scary place of high mountains, brutish people, and tribal grievances rooted in history and myth born of boozy nights by the fire. It's the place where World War I began and where the wars of Europe persist, an ember of hate still glowing for reasons that defy reason it-self."[4] The imagery of savagery and tribalism implies that ethnic conflict is a non-rational activity. The logical extension of this view is that such a phenomenon is not open to rational enquiry and so will not be amenable to rational resolution techniques. Furthermore, if rational techniques to manage conflict are likely to be unsuccessful, then why bother applying them in the first place? For John Burton, even the United Nations holds uni-dimensional views of conflict: "... ethnic conflicts within and between nation-states, war-lord violence and repressive military regimes are viewed by the United Nations as phenomena to be repressed rather than explained."[5]

So while the term "ethnic conflict" is employed in this chapter it should not be taken to mean that the conflicts are sparked by ethnicity. Instead, these are intergroup conflicts that often occur within a state boundary, although they can spill across international boundaries.[6] While issues like group identity often play a major role in such conflicts, to view them solely through the lens of ethnicity or identity might lead to distortion. Conflict itself is an everyday human experience found in the most peaceful of polities and relationships.[7] It is not the preserve of certain ethnic groups or those who have unsatisfied ethnic claims. Indeed, conflict is essential to human behaviour; it becomes problematic, however, when it turns violent. Ethnic conflict is often non-violent. Ethnically diverse, but reasonably peaceful, cities such as Seattle or New York are more common than vio-lent ethnically contested cities such as Sarajevo. Yet when ethnic conflict becomes violent, the violence is often extremely enduring, may adopt peculiar and inherently escalatory forms, and may prove resistant to conflict management strategies.

There is a common perception that what is labelled "ethnic conflict" is very different from other forms of conflict. In fact, it is often entirely rational and revolves around many of the political issues found in stable polities, such as access to political power. The emphasis on security issues often found in ethnic politics may also be entirely rational; if a group feels under threat (real or imagined) then it is logical that the group would take steps to defend its interests. Recognition of the rationality of much ethnic conflict does not in itself deny that there are aspects connected with ethnicity, identity, nationalism, and violence which are difficult to rationalize. Walker Connor's arguments on the "nonrational core of the nation" are persuasive.[8] He notes that nationalism is a mass phenomenon, and often appeals to emotions through symbolism, shared blood, music, or familial metaphors. This aside, there are many aspects of ethnic conflict that are open to rational analysis and which do suggest effective means of conflict management.

Despite grim warnings from the early 1990s, the world is not facing an ethnic Armageddon.[9] Wallensteen and Sollenberg identified a total of 110 armed conflicts in 73 locations in the decade 1989–1999.[10] The number of conflicts has actually been falling since a peak of 55 in 1992. The vast majority have been intrastate and conform to Mary Kaldor's categorization of "new wars". In other words, they are marked by an increased ratio of civilian to military casualties, tend to be of relatively low intensity, and rarely have decisive endings.[11] The new wars are also characterized by large-scale dislocation in the form of population displacement and disruption to society.

Confusing the picture of conflict in the 1990s is the increased prominence and visibility of that conflict. There are a number of reasons for this increased visibility. First, the decline of Cold-War-sustained ideological conflicts has allowed issues of ethnicity and identity to gain greater prominence in national and international politics.[12] Identity politics has been relegitimized in many polities, particularly in societies undergoing political and economic transition, and states have been unable to present their citizens with more immediately rewarding alternatives.

Second, many states have become weaker. This operates in the absolute sense, with a number of African and post-Soviet states suffering from a declining capacity for governance, whether through conflict, economic impoverishment, corruption, or incompetence. Again, the end of the Cold War played a significant role in this process of state-weakening, with superpower client states no longer enjoying privileged access to external sources of support. While few states have collapsed outright, many have experienced a contraction in their capabilities. The trend also operates in the relative sense, with increased transnational flows and means of communication allowing non-state entities to become more powerful and independent of state control. The result has been that many states are more prone to ethnic and identity-linked upheavals.

A third factor contributing to the increased visibility of ethnic conflict relates to an increased democratization of foreign policy processes in many states. Much of this stems from genuine attempts by some governments to make governance more transparent, accessible, and responsive. It also reflects increased pressure from better-informed publics. The revolution in the electronic media means that news and, just as importantly, images of ethnic conflict are now more accessible than ever before. There has also been an increase in the number of non-governmental organizations working in ethnic conflicts and complex emergencies. Jenny Pearce notes that by 1989 there were 700 NGOs in Guatemala and a similar number in El Salvador, over half of which were established after 1985.[13] These organizations and related advocacy groups have become more vocal and many have achieved respectability undreamed of in past decades. Finally, and related to the last point, human rights issues, central in any ethnic conflict, have gained increasing mainstream political attention in recent years.

Contemporary peacekeeping

UN peacekeeping operations have played a significant role in the management of ethnic conflict, mainly through interpositioning between the warring parties. The UN Force in Cyprus (UNFICYP) and the UN Interim Force in Lebanon (UNIFIL) provide two of the most prominent and relatively successful examples. These operations have been criticized for not extending beyond "pacific perpetuation", in that they are merely keeping the warring sides apart and not addressing the root causes of the conflict.[14] They provide little opportunity or incentive for the protagonists to become engaged in a process that would lead to a reduction of conflict. Nor do they have the capacity to penalize those who do not engage in conflict-reducing behaviour. Yet such operations have undoubtedly contributed towards the stabilization of violent ethnic conflicts and have saved lives.[15]

Peacekeeping operations have grown much more sophisticated from the mid-1980s onwards, and have increasingly adopted a civil dimension such as policing and human rights monitoring. There has also been an emphasis on the organization and delivery of humanitarian aid. These changes reflected a need to adapt to the demands of complex emergencies, many related to ethnic conflicts. Confusing the picture was the end of the Cold War and a gradual reordering of a number of the norms that had helped shape the post-war international political system. For example, a loose bipolar system gave way to a loose unipolar system dominated by the USA. In the first half of the 1990s the USA shrank from the position of an emboldened interventionist to that of a neo-isolationist. Norms of the inviolability of state boundaries were also reconsidered, particularly as the Soviet Union collapsed. The key point is that an environment combining pervasive ethnic conflict and a changing international political system presented potential interveners with a number of problems. Those problems that relate to the nature of ethnic conflict will be outlined next.

Violence in ethnic conflict

Ethnic conflict may adopt peculiar forms of violence which necessitate specialized responses from any intervention force. This is not to suggest that violence is somehow "ethnic". According to Brubaker and Laitin, "[t]he 'ethnic' quality of ethnic violence is not intrinsic to the act itself".[16] Instead, the term "ethnic" relates to the interpretation of the violence. Often the interpretations of violence are contested. A violent act may have multiple motivations and interpretations; the perpetrator and victim may variously interpret an action as criminal, political, or random, or motivated by religion, ethnicity, race, or identity. In Northern Ireland, for example, an attack on a Protestant-owned business by pro-United Ireland militants may be publicly justified as an attack on an economic target as part of a wider political or military campaign. The Protestant business owner, however, may rationalize his or her victimization in entirely different terms; as personal, sectarian, or criminal. The chief point is that violence in ethnic conflict is a complex phenomenon. It may vary in scale, complexity, intensity, longevity, number of actors, degree of external involvement, and military sophistication of the combatants.

Another key factor that influences the scale and intensity of violence in an ethnic conflict is the moral or civil code that the combatants adopt during the conflict. For example, in some conflicts efforts are made to avoid civilian casualties. Bad publicity arising from civilian casualties may damage the political legitimacy of a group or risk alienating powerful external supporters, such as a wealthy diaspora community. In other conflicts, civilians are prime targets and civilizing restraints may be absent.

Ethnic conflicts are also fluid, moving through different phases. As a result, the level and intensity of the violence may vary throughout the duration of the conflict due to a range of factors, including political developments between the parties, seasonal changes, or external interventions. Varieties of ethnic conflict and violence mean that there is no template that an international organization such as the United Nations can apply to all cases. Instead, each intervention requires a high degree of specialization, which is both costly and time-consuming. That, of course, also risks accelerating the sense of conflict fatigue within the international and donor community.

Structural violence

Structural violence may take the form of discriminatory judicial systems or partisan security structures. It may include systematic human rights abuses, which are key indicators of the potential for violent ethnic conflict. Those organizations engaged in conflict early warning have been devoting greater attention to such abuses in recent years. Such situations do not call for large-scale interventions such as peacekeeping. Instead, more limited interventions aimed at encouraging democratization or the protection of minorities are more appropriate. Where possible, the United Nations or other organizations perform these roles, but many interventions require the consent of the host government. While some governments, such as in Myanmar, may allow the UN special rapporteur on human rights access to present a report, there is no guarantee that reforms will be implemented. Some 1990s' peacemaking and peace enforcement operations have avoided the consent proviso in large-scale operations that respond to complex emergencies rather than structural violence. They have also been justified in terms of regional and international security rather than on humanitarian considerations.

Low-level violence

A second feature of the violence found in ethnic conflict is that it is often of a low level; involving hate speech, protests, intermittent rioting, or assassinations of selected individuals. The routine and low-profile nature of some of this violence may contribute to its invisibility and seeming "acceptance".[17] Much of this violence is a political and social construct, reflective of the wider political environment. Pervasive and seemingly static political tension is often overlooked by analyses more interested in full-blown conflict with overt violence.[18] A state may operate in a relatively normal fashion for extended periods and in many sectors of governmental interest. There may be underlying tensions that may occasionally become violent, but are, for the most part, contained by the state. The violence may be restricted to one region of the state, thus insulating mainstream politics from its dislocating influences. While the integrity of the state may be strained, it may not be seriously threatened. Again, in a situation short of all-out war, peacekeeping may be regarded as inappropriate. It is also unlikely that the international community would garner the political will necessary for a large-scale intervention in a situation that does not threaten international peace and security or human rights on a mass scale. Low-level ethnic violence has persisted for decades in many parts of the world without significant international attention.

Identity contestation

Third, ethnic conflicts often show strong linkages to identity issues. One group may define itself in opposition to another and perceive gains by the other group as automatically entailing an erosion of its own position. This has significant implications for the conflict and third-party intervention. While identity is unlikely to be the primary conflict cause, the conflict can be articulated in terms of identity. Such conflicts are likely to be long-lasting, with identity-linked grievances persisting across generations. Sensitivity over identity places extra responsibility on any group considering third-party intervention. Gaining access to insurgent groups is particularly fraught with the danger of misperception. Third parties may be accused of providing legitimacy to insurgents simply by making contact with them. On the other hand, an invitation to a third party from a national government may compromise the third party's neutrality in the eyes of an insurgent group.[19] In many ethnic conflicts issues of symbolism become inflated and attain a real political value. As a result outsiders require a high degree of cultural sensitivity.[20] This may be particularly difficult to achieve and maintain in a large peacekeeping operation with a multinational composition. Despite good intentions, it is difficult to guard against ethnocentrism emanating from centralized standard operating procedures and direction from New York. The 1999 Australian-led multinational intervention force in East Timor was criticized by a number of South-East Asian states which called for an Asian-led peacekeeping force.[21] Third-party intervention also risks overlooking indigenous conflict management techniques that have temporarily broken down.[22] It can impose a power framework and an interpretation of the conflict that is at odds with the views of one or all of the protagonists, and make a resolution of the conflict less rather than more likely.[23] Poulton and Youssouf stress that the very language used in political negotiations and peacemaking processes is of Western European origin and is not always applicable outside that region.[24] Referring to the Malian peace process, they point to local sources of reconciliation, such as church leaders, who played a successful role in conflict reduction.

In all conflicts, the protagonists are acutely aware of favouritism displayed by third parties to one side or the other. The presence of identity issues in ethnic conflicts reinforces this awareness. For example, the Multinational Force in Lebanon in the early 1980s, although not sanctioned by the United Nations, claimed neutrality. The US contingent within that force, however, was widely regarded as pro-Israeli, and as such jeopardized the entire mission.[25] More recently, the 1999 NATO-led operation to stop ethnic cleansing in Kosovo had to deal with accusations that German troops would be anti-Serbian while Russian troops who joined its Kosovo Force (KFOR) would be pro-Serbian. Traditional peacekeeping missions emphasized the principle of neutrality, and in the Cold War era a disproportionate number of peacekeepers came from states with neutral security policies, such as Sweden, Fiji, and the Republic of Ireland. In the post-Cold War era, much of this neutrality has become meaningless.[26] States may still be regarded as partisan, according to history, membership in a military or economic alliance, or close relationship with another state.

Questions of neutrality have been raised in the context of peace enforcement missions. NATO's operation in the skies above Kosovo identified the Milosevic regime in Belgrade as the aggressor. It was difficult, however, to separate Milosevic's government from the Serbian people. This was not helped by the emphasis on non-military targets during NATO's bombing raids. When, in June 1999, Kosovo Albanians began returning to their homes, prompting an exodus of Serbs, the international condemnation was much more timid. Perhaps there had been a blurring of the Serb people and the Serbian government in the public mind.

Demography and geography

A fourth feature of ethnic conflict and violence relates to ethnic demography and geography. Ethnic segregation is common in many conflicts, with the city of Jerusalem providing a classic example of near-total ethnic separation. In other conflicts, the situation is not as clear-cut. Populations from different ethnic groups may be mixed. Segregation dating from earlier conflicts may be eroded by intermarriage or normal population flows associated with economic and social development. A resumption of conflict may result in ethnic cleansing or might leave mixed, but conflicting, populations *in situ*. Both situations create specific problems for any peacekeeping force and tend to require policing, civil, and humanitarian dimensions rather than traditional military responses. Rather than separating or interposing between groups, a peacekeeping force is required to operate among groups; a process that is labour-intensive and requires local knowledge. Such close-contact peacekeeping requires difficult decisions, many relating to the above point on neutrality. In the case of Rwanda, a notorious Hutu accused of playing a prominent role in the genocide of Tutsis later held a key position in a UN refugee camp for Hutus.[27] This figure was essentially coopted for the smooth running of the camp, but the case does raise ethical questions and complications for a strict interpretation of neutrality.

The civil dimension

A fifth feature of violence in ethnic conflict relates to the prominent role played by civilians. These types of conflict are often fought in the very territory in which the combatants live. The result is twofold: the blurring of the demarcation between civilians and combatants, and an increase in civilian casualties.[28] That the focus of an ethnic conflict is often a people and a culture, rather than an army, state, or ideology, reinforces the point of the crucial role of civilians in ethnic conflicts. The part-time, organic, and ad hoc nature of many of the armed groups in ethnic conflicts further blurs the distinction between civilians and combatants. In such situations, third-party interventions require an increased civil dimension and an emphasis on the demilitarization of society. The problem of children in conflict is also magnified in ethnic conflicts. This not only applies to the problem of children as direct casualties of war, but also the estimated 300,000 child soldiers engaged in 35 conflicts worldwide.[29] Tackling such problems is difficult, requiring coordination of national and international initiatives, as well as attempts to trigger cultural changes in a diverse range of societies.

Intra-ethnic struggles

Another consequence of the relatively disorganized nature of many ethnic political or guerrilla movements is that leaders may not be in full command of those whom they claim to represent. Insurgent groups may be rapidly formed in response to a drastic situation. Such reactive movements are often defensive, and may not have an agreed philosophy or a particularly well-developed political message. Several groups may claim to represent the same community, and competition between groups can become violent. Ethnic groups have been known to invest as much energy into intra-group feuds as inter-ethnic conflicts. As a result, severe problems can arise during political negotiations aimed at reaching a peace accord. A political leader may negotiate and sign an accord on behalf of a community, but may not be able to deliver the consent of that community.[30] The identification of credible negotiating partners is crucial if negotiations are to attain legitimacy, but in the absence of properly verified elections it can be difficult to assess which group actually represents a community.

The prominence of small arms

The task of demilitarization is heavily influenced by the predominance of small arms in ethnic conflicts. Such weapons are highly durable, portable, and relatively easy to operate. As a result, they may be accessible to large sections of society rather than limited to trained professionals. Their mobility means that there is a risk of weapons reaching other conflicts or criminal networks.[31] According to a 1998 estimate, 95 per cent of war casualties are civilian and 90 per cent of casualties are caused by small arms.[32] The United Nations has a long record of involvement in demilitarization processes and associated processes of demobilization and the reintegration of ex-combatants into society. Most weapons collection programmes involve a voluntary dimension that is linked to a wider peace process or an incentive-led weapons handover, such as a buy-back scheme.[33]

Chronically weak states

A further feature of ethnic conflict is a collapsed or weak state.[34] Many states, particularly those which gained independence during the decolonization period of the 1950s and 1960s, possess arbitrary boundaries and heterogeneous populations. Economic stagnation, among other factors, meant that many of these states had a limited capacity to control and administer the territory over which they gained sovereignty. Indeed, in some cases, economic circumstances made the possession of international boundaries and internal bureaucracies "expensive liabilities".[35] In times of ethnic conflict, a number of these states collapsed entirely, with Somalia and Liberia providing notable examples.[36] A more common pattern was that of the contracting state, with a state's capacity to govern declining over certain territories or functions. Such situations require large, multidimensional peacekeeping forces, although they face the problem of an absence of local sources of authority and stability with which to cooperate. The United Nations and other organizations have faced criticism for responding to collapsed states by attempting to resurrect them without recognizing the structural problems inherent in such states. According to Herbst, "international society has yet to acknowledge that some states simply do not work".[37] Ihonvbere places the blame more locally: "No pro-democracy movement or new political party in Africa has shown any interest in dismantling and reconstructing the unstable, violent, and inefficient neo-colonial state."[38]

There seems to be little international political will to investigate other, non-state, legal concepts. The establishment of international protectorates has occurred in Bosnia and Kosovo; but it is policy-making "on the hoof". Circumstances meant that there was little planning for the creation of these quasi-states. Without determined high-level political action, such temporary dispensations are likely to acquire semi-permanence. A problem with this is that ethnic or identity-linked conflicts are fuelled by uncertainty (of constitutional status or the intentions of opposition groups). A constitutional position which was established on an ad hoc basis may actually contribute to the perpetuation of the conflict.

Intragroup politics

An important and often overlooked dynamic in many ethnic conflicts is intragroup politics. It is particularly important in relation to political élites within ethnic groups and relevant states who can play a leadership role in the escalation or management of a conflict. Many studies of ethnic conflict tend to concentrate on mass-level explanations at the expense of attention to élite decisions. Brown emphasizes the salience of internal power struggles, particularly in cases where a lack of élite legitimacy leads to élite vulnerability.[39] In such situations, weak élites may wish to divert attention from legitimacy problems by "playing the ethnic card" or pursuing ethnically motivated strategies. Tatu Vakanen finds that in situations of "ethnic nepotism", the more a society is ethnically divided, the more political and other interest-related conflict tends to become channelled along ethnic lines.[40] The international community can play an important role in facilitating peaceful transitions within élites or encouraging them to moderate their responses in relation to ethnic issues. Such interventions often call for local knowledge and rely on a level of consent from the élites themselves. They also work best if carried out sensitively on a low-key basis. The United Nations can facilitate such interventions, as was the case with the appointment of a political adviser to the UN Development Programme in Mali.[41] The promotion of often underrated political skills, such as consensus-building, can be extremely cost-effective, with the potential to prevent conflict.

Conflict complexity and public opinion

Another feature associated with, but not exclusive to, ethnic conflict is complexity. Rather than two sides, such conflicts often have multiple protagonists, varying in degrees of significance, militancy, and proximity to the conflict zone. The conflicts are often protracted, with tortuously slow political negotiations, and cease-fires and peace accords are rarely permanent. They are characterized by humanitarian catastrophes, the collapse of civil and political society, refugee flows, outbreaks of disease, and systematic human rights abuses. They demand large, expensive responses from the international community. It is not simply a matter of separating warring factions and brokering a cease-fire followed by a political accord. Instead a more holistic, long-term approach is required; herein lies the problem.

The complexity of these conflicts and years of ambitious UN peacekeeping operations with mixed results have left the international community with a limited political willingness to become involved in such disputes. Few states are interested in open-ended commitments. Even large-scale multidimensional operations have no guarantee of success. The massive UN Transitional Authority in Cambodia (UNTAC) represented a $2.6bn investment on behalf of the international community, yet this did not prevent a coup in 1997.[42] However, success in resolving ethnic conflicts is not simply an issue of capability, but one of fatigue and lack of willingness. Nor is it restricted to the United Nations, with key members of other international organizations also becoming more selective about the conflict situations they want to become involved in. An added problem is that with greater access to information, there is greater public pressure on governments to take action. However, this does not necessarily translate into a demand that their government intervenes on the ground. The NATO-led operation in Kosovo showed that many Western states were prepared to kill, but not to sustain casualties, in the pursuit of international goals. While hard evidence of a "CNN factor" has yet to emerge, it is clear that key governments in the international community are acutely sensitive towards public opinion and domestic political factors in their foreign policy-making.[43] Given that ethnic conflicts rarely offer the prospect of a decisive outcome or a straightforward "just cause", public opinion in key states may err on the side of caution in relation to intervention. Even the repackaging of NATO's 1999 Kosovo intervention as "humanitarian war" had limited effect in persuading Western publics of the need to commit ground troops.

A persistent lack of political will by powerful governments to intervene in far-away conflicts leads to a situation in which interest and involvement in internal conflicts often comes from neighbouring or regional states, which may fan the flames of conflict by supporting particular groups, or by attempting to increase their own sphere of influence. Regional concerns such as refugee flows and the spread of instability are further enticements for regional responses.

The media's role in the coverage of conflicts, alluded to above, has serious implications for peacekeeping in ethnic conflicts. Jean Seaton illuminates the problems in her exploration of the Balkan crisis.[44] Few broadcasting networks or newspapers want in-depth coverage of every war, and due to financial constraints and competition most cannot provide in-depth coverage even if they wanted to. In certain areas, for example Rwanda, Liberia, Bosnia, and Chechnya, the media can act as a powerful spotlight. However, other conflicts are simply bypassed.

Is there a remedy?

Much of the literature on peacekeeping implies that ethnic conflict is the "wrong sort of conflict"; that it has the temerity to be awkward and unsuited to the carefully crafted conceptualizations of peacekeeping that have been pieced together over the last four decades. This clash between the nature of conflicts on the one hand, and the means at the disposal of the international community to deal with them on the other, is likely to persist. Despite its shortcomings, the deployment of multinational peace operations often presents the most effective approach to conflict management. Many conflicts require large-scale interventions and the logistical skills that only military organizations possess. Furthermore, many interventions require the legitimacy that only an almost universal organization such as the United Nations can confer. Yet there are a number of initiatives and skills that can be usefully added to peacekeeping operations in their attempts to deal with ethnic conflict. Some of these initiatives can also operate on a stand-alone basis, and because of their less intrusive nature can precede a peacekeeping operation. Clearly many of these initiatives are dependent on factors that are not easily controlled; particular circumstances or phases of conflict may make them impossible to apply. For example, democracy skills training for politicians or officials may be inappropriate during a period of all-out war.

One initiative should be the compulsory teaching of basic conflict resolution skills to peacekeepers, both military and civilian. These skills need not necessarily contradict the more traditional military skills possessed by many peacekeepers; indeed, they can build upon many of the skills military personnel have already acquired. An introduction to the idea of conflict as an inherently human phenomenon that is not always destructive, and an exploration of the various approaches to a conflict situation, may encourage peacekeepers to think and act beyond a passive peacekeeping role. Pioneering work in this field with the Australian Defence Force by Greg Tillett has produced positive results and has also paid attention to the needs of the peacekeepers themselves.[45]

Other possible initiatives which could be usefully emphasized as part of peacekeeping operations are confidence-building measures. The term is often associated with arms control, whether in relation to threat reduction between nuclear powers or along disputed borders between states. It is also often associated with large-scale, institutionalized schemes. Political confidence-building measures can often operate on a small scale. They are usually low-cost initiatives capable of yielding high results from a small investment of time or political capital. They are intermediate, often occurring before the start of formal negotiations between protagonists. One example was the declaration of a "humanitarian pause" in Aceh from June 2000 onwards. Due to sensitivity over terminology, the protagonists shied away from the term "cease-fire" and agreed upon the alternative term following NGO facilitation. The pause allowed aid to be directed to the region's internally displaced persons and, perhaps more significantly, allowed substantive political negotiations to commence.[46] The key point is that confidence-building measures can be innovative and adaptable to suit particular conflict conditions. Common confidence-building measures include prisoner releases or the lifting of travel restrictions. They can also operate at the symbolic level (again low-cost but high-impact politics) and take the form of meetings between political leaders. Confidence-building measures are not restricted to the élite political level; they can take place within and between communities and thus shore up wider political accords. The United Nations has an immense capacity to facilitate such confidence-building. The low-key nature of this facilitation may overcome possible opposition to more formal or large-scale interventions. Furthermore, many confidence-building measures are not dependent on a cease-fire; they can proceed while violence is ongoing. At the heart of confidence-building measures lies the idea of reciprocity; that concessions will be mutual, cumulatively leading to a reduction of violence.

The notion that the United Nations should encourage governments and parties in conflicts to develop political skills may seem like an odd suggestion. By its very nature, politics in deeply divided societies tends to be partisan; infecting even the most innocuous of matters. Everyday issues, such as healthcare or education, can become political battlegrounds between groups. The United Nations has traditionally shied away from intervention in the domestic politics of member states. But the teaching of basic political and governance skills to government officials and members of new and established political parties offers immense benefits. Of course, such activities may inspire thoughts of Machiavellian political organizers encouraging political parties to be ever more sophisticated in their ruthlessness. Instead, the work can take a more mundane but useful form. For example, an organizer with a background in political organization from a stable democracy may be assigned to a newly formed political party. His or her main task would be to share skills on electoral targeting and/or media management. Much of this work would take place at the local level. The main aim is to relegitimize political activity and to illustrate that the political system can work. Clearly such activities are sensitive and require the consent of the party involved. They can be cost-effective, however, and contribute to conflict prevention. If parties and communities have faith in non-violent and political methods of resolving disputes then violent conflict may be minimized.

Related to the promotion of political skills is democratization. Again this is a long-term, educative strategy that conceptualizes democracy as a process rather than an endpoint. Laurence Whitehead notes that "democracy is frequently established by undemocratic means".[47] Third-party intervention may often be viewed as subverting rather than sustaining democracy. Furthermore, intrusive or large-scale operations result in the establishment of democratic institutions that face problems when third-party support is withdrawn. Premature post-conflict elections can give a democratic veneer to societies with a shallow democratic culture and a poorly developed civil society.[48] A possible remedy lies in building democracy from the bottom up, a process that the United Nations can actively support.[49] The United Nations can encourage constitutional framers to include elements of flexibility into new constitutions. For example, enshrining the right to dissent and to demonstrate in public allows for the possibility for non-violent protest and does not leave the option of violent protest as the only recourse for the disaffected.[50] Democracy need not be a rigid or alien concept. It can incorporate relevant elements from indigenous society and root democratic institutions close to the societies in which they are expected to operate.

Conclusion

There does seem to be evidence of a declining UN involvement in efforts to manage ethnic conflict. Between 1988 and 1998, 36 formal peace accords were reached in 32 states. The United Nations was directly involved in 16 of these accords, the bulk of them between 1988 and 1993.[51] A clear trend of decreasing UN involvement in peace processes is identifiable. A chief reason for this is that member states have become less ambitious in their support of intervention in general and peacekeeping operations in particular. In the early 1990s the United Nations was involved in a number of highly ambitious, large-scale, multidimensional peacekeeping missions that had mixed results. In 1994 there were 17 peacekeeping missions in the field, as opposed to five in 1988.[52] However, the UN's peacekeeping budget dropped from $3bn in 1995 to $1bn in 1998, reflecting a diminished willingness among the international community to become involved in further extensive peacekeeping commitments.[53] Other agencies and international organizations have shown a growing competence in conducting peace operations. Restructuring and a reinvestment of political will in NATO, the Western European Union (WEU), and the Organization for Security and Cooperation in Europe (OSCE), among others, meant that they were newly empowered to perform tasks once reserved to the United Nations. The United Nations also showed a greater tendency to delegate – implicitly or explicitly – to regional organizations, such as the Economic Community of West African States (ECOWAS) in Liberia and the Commonwealth of Independent States (CIS) in Tajikistan.[54]

The United Nations has been criticized as an unwieldy intervention mechanism. Hindered by a slow-moving bureaucracy and consensus-building decision-making processes, it has often intervened late in a conflict, after major fighting had taken place.[55] Single states and smaller organizations possess greater capacity for rapid and decisive intervention, but many lack the UN's authority. Fundamentally, little attention has been paid to the nature of ethnic conflict, and especially to the nature of violence within such conflicts. A more precise understanding of the dynamics behind such violence could help the United Nations and other interested parties to tailor their responses more appropriately. A more careful balance between the military, humanitarian, and political aspects of intervention is necessary. At times, purely military forms of intervention will be required. But in anything beyond the short term, such responses need to be integrated with other forms of intervention that can enable the protagonists to engage in a credible conflict-reduction process.

Attempts by the international community to force protagonists in an ethnic conflict situation to the negotiating table can be counterproductive. Negotiators without faith in the negotiating process are unlikely to have a strong attachment to any negotiated outcome. Nor are they likely to sell any agreement to a sullen invaded populace. More sophisticated approaches by the international community that can encourage protagonists to work towards accommodation and offer credible alternatives to violence or repression may produce dividends.

The trend away from large-scale peacekeeping operations, however, does not mean that the United Nations has no role to play in responding to ethnic conflict. Beginning with its supervision of the 1989 Namibian elections, the United Nations has engaged in a series of "democratic interventions".[56] Many of these interventions were small in scale and carried out by UN agencies in collaboration with NGOs. Capacity-building activities such as post-election institution development or civic education programmes are cost-effective. Such programmes can be flexible, operate at a local level, and remain responsive to community needs. They do not have to wait for implementation until all-out war or the breakdown of society. Sometimes, small is best.

Notes

1. Viva Ona Bartkus, *The Dynamic of Secession*, Cambridge: Cambridge University Press, 1999, pp. 68–72. Interestingly, after noting that the "foundation-stone" of the UN's work is the state, Boutros-Ghali goes on to note that "[t]he time of absolute and exclusive sovereignty ... has passed; its theory was never matched by reality". See Boutros Boutros-Ghali, *An Agenda for Peace*, New York: United Nations, 1992, paragraph 17.
2. Kumar Rupesinghe, "Multi-track solutions to armed conflicts", in *Prevention and Management of Conflicts: An International Directory*, edited by the Dutch Centre for Conflict Prevention in cooperation with ACCESS and PIOOM, Amsterdam: NCDO, 1996, p. 10.
3. "The United Nations in its second half-century", *Report of the Independent Working Group on the Future of the United Nations*, http://www.library.yale.edu/un/unhome.htm/, 1995.
4. Richard Cohen, "Send in the troops", *Washington Post*, 28 November 1995; cited in Michael E. Brown, "The causes of internal conflict", in Michael E. Brown, Owen R. Cote, Sean M. Lynn-Jones, and Steven E. Miller (eds), *Nationalism and Ethnic Conflict*, Cambridge, MA: MIT Press, 1997, p. 3.

5. John Burton, *Violence Explained: The Sources of Conflict, Violence and Crime and Their Prevention*, Manchester: Manchester University Press, 1997, p. 24.

6. Two classic texts on ethnic conflict are Donald L. Horowitz, *Ethnic Groups in Conflict*, Berkeley, CA: University of California Press, 1985; and Joseph Montville (ed.), *Conflict and Peacemaking in Multiethnic Societies*, Lexington, MA: Lexington Books, 1990.

7. John Darby, *What's Wrong With Conflict?*, Occasional Paper, Coleraine: Centre for the Study of Conflict/University of Ulster, 1993.

8. Walker Connor, *Ethnonationalism: The Quest for Understanding*, Princeton: Princeton University Press, 1994, p. 204.

9. Robert D. Kaplan, "The coming anarchy," *The Atlantic Monthly*, February 1994, pp. 44–76.

10. Peter Wallensteen and Margareta Sollenberg, "Armed conflict, 1989–99," *Journal of Peace Research*, Vol. 37, No. 5, 2000, p. 635.

11. Mary Kaldor and Basker Vashee (eds), *Restructuring the Global Military Sector: New Wars*, London: Pinter, 1997, p. 8.

12. Roger Brubaker and David Laitin, "Ethnic and nationalist violence", *Annual Review of Sociology*, Vol. 24, 1998, p. 424.

13. Jenny Pearce, "From civil war to 'civil society': Has the end of the Cold War brought peace to Central America?" *International Affairs*, Vol. 74, No. 3, 1998, p. 599.

14. Pacific perpetuation is addressed in Stephen Ryan, "Ethnic conflict and the United Nations", *Ethnic and Racial Studies*, Vol. 13, No. 1, January 1990, pp. 25–49. See also Burton, note 5, p. 44.

15. For example, it has been claimed that UNIFIL turned back 2,159 infiltration attempts in south Lebanon between mid-June 1979 and June 1982. Ryan, note 14, p. 29.

16. Brubaker and Laitin, note 12, p. 444.

17. Patricia Hill Collins, "The tie that binds: Race, gender and US violence", *Ethnic and Racial Studies*, Vol. 21, No. 5, September 1998, p. 924.

18. See the "five stages of conflict and two crises thresholds" model developed by the Inter-disciplinary Research Programme on Root Causes of Human Rights Violations (PIOOM) in A. P. Schmid and A. J. Jongman, "Violent conflicts and human rights violations in the mid-1990s", *Terrorism and Political Violence*, Vol. 9, No. 4, Winter 1997, p. 167.

19. Rupesinghe, note 2, p. 11.

20. Tamara Duffey, "United Nations peacekeeping in the post-Cold War world," *Civil Wars*, Vol. 1, No. 3, Autumn 1998, pp. 18–19.

21. "Doubts on UN Timor plan", *International Herald Tribune*, 7 October 1999.

22. Hugh Miall, Oliver Ramsbotham, and Tom Woodhouse, *Contemporary Conflict Resolution*, Cambridge: Polity Press, 1999, p. 199.

23. Burton, note 5.

24. Robin-Edward Poulton and Ibrahim ag Youssouf, *A Peace of Timbuktu: Democratic Governance, Development and African Peacemaking*, Geneva: UNIDIR, 1998, pp. 182–188.

25. Robert Fisk, *Pity the Nation: Lebanon at War*, Oxford: Oxford University Press, 1990, pp. 452–453.

26. Michael Cox and Roger Mac Ginty, "Farewell to a beautiful idea: The end of neutrality in the post-Cold War world", in Werner Bauwens et al. (eds), *Small States and the Security Challenge in the New Europe*, London: Brassey's, 1996, pp. 122–136.

27. The case was highlighted by BBC journalist Feargal Keane in *Letter To Daniel: Despatches from the Heart*, London: Penguin/BBC Books, 1996, p. 225.

28. William Eckhardt challenges the notion that there was ever a clear distinction between civilians and combatants in "Civilian deaths in wartime", *Bulletin of Peace Proposals*, Vol. 20, No. 1, March 1989, pp. 89–98.

29. Figures from Save the Children (Sweden) website, http://www.rb.se/childwardatabase/efaq.htm, 1999.
30. John Darby and Roger Mac Ginty (eds), *The Management of Peace Processes*, London: Macmillan, 2000, pp. 256–257.
31. Pierre du Toit examines the example of South Africa in Darby and Mac Ginty, *ibid.*, pp. 46–47.
32. Figures cited in Joseph Di Chiaro III, *Reasonable Measures: Addressing the Excessive Accumulation and Unlawful Use of Small Arms*, Brief 11, Bonn: Bonn International Centre for Conversion, 1998, p. 10.
33. Edward J. Laurance and Sarah Meek, *The New Field of Micro-Disarmament: Addressing the Proliferation and Build-up of Small Arms and Light Weapons*, Brief 7, Bonn: BICC, 1996, p. 26.
34. Much of the discussion on weak states is taken from Jeffrey Herbst, "Responding to state failure in Africa", in Brown *et al.*, note 4, pp. 374–398.
35. William Reno, "War, markets, and the reconfiguration of West Africa's weak states", *Comparative Politics*, Vol. 29, No. 4, July 1997, p. 505.
36. Morten Bøås, "Liberia – the hellbound heart? Regime breakdown and the deconstruction of society", *Alternatives*, Vol. 22, No. 3, July–September 1997, pp. 35–75.
37. Herbst, note 34, p. 390.
38. Julius O. Ihonvbere, "Democratization in Africa", *Peace Review*, Vol. 9, No. 3, September 1997, p. 375.
39. Brown, note 4, pp. 17–20.
40. Tatu Vakanen, "Domestic ethnic conflict and ethnic nepotism: A comparative analysis", *Journal of Peace Research*, Vol. 36, No. 1, 1999, pp. 55–73.
41. Poulton and Youssouf, note 24, pp. 155–157.
42. The figure is reported in "Who speaks for the people?", *The Economist*, 27 January 1996, pp. 55–56. Please also see the chapters in this volume by John Sanderson and Yasushi Akashi.
43. Peter Viggo Jakobsen, "National interest, humanitarianism or CNN: What triggers UN peace enforcement after the Cold War?", *Journal of Peace Research*, Vol. 33, No. 2, May 1996, pp. 205–215; and Piers Robinson, "The CNN effect: Can the news media drive foreign policy?", *Review of International Studies*, Vol. 25, No. 2, April 1999, pp. 301–309. George Stephanopoulous's autobiography reveals how dependent the Clinton White House was on opinion polls: *All Too Human: A Political Education*, London: Hutchinson, 1999.
44. Jean Seaton, "Why do we think the Serbs do it? The new 'ethnic' wars and the media", *Political Quarterly*, Vol. 70, No. 3, July–September 1999.
45. Greg Tillett, *Conflict Resolution Training for Military Peacekeepers*, INCORE Occasional Paper, 1996, http://www.incore.ulst.ac.uk/publications/research/peacekeeping/tillet.htm.
46. The authors are indebted to David Connolly, PRDU, University of York, for this insight.
47. Laurence Whitehead, "The imposition of democracy: The Caribbean," in Laurence Whitehead (ed.), *The International Dimension of Democratization: Europe and the Americas*, Oxford: Oxford University Press, 1996, pp. 59–92.
48. The problems and opportunities of post-conflict elections are covered by Timothy D. Sisk, *Power-sharing and International Mediation in Ethnic Conflict*, Washington, DC: USIP Press, 1996; Timothy D. Sisk and Andrew Reynolds (eds), *Elections and Conflict Management in Africa*, Washington, DC: USIP Press, 1998; Peter Harris and Ben Reilly (eds), *Democracy and Deep-rooted Conflicts: Options for Negotiators*, Stockholm: International IDEA, 1998.

49. National Research Council, *Democratization in Africa: African Views, African Voices*, Washington, DC: National Academy Press, 1992, p. 10.
50. Whitehead, note 47, p. 51.
51. Figures taken from John Darby and James Rae, "Peace processes 1988–98: Changing patterns?", *Ethnic Studies Report*, Vol. XVII, No. 1, January 1999.
52. Duffey, note 20, p. 7.
53. Darby and Rae, note 51.
54. Issues of devolution to regional organizations are covered in Thomas G. Weiss (ed.), *Beyond UN Subcontracting: Task-sharing with Regional Security Arrangements and Service-providing NGOs*, London: Macmillan, 1998.
55. Tinaz Pavri, "Help or hindrance: Third parties in the Indo-Pakistani conflict", *Negotiation Journal*, Vol. 13, No. 4, October 1997, p. 380.
56. Larry Diamond, "Promoting democracy in the 1990s: Actors, instruments and issues", in Axel Hadenius (ed.), *Democracy's Victory and Crisis*, Cambridge: Cambridge University Press, 1997, pp. 329–330.

3

The role of the UN Secretariat in organizing peacekeeping

Hisako Shimura

The United Nations is an international – or, more precisely, intergovern-mental – organization whose main actors are its member states and whose decisions are made by government representatives in political organs, such as the General Assembly and the Security Council. Of the six principal organs, only the Secretariat can be said to have essentially a supporting role, implementing those decisions made by the political organs. The Charter describes the Secretary-General, who heads the Secretariat, as "the chief administrative officer" of the United Nations. However, under the Charter, the Secretary-General has been considered to play a larger political role than his counterpart in the League of Nations or in most international organizations. Certainly, each of the seven individuals who have served as Secretary-General to date has considered that, as the only person who can – and should – speak for the United Nations as a whole, the Secretary-General has the moral duty to defend the principles of the Charter and speak out when necessary on political issues.

Even so, the role of the Secretary-General and the Secretariat in or-ganizing and managing peacekeeping operations (PKOs) can be said to be unusually prominent, and it may exceed anything the founders of the United Nations had envisaged, especially since it concerns the field of the UN's central activity related to the maintenance of peace and security. This fact is related to the circumstances and the manner in which PKOs have developed over the years.

"Traditional" PKOs

As is well known, peacekeeping operations are not based on any article of the Charter. When the Cold War made it impossible to implement the collective security system under Chapter VII, and the "UN Force" envisaged in Article 43 never came into being, attempts were made to give the United Nations, under the constraints of the Cold War, whatever role possible that could limit conflict and contribute to peace.

The first PKO, the UN Truce Supervision Organization (UNTSO), had its origin in a cease-fire that was achieved in the first Middle East war in 1948. Count Bernadotte, the Swedish UN mediator, asked UN Headquarters to send urgently a small group of officers to help him monitor the cease-fire, and Secretary-General Trygve Lie responded by asking Belgium, France, and the USA, members of the Palestine Commission, to make such officers available to the United Nations. Soon after, another similar operation – the UN Military Observer Group in India and Pakistan (UNMOGIP) – was established in Kashmir in 1949 between areas occupied by India and Pakistan. These two set the pattern for the first of the two types of PKOs – military observer groups (MOGs).

When the second Middle East war erupted in 1956, a different, somewhat larger – and the first armed – operation was considered necessary to supervise not only the cease-fire but also the withdrawal of the armies of the UK, France, and Israel that had been deployed in the Suez Canal area. Thus the First UN Emergency Force (UNEF I) was established as the first of the second type of PKOs, namely, a peacekeeping force.

The practical nature and the urgency of the circumstances surrounding the origin of these operations – now called "traditional" PKOs – prompted the Security Council to turn to the Secretary-General and the Secretariat to act quickly to raise and dispatch, with little or no guidance from political organs, the required military personnel, and the practice has continued. UNEF I, the first large-scale PKO, was the brainchild of Lester B. Pearson, then the foreign minister of Canada, and Dag Hammarskjöd, the second Secretary-General of the United Nations, and it established many of the principles and practices on which later operations were based, including the three basic principles of consent, impartiality, and non-use of force. Most of the detailed rules and specific ways and means of quickly setting up and running a PKO emerged from actual practice, in which the Secretariat played a major part.

In 1958, two years after UNEF I began its operation, Hammarskjöd issued a report, commonly called "The Summary Study", in which the principles and *modus operandi* that were applied in later operations were first documented.[1] In it, Hammarskjöd wrote that one of the merits of

PKOs was the fact that their chiefs were appointed by an organ of the United Nations and acted under its authority, and thus the activities of a PKO were administratively tied to the Secretariat and its international status. In practice, too, the actual political and administrative direction of these operations has largely been entrusted to the Secretary-General and responsible departments of the Secretariat. The Secretary-General, for his part, regularly sends reports to the Council and the Assembly and frequently consults them.

There have been 55 PKOs to date, 13 during the Cold War period and 42 since. Each one had to be built "from scratch", quickly, and under pressure, chiefly by a small group of Secretariat officials experienced in setting up and managing these operations.

Planning "traditional" PKOs

When a new PKO is considered necessary, the Security Council normally decides in the first resolution to establish in principle an operation.[2] It then asks the Secretary-General to present a report, sometimes within only 48 hours, containing his detailed recommended plan for the operation. The 13 "traditional" PKOs established during the Cold War era, with the exception of the UN Operation in Congo (ONUC, 1960–1964) and the UN Temporary Executive Authority (UNTEA) in West Irian (1962–1963), as well as about half of the 42 post-Cold War operations, were essentially cease-fire monitoring operations. For these, the mandate and tasks are relatively clear and straightforward. Nonetheless, the Secretary-General, in the light of the conditions on the ground and based on work done in the appropriate units in the Secretariat, must decide on a concrete and detailed plan about how an operation will be carried out. A cease-fire line might have to be drawn or confirmed; a demilitarized zone might have to be established; a timetable for the withdrawal of foreign troops might need to be agreed. These will require careful consultations with the parties to the conflict. A fact-finding mission may need to be sent to the area. Some details may have to be agreed upon after the advance party of the operation arrives in the area.

Once the overall concept of the operation has been decided, the Secretary-General must next decide whether to recommend to the Security Council a relatively small-scale and unarmed military observer group, or a larger and lightly armed peacekeeping force, or, increasingly, a combination of the two. He must also decide on the size of the operation – how many individual officers are needed for a military observer group, or how many infantry and specialized support battalions for a peacekeeping force. He must decide what type and quantity of equipment will be required, including light weapons in case a peacekeeping force is to be established. To the extent possible, plans are made on how the members of the operation will be transported and where they will be based, housed, and deployed in the field. Further negotiations with host governments, which are also normally the parties to the conflict, are necessary on the status of forces agreement (SOFA), including the facilities and services the government is expected to provide to the operation.

Multifunctional PKOs

For the new multifunctional operations that have become common after the end of the Cold War, the task of deciding on the basic concept of the operation and drawing up a detailed plan is a far more complex exercise, even when a comprehensive political settlement, such as the Paris Accords for Cambodia, is already in place to guide it. During the time of the traditional PKOs, the Secretariat unit that was chiefly responsible for these tasks and made recommendations to the Secretary-General was the Office for Special Political Affairs (SPA), which had been developed around Under-Secretary-General Ralph Bunche. He was succeeded by Sir Brian Urquhart, and for 40 years the unit remained a small group of capable and dedicated officials. Their work was assisted by the Secretary-General's military adviser, the sole military officer in the Secretariat, who worked closely with, and later became part of, SPA.

As the number, scale, and complexity of PKOs grew, in 1992 SPA was expanded, in part by incorporating the Field Operations Division (FOD) of the Department of Administration and Management (DAM), which had handled administrative and logistic matters for PKOs. It was renamed the Department of Peacekeeping Operations (DPKO). In 1993 the DPKO was further reorganized, creating a new internal structure including the Office of Operations, the Office of Planning and Support, and the 24-hour situation centre. In addition to expanding the civilian Secretariat staff, the DPKO was further strengthened by approximately 50 military officers temporarily on loan from member states.

For the new, complex operations, military officers and civilian officials from member states who were expected to participate in a forthcoming operation have frequently been invited to join Secretariat staff in the planning process, both to contribute their specialized knowledge and expertise at this stage and to prepare for their duties in the field later. In the planning exercise for the UN Transitional Authority in Cambodia (UNTAC), for instance, General John Sanderson of Australia, who was to command its military component, and Commander Klaas Roos of the Netherlands, the future head of the civilian police component, played a valuable role.

Even with such an augmented Secretariat team, the planning of complex operations was a difficult exercise beset by many shortcomings and long delays. One of the major shortcomings was the lack of adequate expert knowledge and expertise within the Secretariat about the country or region in which a new operation was to be deployed. Yet the complex operations arising from civil wars required such knowledge and expertise to a much greater extent than did the earlier cease-fire monitoring missions. Attempts to remedy these staffing shortcomings were frustrated by increasing pressures since the 1980s to reduce and streamline the Secretariat.

Beyond the challenge of planning such complex operations, member states were asked to increase their commitments – in the form of more military personnel and units, and civilian police as well as a wide variety of other civilian experts and specialists. It turned out to be much more difficult to secure civilian personnel, as most countries had far fewer qualified civilians than suitable military men and women.

To launch complex operations, pre-operation fact-finding missions to the area were essential. For example, although several such missions had already been dispatched by the time the Paris Accords appeared likely, UNTAC required four more missions after the signing of the accords in order to obtain vital information and data that the Cambodian parties had not yet provided. This, of course, greatly delayed the submission of the Secretary-General's implementation plan. Precious time was thus lost in deploying the operation, exacerbating already uncertain conditions on the ground and causing serious problems and severe criticism from all directions.

The Secretary-General frequently consults the Security Council – especially the permanent five – before his/her report is finalized. Eventually, the Council almost always accepts the Secretary-General's report and its recommendations, and it proceeds to adopt a second resolution that officially establishes the anticipated operation along those lines. In recent years, however, the Secretary-General has, on occasion, presented several options for the Council to choose from (such as in Somalia). This gave rise to a certain lack of clarity of purpose and coherence of the proposed operation. In other cases, the Council authorized a smaller operation than recommended by the Secretary-General (for instance, in the former Yugoslavia), creating an operation without the resources needed to achieve its mandate.

Establishing PKOs

Once a new operation is formally authorized, the Secretariat plunges into a period of intense activity. Consultations are held with the representatives of the parties concerned on the detailed implementation of the operation, and on the facilities and services they will provide. A list of potential countries to provide troops and other personnel is drawn up, in consideration of factors such as geographical balance, political neutrality, and past peacekeeping record. This is followed by consultations with each potential contributor.

During the Cold War period it became established practice that the five permanent members of the Security Council – and especially the two superpowers – would not normally provide military personnel to PKOs, so as to keep local and regional wars from becoming entangled in major power confrontations. As a result, a number of "middle powers" were called upon repeatedly to participate in these operations – notably Canada, the Nordic countries, Austria, and some others. Since the end of the Cold War, the permanent five have taken a more active part. At first all five contributed relatively small – and often equal – numbers of military observers, as in the UN Iraq-Kuwait Observer Mission (UNIKOM, 1991 to the present) or UNTAC (1992–1993). This was taken to symbolize their unity and shared political support for the operation, and had a generally beneficial effect. Later, however, they often provided a major and sometimes dominant contingent, as was done by France and the UK in the UN Protection Force (UNPROFOR), or the USA in the UN Mission in Haiti (UNMIH) and the Second UN Operation in Somalia (UNOSOM II). Occasionally, a major power presence has put into question the "UN-ness" of a given operation, or created problems of command and control. While not always with success, the Secretary-General has attempted to keep any one country's share of the military personnel to no more than one-third of the total number.

The overall selection of countries to provide the needed personnel to a given operation is essentially made by the Secretariat in consultation with member states. At the end of the exercise, the Secretary-General presents the Council with a proposed list of countries that will contribute troops and civilian police forces. The Council customarily replies that it "agrees" with the Secretary-General's choice. This exchange is not, however, regarded as the Council's formal approval of the Secretary-General's decision.

Deciding who will head an operation is always an extremely important and delicate task. In a cease-fire monitoring operation, comprised mostly of military personnel contributed by member states, a senior military officer, normally – but not always – from one of the countries contributing troops to that operation, is nominated as force commander or chief military observer by the Secretary-General and agreed to by the Security Council. The choice is often a delicate one, hotly contested by the governments concerned. For the new multifunctional operations, the top official is a civilian called the special representative of the Secretary-General (SRSG), and is sometimes a senior member of the Secretariat and sometimes a distinguished personality outside the UN system. Here again, the decision used to be made essentially by the Secretary-General; lately, however, some member states have been very assertive about their specific preferences.

Parallel to these activities, the Office of Planning and Support of the DPKO decides on the vehicles, prefabricated buildings, and other equipment other than arms (which are brought to the operation by national contingents according to UN specifications) that will be required by the operation. Contracts are given to the most competitive bidders, materials are procured, and arrangements are made for the transportation of personnel and equipment to the theatre of operation.

Another crucial task is the preparation of the budget. This process can formally begin only after the above-mentioned second Security Council resolution is passed, which approves the Secretary-General's report and establishes the operation. When the budget has been formulated, it must be approved first by the Advisory Committee for Administrative and Budgetary Questions (ACABQ) of the General Assembly, then by the Fifth Committee, and finally by the full Assembly. A further delaying factor is that the procurement of equipment can begin only after the approval of the budget. The entire process can be time-consuming, and the Secretariat is caught between the obligation to adhere to these rules and requirements, originally developed for the normal activities of the United Nations but now applied to PKOs as well, and the pressure to deploy the operation as quickly as possible. When UNTAC was launched, the Assembly responded pragmatically to this dilemma: it authorized the Secretary-General to spend $200m of the anticipated $1.5bn budget in advance of its formal approval under the condition that this would not set a precedent. These and similarly creative measures will be needed in the future to establish operations more speedily.

In order to enhance the UN's capacity to set up a new operation quickly and efficiently, in 1994 former Secretary-General Boutros-Ghali established a PKO "standby arrangement system". Under this system, some 70 member states have undertaken to provide, in principle, a total of some 100,000 personnel to future PKOs. However, contribution to these operations is entirely voluntary and even those member states that participate in the standby system decide on a case-by-case basis whether and what to contribute to a specific future operation. The first test case of the system, that of organizing an enlarged operation for Rwanda in 1994, failed when all member states that had registered their willingness declined the Secretary-General's request for troops.

Managing PKOs

After a peacekeeping operation is launched, its day-to-day direction and management is in the hands of the Secretary-General and the Secretariat, who keep in close contact with personnel in the field through coded and uncoded cables, telephone, satellite communication, and, increasingly, computer networks. The creation of a 24-hour situation centre has improved communication. Periodic reports and special reports to the Security Council are prepared for all ongoing operations and for the budgets drawn for each mandate renewal. Security Council members and troop-contributing countries are regularly briefed or consulted; discussions are held with the parties in the field and at UN Headquarters. When problems arise in the field, efforts are made first to resolve them on the spot by negotiation, raising the level of the negotiators in stages as required. If problems cannot be resolved in the field, they are reported to UN Headquarters – first to the DPKO or the Secretary-General; then, if necessary, to the Security Council for consideration and action. The United Nations is, however, handicapped by not possessing either carrots or sticks that can be readily employed to influence the behaviour of parties. All too often, the process ends with a Security Council resolution or statement deploring the situation.

Most PKOs are given relatively short mandate periods, typically six months, and are renewed as needed. Before each mandate renewal, the Secretary-General prepares a comprehensive report on the operation for the last mandate period and submits it to the Security Council with his recommendation for renewal or termination. If renewal is recommended, he will have obtained the consent of the parties and of the troop-contributing countries.

Throughout the Cold War years, the United Nations and the international community were less successful in peacemaking than peacekeeping. This caused many PKOs, such as UNTSO and UNMOGIP, that had been intended to be temporary measures, to continue for decades. Yet an operation, once deployed, cannot easily be withdrawn, for fear of destabilizing an already uncertain condition. Since the end of the Cold War, new operations have generally been of shorter duration, some – such as UNTAC – because they were based on political agreements already achieved, and others – like UNOSOM – because they were withdrawn under unsatisfactory circumstances.

Improving PKOs – the Brahimi Report

Early PKOs were often set up within a remarkably short time, even considering that most of these were relatively straightforward cease-fire monitoring operations and their advance parties were often dispatched from existing PKOs. As the number, scale, and complexity of operations grew quickly after the Cold War, the Secretariat faced mounting problems and delays in organizing and deploying them. Many of these problems required political decisions by the Security Council or the General Assembly to ameliorate or resolve them. Successive Secretaries-General have made recommendations, including regular calls upon member states to pay their assessed peacekeeping contributions in full and on time.

Two major reforms within the Secretariat have already been mentioned: the restructuring of the DPKO in 1992 and 1993, and the establishment of the standby arrangement in 1994. In the early 1990s the DPKO was augmented with military staff, including experts in demining and training, and civilian police personnel. These were on loan from member states. Despite these efforts, in the mid-1990s the great difficulties and failures experienced by peacekeeping operations (especially in Somalia, Bosnia-Herzegovina, and Rwanda) led to severe criticisms and disturbing disillusionment within the United Nations and the wider international community. Against this background, in March 2000 Secretary-General Kofi Annan established an expert panel to make a "thorough review of the United Nations peace and security activities, and to present a clear set of specific, concrete and practical recommendations to assist the United Nations in conducting such activities better in the future".[3] The UN Panel on Peace Operations was chaired by Ambassador Lakhdar Brahimi, former foreign minister of Algeria and special representative of the Secretary-General concerning situations in Haiti and Afghanistan, and consisted of 10 members from 10 countries, each with experience in some aspects of UN peace operations, who served in an individual capacity. The panel submitted its findings in early August 2000. The final report was then issued by the Secretary-General on 21 August 2000, in time to be considered by the Millennium Summit and Assembly.

The report examined both the doctrine and the practice of UN peace operations and presented comprehensive and far-reaching recommendations, addressed both to the member states and to the Secretariat. One of the central points made by the panel is the assertion that peacekeeping and what has come to be called peace-building are inseparable activities, as already demonstrated by the so-called complex peacekeeping operations. In order to plan, set up, and manage such complex peace operations, the panel recommends that integrated mission task forces (IMTFs) should be established for each operation, drawing the necessary staff on temporary assignment from the DPKO, the Department of Political Affairs (DPA), and other departments, units, and agencies concerned throughout the UN system, such as the Office for the Coordination of Humanitarian Assistance (OCHA), the UNHCR, the UNDP, and others.[4] The panel also recommends that the DPA be designated the focal point in the Secretariat for peace-building activities and that the UN's capacity in this field be substantially strengthened.

Earlier, Kofi Annan had already taken steps to foster better coordination and cooperation among departments that are engaged in tasks in related fields. He established four executive committees, including the Executive Committee on Peace and Security (ECPS), where heads of departments concerned meet regularly and discuss issues of common concern. The IMTFs may be considered to extend this concept to the working level. As any bureaucracy, the UN Secretariat is regrettably often prone to interagency rivalries and turf protection. It is important to overcome such tendencies, and if this can be done the performance of their tasks in support of peace operations could be significantly enhanced.

The need to strengthen the Secretariat's capacity to collect and analyse relevant information in order to improve the UN's role in conflict prevention and management is another point emphasized by the panel. To that end, the report recommends the establishment, under the direction of the ECPS, of an ECPS Information and Strategic Analysis Secretariat (EISAS).[5] This unit, combined with much greater use of new information technology, is to serve all departments and units involved in peace and security activities and, as in the case of IMTFs, is expected to promote a closer working relationship among them.

One of the issues of crucial importance is how to plan and deploy future peace operations more rapidly and effectively. The report defines "rapidly" as 30 days from the adoption of the Security Council resolution for cease-fire monitoring operations and 90 days for complex operations.[6] To that end, the report calls for strengthening and refining the existing standby arrangement by setting up a roster of 100 military and 100 police personnel who are carefully preselected and able to join the UN Secretariat team on seven days' notice to participate in the planning and start-up of a new mission.[7] A roster of future SRSGs, force commanders, police commissioners, and other civilian specialists is also called for.[8]

At present UN practice regarding budget preparation, as well as the rules and regulations on financial and procurement matters that were originally designed for the general activities of the organization, are applied to peace operations as well, significantly delaying the process of organizing new missions. The panel's report recommended that these rules be adjusted to allow peace operations to be set up more rapidly, and to delegate greater authority from the Department of Management to the DPKO and field missions themselves. These changes, however, will require decisions by the General Assembly.

The report calls for significantly strengthening the DPKO, as the unit principally tasked to plan and support peace operations, in terms of both its staff level and financial base. It points out that the cost of UN Headquarters support for peace operations, centred in the DPKO, is currently only some 2 per cent of the cost of operations themselves, an unheard-of ratio. Some 85 per cent of DPKO staff are now financed from budgets of ongoing operations and must be authorized annually. The report recommends that DPKO resources be strengthened and the bulk of its costs be financed by the regular budget. It asserts that, while the staff level of the DPKO and other related units should "expand and contract to some degree in relation to the level of activity in the field",[9] after 52 years of peacekeeping this activity should no longer be treated as a temporary one but as a continuing and central task of the organization. This call is coupled with the recognition that both the Secretariat staff and mission personnel in the field must achieve a high standard of quality in performance and accountability, while at present the level is uneven. Managers should reward quality performance and weed out incompetence. The report calls on them to "keep in mind that the United Nations they serve is *the* universal organization. People everywhere are fully entitled to consider that it is *their* organization, and as such to pass judgment on its activities and the people who serve in it."[10]

The Brahimi Report and its recommendations are now before the member states, while the Secretary-General has already indicated that he will undertake to implement those recommendations that are within his authority. One can only hope that the lessons of the past will have been well learnt and appropriate action will be taken, so that in the future the Secretariat will be in a better position to support these vital activities of the United Nations.

Notes

1. UN Doc. A/3943, New York, United Nations, 9 October 1958.
2. Two of the 55 PKOs have been created by the General Assembly, the other 53 by the Security Council.
3. *Report of the Panel on United Nations Peace Operations*, A/55/305-S/2000/809, New York: UN General Assembly/Security Council, 21 August 2000.
4. *Ibid.*, paragraph 202.
5. *Ibid.*, paragraph 68.
6. *Ibid.*, paragraph 88.
7. *Ibid.*, paragraphs 110 and 125.
8. *Ibid.*, paragraphs 96 and 130.
9. *Ibid.*, paragraph 176.
10. *Ibid.*, p. xiv.

4

Policing the peace

Michael O'Connor

Most of the peacekeeping operations conducted in the past 12 years have attempted to deal with internal conflicts rather than the more traditional commitment to establishing peace between warring states. In these cases, the United Nations has sought to find a formula that would justify intervention in agreement with the UN Charter's unequivocal statement of respect for national sovereignty.[1] Usually, the formula is based on an invitation from the parties to the conflict to supervise a peace agreement reached under the auspices of the United Nations or an ad hoc international body.

All too often, agreements have proved to be extremely fragile and the peacekeeping mission has been unable under its mandate to prevent or put an end to the outbreak of violence. In the process, peacekeepers have been killed or taken prisoner, sometimes in substantial numbers. And every time such a breakdown occurs, the authority of the United Nations is further diminished. Sometimes it seems that some factions are only too ready to use violence to defy the authority of the United Nations because they recognize that they are immune from real sanctions and that the peacekeepers are less of a threat than their immediate antagonists. Current activities of the militias in East Timor and the insurgents in Sierra Leone are cases in point.

With the benefit of hindsight one also cannot but recognize the flaws in the agreements and mandates that have so often failed to deliver peace and stability. But if the international community declines to learn from those failures, there can be no justification for criticism of those UN members who refuse to contribute either money or personnel to current or future operations. Indeed, without such reform, the number of such backsliders may well increase in the future. The objective of this chapter is not so much to tease out the reasons for failure in peacekeeping operations, but to propose a number of principles that should guide operations in the future so that the United Nations is able not only to operate effectively but to gather and sustain the necessary political support for its primary task, "to maintain international peace and security".[2]

While the massive volumes of material published by the United Nations itself and many analysts around the world examine at length the causes of peacekeeping failure or operations' inadequate performance, they often fail to offer operationally credible alternatives. For the sake of effectiveness, a new paradigm is required – even if it does confront some long-standing traditions.

The following discussion will suggest that, especially in the case of internal conflicts, traditional peacekeeping should be abandoned in favour of peace enforcement, where the military component acts as a law enforcement constabulary under a dominant and impartial political authority rather than as a force interposed between warring factions and monitoring an unstable peace agreement.

The growth of community

One of the significant characteristics of the upsurge in UN-mandated peace operations, especially since the end of the Cold War, has been the focus on intrastate rather than interstate disputes. There are a number of reasons for this change, such that interstate conflicts are now less likely than they have been for generations, if not centuries. There is now a well-established system of interstate relations moderated in part by the growth of international political organizations at the global and regional levels. The work of these organizations in building peace and cooperation is further facilitated by the communications revolution, which assists conflict resolution before disputes get out of hand. This structural change is, oddly enough, supported – perhaps driven – by the development of modern, accurate, and highly destructive conventional weapons that make warfare between states incomparably more expensive than it used to be. Moreover, the end of the Cold War has virtually put an end to conflicts between smaller states where one or more sides have been backed by Cold War antagonists, raising the stakes for intervention and, potentially, conflict escalation.

On the other hand, the lack of such backing has revealed the political weakness of many smaller states beset by internal division. For all sorts of reasons, which are usually easily identifiable but not especially relevant here, this has led to an explosion of internal conflicts in which the state authorities may be a party, or at least incapable of establishing order in the face of that conflict for the benefit of the citizens for whom they have the primary responsibility.[3] Given that those state authorities are also the holders of the state's representation in the global and regional organizations, there is then an in-built obstacle to any external intervention in the interest of the citizenry except on terms acceptable to the state's leaders.

At the same time, the communications revolution, with its often colourful and near-instant global transmittal of the chaos and misery that results from such conflict, increases the pressure for international intervention. Similarly, the publicity operations of humanitarian agencies reinforce that pressure so that the global community is no longer ignorant of and to the sufferings of others. There is therefore the growing maturation of a global society, which is in conflict with the tradition of state sovereignty.

Historically, communities have grown progressively in stages from isolated families to local, regional, and national communities that are characterized by shared interests and structures of government. Following the disasters of the First and Second World Wars, deliberate attempts were made to establish a global system that would reflect interests shared by the whole of humanity, particularly our common interest in maintaining peace. The United Nations is the current manifestation of that aim. In recent years, the communications revolution has compressed time and space to such an extent that the notion of a global community is no longer as remote a concept as it was in 1945. Communities of interest groups, such as multinational companies, trade union organizations, and professional, human rights, environmental, and humanitarian groups, are emerging and transcend traditional national boundaries. They create growing pressures for a range of international agreements and the structures associated with their implementation. The United Nations, which sits somewhat uneasily at the summit of this evolving system, is also, through the Security Council, the only organization charged with maintaining "international peace and security".[4]

A core element in any security structure, be it local, regional, national, or international, is a system of law and its administration. Indeed, without the foundation of a body of law accepted by and governing relations between people and organizations, the legitimacy of society is open to question. Security issues will be decided in an arbitrary fashion and subject to political pressure by those powerful enough to coerce in their own interest. At the same time there is a growing body of international law and the associated judicial structures. Of course, countries suffering from internal conflict have their own domestic laws, albeit their enforcement is all too often non-existent or capricious.

Central to any system of government by law is an enforcement mechanism, as no society in history has ever been able to eliminate the law-breaker. In the Western tradition, the figure of Justice is a woman, blind-folded so as to be unable to distinguish between the parties, and bearing in one hand a set of scales which represents the role of justice in deciding issues on the basis of equity. But in the other hand, Justice bears a sword representing the authority to enforce decisions made by law. If it lacks a structure of enforcement without fear or favour and owing allegiance only to the law itself, the rule of law becomes subject to structures of power rather than of right. On the other hand, an enforcement process that is not backed by a structure of law and authority is merely vigilantism, neither authorized nor legitimate. This notion of justice according to law also confronts the treasured UN tradition of political impartiality. Justice is not always impartial because it is rooted in law. It must always be partial to and protect the party acting within the law against the law-breaker.

The Charter of the United Nations established the Security Council to be the organization's enforcement authority. However, the Council rules by political consensus rather than by impartial enforcement of a body of law. This is its fundamental weakness because, in many cases, its authority is based upon a consent that is all too often withheld or withdrawn at some stage in its operations. Nevertheless, it is also true that the authority of the Council has been upheld often enough for it to have acquired some permanent standing. The challenge for the future in a world that is shrinking and where the authority and legitimacy of the nation-state are diminishing is to ensure that the Council's future activities enhance its authority.[5]

Peacekeeping or peace enforcement – does it matter?

Much of the debate about the authority for UN intervention and the nature of that intervention revolves around the difference between traditional peacekeeping, authorized under Chapter VI of the UN Charter, or peace enforcement, authorized by Chapter VII. Traditional peacekeeping normally depends upon the existence of a genuine (as distinct from a tactical) political agreement between two states in conflict or between parties to a conflict within a state. The peacekeeping operation is concerned largely with monitoring this agreement. To a large extent, the peacekeeping operation is part of an overall package of assistance to a peace process facilitated by the United Nations.

By contrast, Chapter VII enforcement operations are based upon a response to an agreed threat to international peace. Almost implicit in the concept is a large-scale conflict between states that has an impact beyond the immediate area of the conflict. For a range of reasons, the United Nations has traditionally been ineffectual in peace enforcement. One reason has been the difficulty of gaining consensus among the permanent members of the Security Council, or at least enough of a consensus to avoid the use of a veto. But a further limitation has been the inability of the United Nations to deploy a credible and capable force without the leadership of a permanent member, usually the USA. Peace enforcement tends therefore to be carried out by contract, as it were, under a mandate over which the Security Council has little or no control. Moreover, once a mandate has been issued, it is virtually impossible for the Security Council to withdraw it because the veto power then operates in reverse to sustain the mandate.

In the case of intervention in an intrastate conflict, the Security Council has been compelled to go beyond its powers under the Charter's Chapters VI and VII. In most cases, Chapter VI does not apply because no peace agreement exists. In extreme cases, such as Somalia, the United Nations has operated or authorized operations in a country where no one of a number of claimants could seriously be regarded as the state authority. In such cases, the Council has resorted to artifice: simply asserting, for example, that a threat to international peace exists; or basing the deployment of a force upon support for humanitarian operations such as famine or natural disaster relief. Such expedients are risky not least because, as they base the authority of the United Nations on political expedience rather than law, they diminish the long-term authority that the United Nations ought to build. The fact that such interventions ordinarily stem from political pressure by individual state members on the United Nations to appear as if they were doing something is not a sufficient justification for intervention. In a practical sense, too, such intervention may well exacerbate a conflict, especially if, in trying to be impartial and minimalist, the intervention is ineffectual. A more soundly based justification is required if intervention is to be effective in the longer term.

In fact, the Charter offers a means of establishing UN authority in an intrastate conflict through Chapter XII, the international trusteeship system. In particular, Article 77.1(c) provides for a trusteeship to apply to "territories voluntarily placed under the system by states responsible for their administration". No limit is placed on the extent of the state territory that can be placed under trusteeship. The effect is to transfer authority for the government of the territory to the United Nations. The basic principle is that intervention is founded upon consent, but also a transfer of authority from the state to the United Nations until the United Nations itself surrenders that authority. Clearly, the consent principle is fundamental to the transfer of authority as long as the state concerned is not expelled or suspended from membership of the United Nations. However, it is always within the competence of the United Nations to persuade the state concerned to accept a trusteeship agreement. Such an arrangement might have been useful in parts of the former Yugoslavia.

Enforcing the peace

Re-establishing or building peace through enforcement is arguably more often necessary than not. What is important is to remain committed until the goals of the enforcement action are reached, rather than to set the limited and relatively simple objective of only ending violence. In several cases throughout the 1990s, the peace process failed because of this fundamental flaw. Thus, in the most extreme case in the Persian Gulf, simply expelling Iraq from Kuwait has done nothing to create peace in the region. The regional and global community is still faced with a continuing and intractable threat to peace and security.

In the former Yugoslavia and through large parts of Africa, peace operations have failed, and even where an uncertain truce exists it is sustained more by the threat of force than any persistent search for genuine peace and security. In many cases, well-armed and well-supported insurgents and governments seem content to wait out the various misnamed peacekeeping forces, believing that costs and weariness will cripple their determination. In the process, they use well-tried tactics of harassment to raise the political and financial costs of the peace operation while risking little from poorly conceived strategies. Leaving aside for the purposes of this chapter the political difficulties of authorizing enforcement action, there is a need to reassess the conceptual and organizational basis of peace operations to give them a better chance and, just possibly, encourage politicians and diplomats to believe and invest in their eventual success.

It is hardly novel to suggest that peace operations must incorporate and integrate three levels of action: the military to stop the fighting and disarm the combatants; the police and judiciary to re-establish a system of justice; and the community development personnel to rebuild and develop political systems, the economy, and social/civic structures. What does seem to be novel, at least in many peace operations, is a commitment to a coordinated strategy to achieve well-defined and sustainable objectives. In Somalia, for example, the initial objective was simply to provide humanitarian assistance in the face of famine. Yet it was soon apparent, at least to personnel in Somalia, that such an objective could not be achieved, much less sustained, without the use of force to neutralize the competing militias and bandits, and a further programme to rebuild the shattered institutions of society.[6] Without making and sustaining a commitment to the total package, peace operations become little more than well-meaning public demonstrations of concern by the international community.

In the general theory of modern policing, especially as developed in the common law societies, the goal is to keep the peace among the citizenry. This is something more than law enforcement, in that it validates intervention in a dispute to contain it so as to prevent a breach of the law. In the same way, society grants to the "peace officer" authority to use force to prevent a breach that it does not allow to the ordinary citizen. It is not an authority that is unaccountable; on the contrary, the police officer is solely and personally accountable. Translated into international peace operations, this suggests that wider authority should be given to UN forces at the outset of a mission. How this authority translates into action will be discussed further below. It does suggest, however, that the use of military force in peace operations should be driven more by concepts of law enforcement than of defeat of a designated enemy. It may also suggest that, in the context of traditional peacekeeping, the use of military forces should be kept to the absolute minimum, with more reliance being placed upon police or gendarmerie. Obviously, in more violent and extensive conflicts, military forces will have to be used because of their greater coercive power. But where coercive power is less important, military units should only be used where they have skills not otherwise available. Even in such cases as mine clearance, the use of competent civilian contractors, often ex-military personnel, may be preferable because they are less threatening. Expediency should not be a determinant in the decision to deploy military forces. That said, many of the peace operations of the past decade have demanded the use of military force. The key questions are what sorts of forces should be used, and how should they be organized?

At the outset of an operation, when the task is to put a stop to violence by the use or threat of use of force, the international force must have superior combat power as well as the freedom and determination to use it. The commitment of armed forces, whatever their mandate, represents a significant escalation that compels the various warring parties to reassess their own strategies. That reassessment, based on the capabilities and intentions of the intervention force, has a vast range of possible conclusions. At the extremes, they will, on the one hand, surrender and cede hostilities, or, on the other, combine however temporarily with their enemies to defeat and expel what they regard as an invader. If the re-establishment of peace is to have any chance, the intervention force must be able to persuade the parties that it can and will end hostilities. Many of the failures of peace operations can be attributed to the lack of capability and intention on the part of the intervener. Equally, successes such as that in eastern Slavonia in 1996 are a product of a manifest capability and intention to assert control.[7] As a broad matter of principle, an intervention should be supported by a mandate that denies all organizations except the intervention force the authority to maintain combat forces.

Clearly, any decision to intervene to put an end to conflict must be based on a worst-case assessment of various possibilities. One of the clear lessons to be learned from enforcement operations over the past decade is that the good faith of the parties cannot be taken for granted. Truce agreements, cease-fires, and similar accords are all too often tactical expedients accepted only to permit resupply or rest of tired forces, or an attempt to extract political advantage from a temporary tactical success. All too often, those negotiating for the conflicting parties are not able to control forces that owe only limited allegiance to their nominal political masters, or which may even control the political structures. Such agreements must be viewed by peace negotiators with the utmost scepticism and should not be allowed to determine the composition or posture of the intervention force.

Similarly, once a decision to intervene has been taken, the United Nations must ensure that proper operational priorities are established and maintained. In Bosnia and Somalia, for example, priority was given to humanitarian aid, and military force was deployed primarily to protect aid organizations and not to bring an end to fighting. As indicated above, there are three main fields of endeavour in a peace operation, each with its own peculiar requirements, but none can proceed unless fighting is ended and the parties' combatants are neutralized – either through comprehensive military defeat in the field, disarmament, interdiction of supplies, cantonment, or disbandment. Two elements of a peace operations paradigm are crucial in this context: the peacekeeping soldier and the military organization of peace operations.

The peacekeeper

In an internal conflict, the military operational focus must always recognize that, while priority has to be given to ending the fighting, the command and the individual troops must pay close attention to the welfare of the ordinary people, who are not only the principal victims of the fighting, but whose support for the overall peace process is crucial. Moreover, in crude military terms the local population is a prime source of tactical intelligence.[8] If the local community sees the interventionist troops as effective protectors, they will supply information about enemy strengths and movements as well as information about pending operations. A peace force that fails to cultivate and neglects this asset will be hamstrung. Thus any policy of non-fraternization or non-involvement with the local community will doom the operation. Soldiers who are very committed as individuals to voluntary aid and relief work over and above their mission will contribute to a perception of them as helpers, often in contra-distinction to their oppressors. By contrast, the American policy of strict non-fraternization reinforces a view that all soldiers, regardless of nationality and uniform, are equally poorly prepared to cultivate friendly relations with their hosts.[9]

The individual UN soldier is the person with whom the local community comes mostly into contact. Manning his roadblock or leading an anti-bandit patrol, the young lieutenant or corporal is the key element of the peace operation. Very often young and experiencing his first encounter with a foreign environment and community that are at least initially both alien and dangerous, he is working under great stress in circumstances where more experienced and senior leaders are not readily available. His reaction to incidents can have far-reaching effects for good or otherwise on the success of the mission. But if he combines manifest military professionalism with a genuine and personal concern for the simple welfare needs of the local civilian community, he will contribute greatly to the success of the mission. He is at once "ambassador, peacekeeper, teacher and soldier".[10] For success, then, the policy of drawing peace operations troops from a wide range of countries with varying cultures and military skills demands a review if modern peace operations are to be successful.

Many cultures throughout the world value some variation of the tradition of knightly chivalry that combines military skill with a predisposition to protection of the weak. It is a tradition all too often honoured in the breach as well as being foreign to some cultures, but it does offer a guide to the type of troops that should be sought for peace operations. Arguably, relatively few military forces in the world combine high professionalism with an inherent as well as fostered cult of protection of the defenceless. In some cases, a cultural commitment to protection of the weak is actively discouraged within the military profession because it is perceived to be a source of weakness rather than strength. In some cases, of course, it has proved impossible to overcome cultural mores by military training. Early in the US deployment to Haiti, a young American military police lieutenant contravened his orders, training, and rules of engagement to intervene forcibly to prevent the murder of a Haitian civilian by government thugs. Paradoxically, this had dramatic and positive results by forcing a change in the rules of engagement and the perceptions of the intervention force by all parties in Haiti.

Other cultures simply do not value assistance to the weak and helpless. Without being specific as to country, one senior officer in an interview expressed puzzlement at the idea. He simply could not conceive that such behaviour had any social or military value to the operational task. In any case, he argued, language difficulties made such behaviour impossible. By contrast, the commandant of Malaysia's Peacekeeping Training Centre commented that the ordinary soldier quickly picked up enough of the local language to be able to relate comfortably to the local community if he was encouraged to do so.[11]

Some of the great religions that underpin culture are valuable in fostering chivalry. Both Christianity and Islam have clearly articulated doctrines on the limits of justifiable homicide and just war as well as protection of the weak. These teachings, not always honoured, nevertheless reinforce the vital distinction between the law-abiding citizen in need of protection and the law-breaker whose activities must be contained. In seeking national contingents for peace operations, the United Nations and regional organizations sponsoring such operations need to look for such religious and cultural underpinnings. Sound practices can be instilled by generalized as well as mission-specific training and education, but only up to a certain point without that cultural underpinning.[12]

The second element is military professionalism. Peace operations, especially in peace enforcement, demand highly skilled combat soldiers. Even if their skills are not required in all circumstances, they may be in some. By their lack of effectiveness, poorly trained and led troops have only limited value for the force commander, and in extreme cases may become a severe embarrassment and liability. More to the point, the presence of well-armed and well-trained troops, with the scope and ability to interpret the rules of engagement flexibly, will tend to overawe the often ill-trained near-bandits who make up both the insurgent groups and government forces in many if not most countries suffering internal conflict.

The variation in military professionalism around the world is vast. It ranges from the high-technology military force built upon the so-called revolution in military affairs in the USA to what might politely be described as bandits in uniform, skilled only in oppression of the defenceless. Even among those accepted for peace operations, the variation in military skills is substantial, with one very professional and experienced peacekeeper[13] describing various national contingents as "professional", "good but rigid", "hopeless", "patchy", "good but dependent upon a single senior officer", "hopeless and apprehensive", and "flashy". Even among the most professional, the lack of a sound concept of operations or operational doctrine can vitiate the capacity for effective peace operations. The USA, for example, has been working hard at producing a doctrine for what it calls "operations other than war", but a number of factors combine to reduce their effectiveness substantially. American concepts are heavily oriented to the use of technology and rigid adherence to doctrine. Soldiers are actively discouraged from fraternization with the local population, and from tactical and operational flexibility. Moreover, the intense political sensitivity to casualties tends to make the Americans concentrate more on force security than operational effectiveness.[14]

Selection of contingents for peace operations has to become more selective. One mark of a sophisticated society is the division of labour within the society. Gardeners are not used as policemen; both need special and unique skills and training to do their jobs properly. So it should be for troops selected for peace operations. They must be selected on the basis of military professionalism and cultural commitment to respect for human rights and protection of the weak and defenceless. This will be politically sensitive, but failure to do so threatens the success of the mission, especially in the more demanding missions.

Other factors come into play when selecting national contingents. For example, selecting contingents for deployments to countries with a history of pre-independence colonialism suggests that the former colonial power should not be asked to provide troops. Even where the country itself has no continuing interest in its former colony, the perception that it may do or a history of bitterness will taint and limit the effectiveness of the whole force.

Apart from the issue of competence, the policy of the USA that its troops may not serve under foreign command effectively transfers authority and responsibility for the mission to that country. As the world's foremost military power, American support and leadership are pre-eminently essential for the success of a major mission such as the expulsion of Iraq from Kuwait. On the other hand, the weaknesses of American policy and doctrine forced the abandonment of UNOSOM II, the continuing attempt to bring peace to Somalia in 1995.

As well as professionalism and cultural factors, similar traditions and military doctrines and the extensive use of a common language, although less important, are factors that should be taken into account when constructing a peace operations force. Similar considerations apply to police contingents, with the further element that familiarity with the target country's basic legal system would be an advantage.

While much of the success of a peace operation thus depends upon the quality of the individual personnel – military, police, or civilian – there is clearly a range of factors that must bear on the selection and operations of the national contingents and the force itself. This calls for an assessment of the existing UN command system. The remainder of this chapter will focus on the command and control of the military component of peace operations, with only passing reference to the military/police/civilian interface.

Organizing for peace operations

There is no particular mystery about military command and control. Systems vary in detail and effectiveness, but overall they are very similar. What the United Nations has failed to do is design and adopt an effective system. In part this is due to the traditional sensitivity of an organization devoted to peace in dealing with structures devoted to the precise application of physical force. Nevertheless, the UN Charter itself as well as experience in many peace operations, especially in the 1990s, clearly anticipate the use of military forces to enforce or support peace operations. Article 47 of the Charter establishes a Military Staff Committee comprising the chiefs of staff of the five permanent members of the Security Council to advise the Council and Secretary-General on the use of military forces. Article 47.3 gives the responsibility for the strategic direction of UN forces to the committee but clearly indicates that this is a temporary arrangement.[15] In fact the Military Staff Committee is widely regarded as moribund, partly as a result of the Cold War experience, which prevented cooperation among the chiefs of staff, and partly because its structure is fundamentally clumsy.

Although not provided for in the Charter, there is a military adviser who normally ranks as a lieutenant-general. However, his authority is doubtful. Although strictly speaking he is the adviser to the Secretary-General, in practice his chain of command is through the Under-Secretary-General for Peacekeeping Operations. Similarly the military officers in the Department of Peacekeeping Operations (DPKO) are scattered through the various divisions of the department and appear to have dual lines of responsibility to the military adviser and the Under-Secretary-General. Given the hard lessons that have been learned through the 1990s, the time is surely ripe for the establishment of a more effective system for the command and control of UN military capabilities.

Technically the problem is simple, although the political obstacles are profound. What the United Nations needs is a professional military staff under the control of the military adviser, who would be directly responsible to the Secretary-General for the development of military policy and the strategic command of the military aspect of peace operations. Moreover, being more than an adviser, his title should be changed to chief of staff. A professional military staff would have to be appointed to take responsibility for the whole range of strategic and operational-level military command. Of course, the military component of any particular operation would be subordinate to the political authority established by the Security Council, but the selection of contingents, their equipment and logistic support, training and doctrinal development, and other aspects of strategic command would be the responsibility of the UN's military staff.

The chief of staff ought to be selected from a shortlist of senior professional soldiers in the member countries of the United Nations. But, upon selection, he should be required to resign his commission in his national military organization and become an international soldier with allegiance only to the United Nations. It would be for decision then whether his appointment would be for the traditional fixed and short term or whether he would hold the appointment at the pleasure of the Security Council or Secretary-General. The actual selection of the chief of staff is one task that could usefully be assigned to the Military Staff Committee, subject to endorsement by the Security Council.

The staff, on the other hand, should comprise national officers released for duty with the United Nations under arrangements formally negotiated with their home governments. They would staff the usual branches, including intelligence, plans and operations, training, and logistics. An important non-standard branch would be responsible for civil/military operations, handling such issues as the interface with police and civilian operations as well as military assistance like mine clearance and civil aid for these operations.

Such a structure need not be large because it would be concerned more with policy and administration rather than the conduct of operations. The latter task would be the responsibility of the individual operation's force commander and his staff. A critical element, however, would be the intelligence branch. The United Nations traditionally has shown a reluctance to seek and use intelligence except at the diplomatic level. On the other hand, the lack of adequate intelligence, political, military, and economic, has contributed to serious problems in a number of missions, most notably in Africa.

A military staff intelligence branch would not be structured to collect covert intelligence. Much of the data it would need would be available in the public domain, while other material may become available from member states as a result of formal agreements. The early warning of potential commitments would come from the Political Affairs Department of the United Nations, but the military branch would be required to assess the military capabilities of the parties to the conflict as a basis for advice to the plans and operations branch. It would, of course, be an important source of information to the mission commander and his staff as well as drawing data and analysis from the mission's own intelligence branch.

The plans and operations branch would, above all, be responsible for selecting contingents from those countries considered willing and able to provide suitable troops. The branch would necessarily specify the types of military capabilities required for specific missions, and arrange for deployment to the areas of operation. As indicated above, this task would, at least for the more demanding missions, abandon the practice of drawing contingents from a wide range of sources. Selection would be on the basis of military competence for peace operations in accordance with stringent criteria.

These criteria would be established by the training and doctrine branch.

Developing a modern peace operations doctrine for military contingents poses a substantial challenge for a highly professional staff. Much good work is being done by some member countries in their peacekeeping training centres and by existing military staff. However, the importance of recognizing the vastly different levels of capability of potential national contingents and the implications of this for effective operations is still not fully appreciated.

The doctrine branch will also be responsible for establishing training programmes for troops and commanders. The actual training will be carried out by national armed forces, while the UN military staff should be responsible not only for certification of the national training centres but also the regular validation of their programmes.

The logistics branch will be responsible for arranging transport of the national contingents, their equipment if upgrading is required, and the timely resupply of basic essentials such as food, fuel, spare parts, and ammunition. Even if the actual logistic support is provided by national authorities, it will be necessary for the UN staff to ensure that those authorities are doing their job. In effect, the United Nations must take responsibility for the effective support of any mission it authorizes.

The provision by the United Nations of an effective military staff to plan, support, and oversee operations based upon a sound doctrine will generate confidence in the peacekeeping role of the organization. It will ensure that missions are backed by effective military forces that cannot be seen by the conflicting parties as vulnerable, and it should lead to an improvement in the professional competence of those national armed forces selected for peace operations.

Obstacles

Any serious examination of the UN's role and capability in the field of peace operations quickly identifies an extensive range of obstacles – some obvious, some more or less unstated. Coupled with these obstacles is a reluctance to confront and overcome them, even though failure to do so not only threatens the organization's effectiveness but also leads key countries to abandon support for the United Nations. The USA is only the most obvious of these, but others, including Australia, have become disillusioned to the extent of reducing their commitments to token levels.

Problems with the doctrine of sovereignty operate at different levels. The question of the authority of the United Nations to intervene in an intrastate conflict has been discussed above. While intervention can often be justified on political grounds, doing so on legal grounds is much more difficult as long as the doctrine of national sovereignty remains supreme.[16] The permanent members of the Security Council exercise considerable influence and, sometimes, power. There is very little consistency or predictability about the way in which they operate, so that, by changing their minds for whatever reason, they are able to cripple a mission that has already been launched. On the other hand, many of the smaller nations seek out opportunities to assert their sovereignty even where their real interests are not directly affected. Upon the request of a number of smaller countries, led by the Bahamas, the DPKO in 1998 replaced some 100 professional military officers working in the DPKO on secondment from their own governments with officers employed under contract after open tender and paid for by the United Nations. This was partly an exercise in third world, anti-Western assertiveness and partly an opportunistic bid for greater access to the UN gravy train. But the effect has been not only to rob the United Nations of a low-cost professional staff but also to discourage further those countries whose professional military forces are the most necessary for the success of peace operations. It is noteworthy that the General Assembly resolution to dispose of this group was adopted without a vote, suggesting that those countries which provided and paid for the capability were fundamentally disillusioned.[17]

As suggested above, the doctrine of impartiality is an obstacle to peace enforcement based upon the rule of law. The law cannot be impartial between on the one hand those who submit to and respect the law, and on the other those who defy the law when it suits them. In such cases, impartiality is a weapon that does not serve justice. However, with the establishment of the International Criminal Court, the potential exists for that court in conjunction with the International Court of Justice to make determinations on the lawfulness or otherwise of individuals, groups, and activities that affect security. In some senses, however, the doctrine of impartiality offers the United Nations and its agencies the opportunity to avoid making judgements that it ought to make if its peacemaking role is to be effective. Peace is not achieved by refusing to make judgements between lawful and unlawful actions, and the international community must soon accept that there are individuals, groups, and nations that are unwilling to accept the rule of law.

If that is naive, even more so is the belief that diplomatic practices and diplomatic credulity are often in themselves obstacles to peace operations. In Bosnia, for example, and more recently in Kosovo and Angola, the process of negotiating deals – cease-fires, withdrawals, truces, or whatever term is preferred – with individuals or groups that have frequently demonstrated a contempt for those deals may be good for newspaper headlines. However, these deals achieve little beyond the death of more innocents. Their tendency to agree to the deployment of unarmed military and, increasingly, civilian observers simply adds more potential hostages to the chessboard while creating an illusion of achievement.

The Security Council and the UN Secretariat need to review the process of developing mission mandates and rules of engagement. There is a tendency to micro-manage these from New York and to be too specific in detail. This can lead to substantial difficulty for a mission in the field that tries to deal with a fast-developing situation, such as the one in Rwanda. Similarly, micro-management of the UN Protection Force (UNPROFOR) mandate in the former Yugoslavia resulted in nine changes between June and December of 1992.[18] Mandates and rules of engagement need to be more directive than specific, giving the UN special representative and the force commander in the field greater autonomy in making changes. Similarly the military commander must have some freedom to modify rules of engagement so that he can protect not only his own force but also the overall mandate and the non-combatant civilian population.

Conclusion

This chapter has not attempted to examine the issue of resources for peace operations. That issue is large and complex, and some innovative ideas have been floated in the international community. The problem is bound up with the overall question of reform of the United Nations. Beyond noting here that it is important in the context of peace operations, it is worth emphasizing the point that key nations are increasingly reluctant to contribute to peace operations because of uncertainty about their objectives and the traditional lack of professionalism in managing them effectively.

In any peace operation, much depends upon political will and persistence. If the package is committed, it has to be on the understanding that it is there for the long haul, casualties and cost notwithstanding. Contributing countries have to be confident that their forces will be professionally supported and commanded, and that the mission has clear and achievable objectives that are not subject to political whims. If the commitment and the professionalism are lacking or if the mission is judged unlikely to be successful, it is better not attempted.

Notes

1. Charter of the United Nations, Articles 2 and 78 (hereafter referred to as the "Charter").
2. Charter, Article 1.1.
3. Ninety-one out of 96 conflicts between the end of the Cold War and 1996 were interstate in nature. See Connie Peck, *Sustainable Peace*, Lanham: Rowman and Littlefield, 1998, p. 25.

4. Charter, Article 1.1.
5. This chapter does not look at the issue of Security Council reform. Although it is an important issue, its delay does not necessarily deny legitimacy or effectiveness to the Council or the United Nations.
6. A very readable account of the Australian experience in UNITAF, the US-led Unified Task Force, is contained in Bob Breen, *A Little Bit of Hope*, Sydney: Allen & Unwin, 1998. See also the more exculpatory UN Blue Book Series Vol. VIII, *The United Nations and Somalia, 1992–1996*, New York: United Nations, 1996.
7. *Lessons Learned July 1998 – The United Nations Transitional Administration in eastern Slavonia, Baranja and Western Sirmium (UNTAES) January 1996–January 1998*, New York: United Nations, Lessons Learned Unit, Department of Peacekeeping Operations, 1998.
8. See especially Breen, note 6, Chapters 3, 4, and 9.
9. Interview with Lieutenant-Colonel Phil Wilkinson, staff officer, Peace Support Operations, Ministry of Defence, London, 29 October 1988.
10. *Ibid.*
11. Interview with Lieutenant-Colonel John Derick Osman, Kuala Lumpur, 9 November 1998.
12. The training manuals and publications produced for all peacekeeping soldiers by the UN Department of Peacekeeping Operations are technically excellent, but they assume an underlying cultural predisposition of respect for the weak and defenceless.
13. The person shall remain nameless for obvious reasons.
14. Osman interview, note 11, validated by Wilkinson, note 9.
15. The second sentence of Article 47.3 states: "Questions relating to the command of such forces shall be worked out subsequently." Almost 56 years later, "subsequently" is yet to arrive.
16. Article 2.1 of the Charter emphasizes the principle of sovereign equality. Any attempt to bypass the principle by using Articles 5 and 6 carries political risks that the United Nations has been reluctant to confront.
17. General Assembly Resolution A/Res/53/11.
18. Interview with Lieutenant-General Satish Nambiar, New Delhi, 11 November 1998.

Part II

Regional experiences

5

Regional peacekeeping in the CIS

S. Neil MacFarlane

Through the decade of the 1990s there has been considerable analysis of regional options for peace-related operations. This reflects several factors. In the first place, the UN Charter privileges regional responses to threats to peace and security.[1] In addition, in the 1990s regional responses were seen as a way to reduce the burden on the peacekeeping capacities of the United Nations itself.[2] Many also argued that regional organizations may be more effective, given their knowledge of the ground and the fact that their members are likely to have sufficient interest in the maintenance of peace in their backyard to be willing to deploy the resources necessary to keep the peace. The 1999 Australian deployment in East Timor illustrated the point. The decade also produced a wealth of experience of regional peace operations. Major examples include the activities of the Economic Community of West African States (ECOWAS) and its peacekeeping force, the Economic Community Monitoring Group (ECOMOG) in Liberia and Sierra Leone; the work of the Organization of American States (OAS) in Central America; that of the Conference (since 1994 Organization) for Security and Cooperation in Europe (C/OSCE) in Central and Eastern Europe; and that of the North Atlantic Treaty Organization (NATO) and its partners in Bosnia and Kosovo.

One of the more sustained regional efforts to keep the peace in the 1990s was that of Russia and the Commonwealth of Independent States (CIS) in dealing with the security problems raised by the collapse of the USSR.[3] This collapse was accompanied by substantial civil conflict in four republics: Moldova, Georgia, Azerbaijan, and Tajikistan. Russian forces – operating either bilaterally on the basis of agreement with the parties or multilaterally under the mantle of the CIS[4] – took on peacekeeping roles in three of the four states between 1992 and 1994, Azerbaijan being the exception. In each instance they remain on the ground at the time of writing.[5] Complex relationships have developed between Russian forces and various observer missions mounted by international organizations. In Moldova, the peacekeeping mission has coordinated its activities with the OSCE Mission of Long-Term Duration in Moldova. In Georgia, the Russian-led peacekeeping operation in South Ossetia is observed by military staff in the OSCE Mission of Long-Term Duration in Georgia. In Abkhazia (Georgia), personnel of the UN Observer Mission in Georgia (UNOMIG) perform a similar role. The split of responsibility between the OSCE and the United Nations with regard to Georgia's civil conflicts is based on an understanding between the two organizations reached in 1993.[6]

The "subcontracting" of peacekeeping roles to regional organizations, or for that matter major regional states, presumes that in their efforts to manage conflict they will serve the broader UN purpose of enhancing peace and security through the peaceful resolution of conflict, and that in so doing they will conform to UN peacekeeping norms. In addition, beyond the specific norms governing the rules of engagement and the political disinterestedness of peacekeeping operations, there are important human rights and other humanitarian norms at issue in peacekeeping operations. The chapter examines the extent to which Russian and CIS peacekeeping meets these tests. It begins with a discussion of several potential problems in the reliance on regional actors for peace-related operations. This is followed by an analysis of evolving Russian objectives in the former Soviet space. The chapter then turns to a brief empirical account of Russian experiences of peace operations in the region. It concludes with an assessment of patterns evident in and lessons that might be drawn from this accumulation of experience. The chapter does not discuss the issue of Chechnya (or, for that matter, North Ossetia and Daghestan). The latter operations – although sometimes characterized by Russian analysts as peacekeeping (*operatsii po podderzhaniu mira*) or peacemaking (*mirotvorchestvo*) – occur within the domestic jurisdiction of the Russian Federation and range between counterinsurgency and full-scale conventional war. As such, they are obviously not relevant here. The chapter also does not discuss the conflict in the breakaway Azerbaijani region of Nagorno-Karabakh. Although Russia has been heavily involved in the process of mediation of this conflict, and was instrumental in achieving a cease-fire in May 1994, no peacekeeping mission has ever been deployed.

Problems in regional peacekeeping[7]

The potential advantages of reliance on regional actors for conflict management are reasonably clear in deductive terms. As already noted, such strategies reduce burdens on the United Nations. Regional organizations are more likely to provide the resources necessary for regional peacekeeping, since their interests are directly engaged. Regional actors know the players in local conflicts, and hence may be capable of more effective mediation. Response may be easier politically, since multilateral response is less likely to be hamstrung by extraneous issues unrelated to the conflict in question, such as, for instance, China's role in complicating UN responses in Haiti and Guatemala, and also their withdrawal of support for the UN Preventive Deployment (UNPREDEP) in Macedonia, all of which seem to have been related to the policies of the states in question regarding Taiwan, or the implicit US veto of any substantial response to Rwanda's genocide, which reflected the unhappy American experience in Somalia six months earlier.

The potential disadvantages are equally clear in the abstract. In the first place, the fact that regional actors' interests are directly engaged in a local conflict may be as much a complication as it is a facilitating factor. Particular states in the region may have taken sides in the conflict in question. They may see the conflict to be tightly tied to wider regional competition for power. It is clear, for example, that Nigerian support for Samuel Doe and francophone states' support of Charles Taylor greatly complicated the ECOWAS response to the civil war in Liberia. Moreover, distributions of power in specific regions are often asymmetrical, and regionally dominant states often treat regional organizations as instruments of regional hegemony. Nigeria's hold on ECOWAS is again a good example, as is the traditional American approach to the OAS. The experience of CIS peacekeeping displays similar patterns. As is evident below, "CIS" peacekeeping largely reflected particular Russian interests that may or may not have coincided with the broader search for peace. The organization was used as a fig leaf to legitimize these interests. That is to say, there is reason to believe that the impartiality frequently deemed necessary in peacekeeping and mediation may be more difficult to achieve at the regional than at the global level. In this respect, the notion of "subcontracting" is somewhat problematic. Regional peacekeeping efforts generally emerge not from a deliberate devolution of responsibility from the United Nations to the regional organization or power in question. Instead, they emerge for the most part out of the (often self-interested) policy agendas of regional actors who then seek legitimization for their activities from the United Nations. To cite two examples, ECOWAS intervention in the Liberian civil war and Russian intervention in the war in Abkhazia both predated Security Council approval of the operations.

Outside Western and Central Europe, the administrative, financial, and military and logistical capacities of regional organizations to manage conflict leave much to be desired. Moreover, the effectiveness of regional cooperation rests importantly on the effectiveness of states that make up regional organizations. In some regions (such as Africa) weak states predominate, limiting the potential for regional cooperation. This problem has specific relevance to the former Soviet Union. The non-Russian newly independent states have generally lacked the financial capacity to contribute to post-Soviet peacekeeping. As for Russia, peacekeeping and conflict-resolution activities in the ex-Soviet space have been matters of significant internal dissension and the focus of sustained struggle between various centres of power over policy (for example, the Ministry of Foreign Affairs and the Ministry of Defence). This has made interaction between international organizations and the Russian government peculiarly frustrating.

Discussion of the advantages and disadvantages of regional approaches to peacekeeping raises the question of whether cooperation between the United Nations and regional organizations might not permit the international community to benefit from these bodies' comparative advantages as producers of regional security while mitigating their disadvantages. The problem of impartiality can be addressed to some extent through observer missions that enhance transparency and socialize regional military forces into international norms. The CIS provides two examples where UN forces played such a role – UNOMIG in Abkhazia and the UN Mission of Observers in Tajikistan (UNMOT) – while the OSCE (formerly CSCE) has played a similar role in Moldova and South Ossetia. External financial, capacity-building, and logistical support can compensate for the shortcomings of regional bodies in these areas. Experiences in West Africa and the former Soviet Union suggest, however, that the international community has yet to realize the full potential of such collaboration and task-sharing.[8]

The above analysis allows the identification of a number of deductive propositions of specific relevance to Russian and CIS peacekeeping that are tested in the pages that follow. This characterization of the advantages and disadvantages of regional peacekeeping would lead us to expect that such forms of peace operations would be less impartial, more forceful, more self-interested, and less reflective of and constrained by international norms related to intervention and consent, legitimacy, the use of force, and humanitarian action.

Peace operations and Russian objectives in the former Soviet space

The weakness of the Russian state, the disorganized quality of policy-making, and the obvious and rancorous dissensus over foreign policy and military issues that characterized much of the period since 1991 make it difficult to speak with confidence about Russian objectives in the other newly independent states. Generalization was particularly problematic in the early years, when discourse on foreign policy was divided into liberal Westernizing, nationalist-communist, and Eurasian schools of thought.[9] However, by late 1992 and early 1993 a consensus on aims appeared to be emerging, at least in the so-called "near abroad".

The former Soviet periphery of Russia had been largely neglected in the first months after the collapse of the USSR. Policy was dominated in the first instance by coping with pressing domestic issues of reform and by the clear desire to sustain close and cooperative relations with the West. The latter was a product not merely of the evolution of foreign policy during the Gorbachev era, but of the perception of a clear need for a continuing stream of Western assistance in the early phase of transition. However, by late 1992 it was clear that Russian perceived interests were heavily engaged in the Federation's neighbouring states. This was most obvious for the nationalist/communist fringe who had not reconciled themselves to the loss of empire and saw the independence of the other former Soviet republics as a temporary inconvenience.[10]

For less extreme groups, more concrete issues prevailed. In the first place, the dissolution of the USSR had left some 25 million Russians outside the Federation. Their security was widely considered to be a matter of legitimate interest for the Russian state, not only as a result of kin-country loyalty with a diaspora in difficult circumstances, but also because failure to address the fears of these groups could (and in the case of Central Asia did) result in a massive return of ethnic Russians, a prospect with which the Russian Federation was hardly in a position to cope.

Instability in the other newly independent states produced other negative externalities for Russia, including criminal activity and arms and narcotics traffic. Finally, for geopolitical reasons, many in Russia were concerned about the security implications of the possibly growing influence of other major regional powers (such as Turkey and Iran) and extra-regional powers (such as the Western states) in proximity to Russian borders. Such concerns extended to the possibility of direct military roles for international organizations such as the United Nations and the C/OSCE. One influential analysis of Russia's interests argued quite directly in 1996 that "it is definitely not in Russia's interest to see outside mediation and peacekeeping operations on the territory of the former Soviet Union".[11]

This was linked to a further and more practical reasoning: the ground and air defence and border control infrastructures inherited from the USSR were located for the most part in the non-Russian republics. To the extent that the Russians took defence and border control seriously, they could either seek to control these facilities outside their borders or they could invest in the creation of replacements within Russia. The latter option was prohibitively expensive. Concerns over the role of Turkey – and more particularly Iran – were linked to fears of the spread of Islamic fundamentalism in the ex-USSR. These concerns focused also on the on-going civil conflict and growing influence of Islamists in Afghanistan, and the close links between political and military trends in Afghanistan and Tajikistan.[12] In view of the incursions of militants of the Islamic Movement of Uzbekistan (IMU) in Kyrgyzstan in 1999 and 2000, the threat of "Islamic" extremism in the former Soviet south has taken on new salience in Russian foreign policy under President Putin.

Concern over the accretion of outsiders' influence in the region was not limited to the political/military and ideological spheres. Russian political élites also perceived a clear interest in retaining access to the region's resources (for example, Caspian Basin energy reserves) and a degree of control over their development. Their diplomacy displayed a deep sensitivity to the expansion of Western public and private efforts to integrate these resources directly into broader world markets. This was evident, for example, in their sustained efforts in 1993–1996 to sabotage negotiations on joint ventures between Azerbaijan and Western energy firms and prevent the development of pipeline alternatives to existing lines through the Russian Federation, and the Russian position in the long-standing dispute over ownership of the Caspian Sea floor.

Russian policy towards the other newly independent states was driven not only by a rational strategic calculus. There was an important domestic dimension as well. A growing segment of Russian political opinion profiled government failures to address the historical legacy and interests of Russia in the "near abroad" in its general critique of Russia's foreign policy. To the extent that leaders sought to deflect this criticism, they had to be seen to be acting in defence of these perceived interests.

Peace operations responded to most of the major concerns outlined above. The deployment of Russian forces in such missions was a means of containing instability and spillover. It contributed to sustaining Russian influence in affected states. And it served as a means to preclude strategic penetration of the region by outside powers and organizations. As shall be seen in the next section, however, Russian policy on peace operations evolved over time in important ways.

The Russian and CIS experience of peacekeeping in the newly independent states

As noted in the introduction, there are four major instances of Russian use of force in peacekeeping in the former Soviet space. All were responses to civil and ethnic strife in the early days after the collapse of the USSR.

Moldova

The first case for consideration is that of Moldova.[13] In this instance, the russophone minority was alienated from the Moldovan mainstream in 1989 by the growing "Romanian" nationalism of the majority's popular front. This culminated in 1990 with the passage of Moldova's language law, which established Moldavian as the state language and the Latin alphabet as the official form of writing. It also specified the Romanian identity of the Moldavian language and thus underlined the pan-Romanian proclivities of the majority.

The Russian minority constituted 12.2 per cent of the total population. On the left bank of the Dnestr River, Russians constituted 25 per cent of the district's 546,000 people, while Moldovans constituted 39.9 per cent and Ukrainians 28.3 per cent. Although Transdniestr was therefore hardly a Russian region, the picture is somewhat different if one looks at urban population. The district's capital, Tiraspol, for example, had 82,400 Russians and 64,200 Ukrainians out of a population of 198,500.[14] These groups constituted the core of a subsequent secessionist movement.

Anger over the language law and a general sense of insecurity amongst the Slavic minority population produced a revolt in 1990 when the Transdniestr Republic was declared by regional authorities. A year later, the region defied the Moldovan government by participating in the spring 1991 referendum on the fate of the USSR and voted massively in support of a reconstituted union. The region also backed the August 1991 coup in Moscow.

This produced war between March and June 1992, as the *de facto* authorities of the Transdniestr Republic sought to consolidate their control over their bank of the Dnestr River. Secessionist forces were fortunate in the presence in their territory of the former Soviet 14th Army. The war stocks of this formation were sufficient to arm a force of some 200,000 soldiers. They were repeatedly raided by Transdniestrian forces, losing some 20,000 small weapons in 1991–1992. Officers from the 14th Army – often Russians permanently resident in the area – were seconded to or defected from the 14th Army to Transdniestrian units. When secessionist forces crossed the Dnestr River to secure the city of Bendery in mid-1992, they were assisted by the 14th Army. Russian politicians and policy-makers repeatedly voiced their opposition to Moldovan Romanianization and their support for their kin in Transdniestria.[15]

Matters changed gradually after Moscow reasserted control over the 14th Army in April 1992, and later when Moscow appointed General Aleksandr Lebed to command the force in June 1992. The 14th Army intervened directly in the conflict, interposing itself between the parties after Transdniestrian forces had consolidated control over the left bank as well as the city of Bendery. Russian forces shifted to a policy of "armed neutrality", and Lebed redefined the mission to "deter the outbreak of combat [and] to create the conditions for the cease-fire and thereafter guarantee the cease-fire agreement".[16]

A cease-fire agreement followed on 21 July 1992 with an agreement between Russian President Boris Yeltsin and Moldovan President Segur on a cease-fire, the establishment of a security zone along the front line, and the insertion of a peacekeeping force, originally composed of two Transdniestrian, two Moldovan, and five Russian battalions (approximately 2,000 men, originally drawn from the combatants themselves). In addition, the agreement provided for a Joint Control Commission (JCC) composed of six Russians, six Moldovans, and six representatives of Transdniestria. Since 1993, the peacekeeping operations have been observed by a mission of the C/OSCE. OSCE access to the proceedings of the JCC has been limited, but the organization has played a constructive role in promoting the process of negotiation and has had a significant reassuring influence on the Moldovan side, not least by reiterating OSCE commitment to the norm of territorial integrity.

The deployment of peacekeepers produced lasting stability, despite the occasional incident and despite the downsizing of the Russian component of the force by approximately 50 per cent in November 1994.[17] However, the parties had great difficulty in translating the cease-fire into an agreement on political settlement. In this effort, the Russians were hamstrung by the connection between the fate of Transdnestria and their own domestic politics. On the one hand, the Transdniestrians proved deeply problematic for the Yeltsin government by providing a rallying point for the neo-fascist and communist opposition, and actually intervened in Russian politics on behalf of Yeltsin's adversaries. Transdniestrian volunteers, for example, assisted in the defence of the Russian Duma against the assault by forces loyal to President Yeltsin in 1993. On the other hand, any compromise on the question would be exploited by the Russian right to challenge the government's patriotic credentials.

South Ossetia (Georgia)

The gradual descent of South Ossetia into war began in approximately the same period and for more or less the same reason. South Ossetia had been an autonomous *oblast* in the Soviet period with a population that was approximately two-thirds Osset. The decay of the USSR was accompanied by the blossoming of extremely chauvinist forms of Georgian nationalism. Ultimately, when Georgia's nationalist opposition won power in 1990, South Ossetia began its movement towards secessionism by unilaterally upgrading its political status to "republic". This action was rejected by the Georgian government, which retaliated by unilaterally abrogating the region's autonomous status. The situation deteriorated rapidly into war, with Georgian paramilitaries and defence units seeking to extinguish the rebellion while the South Ossets resisted more or less successfully with considerable assistance from their ethnic kin across the Russian border in North Ossetia, and, some say, with help from Soviet military units stationed in the region. Efforts by the central Moscow authorities to stabilize the situation through the deployment of Interior Ministry forces failed miserably. Fighting continued inconclusively into 1992, with the Georgians being distracted by a deepening civil conflict between supporters and opponents of President Zviad Gamsakhurdia that culminated in the latter's overthrow in January 1992. Eduard Shevardnadze returned to Georgia in the spring of 1992 as head of state, but lacked the authority to prevent a final attempt by Georgian forces to resolve the South Ossetia question by force. Russia responded with an ultimatum to the Georgian authorities, insisting that they agree on a cease-fire and apparently threatening to bomb Tbilisi if they did not.[18] The result was the June 1992 cease-fire agreement.

Here too, one result was the deployment of a mixed peacekeeping force comprising North Ossetian, Russian, and Georgian units. As in Moldova the deployment of a peacekeeping force was accompanied by the establishment of a tripartite Joint Control Commission (JCC) to discuss problems related to the cease-fire and (ostensibly) to smooth the path towards a political settlement. Since 1992 this force has also been observed by an OSCE mission, which enjoys access to JCC negotiations. Relations between OSCE military observers and the peacekeeping force have on the whole been good, and a certain degree of norm transference has occurred. With the passage of time, the practice of Russian and other peacekeepers has come to reflect international norms more closely. However, in a number of areas there are obvious problems. For example, Russian and other peacekeepers for some time extracted protection money from civilians seeking safe passage through the area, as well as from traders in the Tskhinvali market. There are reports that peacekeeping units are increasingly involved in trade in contraband goods across the frontier between South and North Ossetia.

Although no obvious progress has been made towards a formal resolution of the conflict, there has been significant improvement in relations between local Georgian and Osset communities and a palpable improvement in the overall atmosphere. UN agencies (and most notably the UN Development Programme – UNDP) have facilitated this change by funding and coordinating the development of cooperative economic ties between the two sides in the hope that this will spill over into the political process. In the meantime, Track II activities organized by the OSCE and NGOs have contributed substantially to building confidence between the two communities. The growing stability of the security situation has permitted a reduction in the size of the Russian force in the region from around 1,000 in 1992/1993 to approximately 500 in 1999.[19]

Abkhazia

The origins of the war in Abkhazia were roughly similar to those in Moldova and South Ossetia: the insecurity of ethnic minorities in the face of resurgent majoritarian nationalism, and the rash acts of central government officials in exacerbating an explosive situation. Hostilities began with an (apparently unsanctioned) effort by Georgia's minister of defence to take over Sukhumi in August 1992 after the Abkhaz Supreme Soviet had voted to return to the jurisdiction's 1925 Constitution, which identified Abkhazia as a sovereign union republic outside Georgian jurisdiction. The Abkhaz leadership withdrew to the north, reconsolidated, and launched attacks on Georgian forces, taking the city of Gagra in October 1992. In 1993, Abkhaz forces gradually advanced southward, benefiting from a substantial influx of Cossack and north Caucasian volunteers from the Russian Federation, from material taken from Russian Army war stores, and from the occasional assistance of the Russian Air Force. By July 1993 they had advanced as far as the Abkhaz capital, Sukhumi. The Russians – having mediated two unsuccessful cease-fires in September 1992 and May 1993 – tried again, producing an agreement on 27 July 1993 involving the withdrawal of Georgian forces from the region, the surrender of heavy weapons by both sides, and the insertion of a Russian monitoring force to oversee the process. In mid-September 1993, the war resumed. The Georgians, caught off-guard in the midst of their withdrawal, retreated rapidly. Their position was worsened by the outbreak of a rebellion by supporters of former President Gamsakhurdia in Mingrelia, which risked cutting the front off from central Georgia. By the end of September, Abkhazia had been cleared of Georgian forces and of the great majority of the region's Georgian population.

At this stage, Georgia's President Shevardnadze capitulated to Russian pressure to join the CIS and agree on Russian base rights in Georgia. Russian forces then intervened to put down the rebellion in Mingrelia, and interposed themselves between Georgian and Abkhaz forces along the Inguri River and in the Kodori valley. This was followed in May 1994 by an agreed cease-fire between the parties, again mediated by the Russian Federation although with some UN involvement. Unlike in the Moldovan and South Osset cases, the Russians consciously sought international legitimacy for this initiative by obtaining a multilateral agreement on the mandate from the CIS and seeking the approval of the UN Security Council, which was forthcoming in July 1994 in Security Council Resolution 937. It is noteworthy that the UN mandate – and, for that matter, the formal mandate from the CIS – post-dated the deployment by several months. In fact, the CIS mandate post-dated the relevant UN resolution sanctioning CIS intervention.

The United Nations had deployed a small observer force (UNOMIG) to Abkhazia in the late summer of 1993. When Russia inserted several thousand Russian peacekeepers in 1994, UNOMIG was expanded and its mandate enlarged to monitor the cease-fire and the heavy weapons exclusion zone, and to observe and liaise with Russian peacekeepers. Since that time the cease-fire has been maintained, although there have been several serious incidents in the security zone established by the agreement. In early 1995, for example, several people were murdered by Abkhaz police personnel in the town of Gali. CIS peacekeepers and UN observers made no effective effort to intervene in these attacks against civilians, despite the provision in both their mandates to contribute to conditions conducive to the return of displaced persons.

A far more serious incident occurred in the spring of 1998, when Abkhaz authorities reacted to the growing spontaneous return of displaced Georgians into southern Abkhazia – and to attacks on Abkhaz positions and personnel by "partisans" accompanying and sheltering among the returnees – by forcibly expelling several tens of thousands of civilians from the Gali district and destroying their homes and property, much of which had been provided under humanitarian assistance and transitional programmes of UN agencies. Again, there was little effort on the part of those responsible for security in the security zone – the CIS Peacekeeping Force (CISPKF) – to interfere. On the other hand, there have been moments when Russian forces took the protection function more seriously, as, for example, when CISPKF troops shadowed Abkhaz militia during their patrols in the security zone after the March 1995 incidents. Such activities were curtailed in 1996, however, when CIS forces began to take significant casualties, and as the size of the Russian force declined considerably, reducing its capacity to control its environment of operations.[20] It is also noteworthy that, apart from a few difficulties early on, humanitarian agencies and UNOMIG report few problems in their interactions with CISPKF in the security zone.

Beyond these specific instances, it is clear that early in the CISPKF deployment Russian forces displayed a considerable lack of discipline in

their approach to their mandate. Russian forces participated in the looting of property and took bribes from civilians in return for permission to
pass from Georgian to Abkhaz-controlled territory.

All of this said, the deployment has been successful in stabilizing the
cease-fire, although neither side had much incentive to continue the war.
The Abkhaz had attained their military objectives. The Georgian military
was not (and is not) in a position to contest the outcome.

Tajikistan

The case of Tajikistan differs from the others in that it has no obvious
ethnic origin. Instead, the lines of conflict were drawn regionally, with
Leninabad and Kulyab factions struggling for power with Garmi and
Gorno-Badakhshan groupings. This struggle evolved later to divide the
Kulyabi and Leninabad alliance.[21] In the course of time the influence of
Islamic groups within the opposition grew, diluting somewhat the regional
focus of the conflict.

The Tajik conflict was also the most substantial, both in terms of casualties (some 30,000 were killed in 1992 alone), and in the size of Russian
operations (which peaked at around 25,000 troops). Another difference
was that the Tajik peace operation included units from other CIS states.
According to the 1993 agreement mandating the operation, the force was
to be 50 per cent Russian, 15 per cent Kazakh, 15 per cent Uzbek, 10 per
cent Kyrgyz, and 10 per cent Tajik.[22] A fourth difference was that, in this
instance, pressure for intervention came just as much – if not more –
from the Central Asian republics, and particularly Uzbekistan, as it did
from Russia itself. Finally, the Tajik operation was distinctive in that at
one stage it spilled over into a neighbouring state outside the former Soviet
Union. This reflected the close connection between processes of conflict in
Tajikistan and the neighbouring Afghan civil war. Russian leaders and
their Central Asian counterparts were deeply concerned about the potential of the war to facilitate the spread of radical Islam throughout the
Central Asian region.

As in the other cases, the conflict's proximate roots lay in the collapse
of the USSR. Rakhmon Nabiyev's Leninabadi faction won elections in
November 1991 and set about eliminating opposition both in the Supreme
Soviet and in the government. This destabilized the delicate interregional
balance within the structures of power and produced large demonstrations in Dushanbe in March 1992, principally by the Garmi and Gorno-
Badakhshani opposition. These were met by counter-demonstrations
mounted by Leninabadi and Kulyabi loyalists, to whom the government's
security service distributed weapons in May. Despite Nabiyev's acceptance of a coalition government in which 33 per cent of positions were

held by the opposition, the mutual arming of factions led to civil war in May, much of the south of the country being devastated in the summer of 1992, with 70,000 refugees fleeing to Afghanistan. By this time some 500,000 people had been displaced by combat. In November 1992, the coalition government was deposed and Emomali Rakhmonov took power.

Matters were complicated here as elsewhere by the presence on the ground of units of the Russian armed forces. The 201st Motor Rifle Division (MRD) was stationed in Dushanbe and substantial numbers of Ministry of International Affairs (MVD) troops guarded the border between Tajikistan and Afghanistan. Although the Moscow government remained neutral, if not indifferent, to the conflict in its early stages, the 201st MRD intervened in the conflict early on by providing weapons to the supporters of Nabiyev.[23] On 19 September 1991 the Tajikistan government requested the assistance of the 201st MRD in guarding public buildings and the Russian force accepted this role, although continuing its informal support of the ex-communist Rakhmonov faction. Once Rakhmonov took power he was immediately recognized officially by the Russian Federation, and Russian assistance became a matter of official policy.

The deterioration of the situation led to a number of meetings between Russia and the other Central Asian states. In September 1992, the presidents of Russia, Kazakhstan, Kyrgyzstan, and Uzbekistan jointly declared their intention to intervene if there were no cessation of hostilities. In November 1992, Russian foreign minister Andrei Kozyrev met with the Central Asian signatories of the Tashkent collective security treaty to discuss the war in Tajikistan. They agreed that the 201st MRD should remain in Tajikistan and pursue peacekeeping operations until such time as it could be joined by a proper CIS force, with Kazakh, Kyrgyz, and Uzbek units linking up with the Russians who were already in place.

After a lull in late 1992 and early 1993, Russian border forces were attacked from Afghanistan, with 24 deaths resulting. This produced a near war between Russia and Afghanistan, and Russian bombing of targets inside Afghanistan. In this context, Boris Yeltsin declared that the southern border of Tajikistan was in fact the southern border of Russia. A CIS agreement on collective peacekeeping forces followed in September 1993, providing grounds for the establishment of a CIS force on Tajikistan's territory. The agreement is striking in that it expands considerably the term of reference of peacekeeping, strengthening the capacity of the force commander for independent, coordinated action, and permitting the use of force without prior authorization in extraordinary circumstances.[24]

On the other hand, as Lena Jonson points out, the border incident made it clear to Russian leaders that "military means were not enough" and that force had to be accompanied by diplomatic initiatives.[25] Consequently, Moscow began a long effort to bring the parties to agreement on a political

settlement. However, the Russians jeopardized their credibility as média-
tors by continuing to support the government side strongly in the civil war.

By 1995 the war had reached a stalemate. The opposition was not in a
position to defeat a government benefiting from external military support.
The government, in turn, was unable to eliminate the opposition without a
substantial increase in external support. This the Russians were unwilling
to provide, given their increasingly painful engagement in Chechnya, their
deepening budgetary problems, and the reflection of the latter in the
atrophy of Russian military capability.

The growing political and financial costs of the operation and the
shadow of Chechnya ultimately produced a change in Russian (and CIS)
policy towards the conflict. In January 1996, Boris Yeltsin declared that
Russia "cannot endlessly carry Tajikistan when our own people are dy-
ing".[26] The states participating in the peace operation all began to pressure Rakhmonov to compromise. A falling out between the Kulyabi and
Leninabadi factions strengthened Rakhmonov's incentive to negotiate
further. The result was a shift to accommodation with the opposition that
ultimately produced a peace agreement in June 1997. The conclusion of
the agreement, however, hardly stabilized the country. Tajikistan has
been plagued since 1997 by factional infighting, banditry, and delays in
the implementation of the accord, which gave the United Tajik Opposition (UTO) 30 per cent of the positions in government.

Unlike the other cases, this shift in Russian policy has not been accompanied by any significant reduction in Russian peacekeeping and border
troops in the country. The former dropped from 6,500 to 6,000 and the
latter from 16,500 to 14,000 personnel from 1992 to 1999.[27] This reflects
the fact that Russian strategic interests in Tajikistan (stability in Central
Asia and border control of the Afghan frontier) are more substantial and
more directly related to the presence of numerically significant combat-
capable forces than are those in the other conflicts.

The final issue regarding Tajikistan peace operations concerns the role
of the United Nations. As in the case of Georgia, UN activities were coordinated by a special representative of the Secretary-General and the
United Nations placed a small force on the ground to observe CIS peacekeepers' activities. Both the UNHCR and the OSCE monitored the needs
of internally displaced persons (IDPs) and attempted with some success
to perform a protection role. Although these activities by international
organizations enhanced transparency, there was no obvious constraining
effect on the behaviour of the parties in the conflict. With the passage of
time they faced increasing problems of security, culminating in the withdrawal of UNMOT in 1997 owing to the murder of several military observers. And although UN mediation was useful in maintaining channels
between the parties and in facilitating negotiating sessions, as Jonson

argues, the key factor leading to the agreement was the change in Russian policy and the pressure that Russia applied on the Tajik government to make concessions to the opposition.[28]

The cases discussed above display similarities not only with regard to their causes but also concerning the evolution of the Russian response.[29] Russian policy moved from incoherence immediately after the Soviet collapse, through a phase of military assertion (1992–1993) as it attempted to recover control in the former Soviet space, to an increasing emphasis on political solutions in 1995–1996. The move from the second to the third phase resulted in considerable measure from the impact of the Chechen war on Russian prestige and self-confidence, and from the deepening military difficulties the country faced as the decade progressed, of which the debacle in Chechnya was a manifestation. The shift towards a greater emphasis on the quest for political settlement, evident not just in Tajikistan but in the accords proposed in Moldova and Georgia, was accompanied by a gradual downsizing in Russian peacekeeping forces with the exception of Tajikistan.

For various reasons, these settlements have proven very hard to achieve. This brings us to the current phase, which seems to be one of drift. Russia appears incapable of resolving or unwilling to resolve the conflicts in which it has become involved by force. It also appears to be incapable of mediating durable political settlements. And it appears to be incapable of extricating itself from its peacekeeping commitments.

Patterns in Russian peacekeeping behaviour

Impartiality

Several patterns are evident in the Russian experience of peacekeeping across the four cases. The first concerns impartiality. Impartiality has traditionally been conceived to be a critical precondition for success in peacekeeping operations. As noted in an earlier section of this chapter, there are ample reasons to expect that impartiality would be difficult for Russia in its peace operations in the former Soviet space. The empirical record substantiates this deductive proposition. In the case of Moldova, prior to the insertion of peacekeepers, Russian forces armed and supported the secessionist party. Russian statesmen voiced support for the secessionist project. The insertion of peacekeepers followed the consolidation of control over the left bank of the Dnestr River by the proponents of secession, thereby securing that consolidation. The construction of the JCC resulted in disproportionate representation for the secessionist party and ensured that no outcome unacceptable to Russia would emerge.

In South Ossetia, the Osset side benefited from considerable assistance (*matériel* and personnel) from the Russian jurisdiction of North Ossetia, and allegedly from direct Soviet and then Russian military support.[30] In Abkhazia, Russian forces and volunteers participated in the conflict on the Abkhaz side prior to the conclusion of hostilities, while the July 1993 cease-fire agreement was implemented in such a way as to leave the Georgians at a conspicuous military disadvantage once hostilities resumed. In Tajikistan, Russian (and Uzbek) forces supported the government side in the competition for power in 1992 prior to undertaking a "peacekeeping" mission in that country.

On this vector, then, Russian behaviour confirms the expectation of self-interested bias quite consistently and underlines the doubts in this regard with regard to regional-power peacekeeping. On the other hand, impartiality may be neither necessary nor desirable in international mediation.[31] Instead, it may be more effective to pressure one side or another towards compromise even if this constitutes a departure from impartiality. The same might be true of peace operations. And, indeed, in several instances Russia appeared to be manipulating the parties more or less successfully towards peace. The obvious example here is Russian policy towards the Tajik conflict after 1994.

However, there are three necessary conditions for success in "partial" peacekeeping. Each is to some extent questionable in the Russian/CIS context. In the first place, to sustain credibility, the objective of such manipulation must be settlement *per se*, rather than more self-interested concerns (such as influence over one or the other parties on other issues). Russian policy does not meet this test. Second, the powerful mediator must have the capacity to sustain the policy. Russian capacity has declined both generally and in each of these fields of operations. And thirdly, this approach to mediation is likely to require consistency in strategy over a considerable period of time. In the Russian domestic policy-making environment of the 1990s, this consistency has been difficult to sustain.

Legitimacy

Given the Russian Federation's position on the illegitimacy of NATO's 1999 operations in Kosovo in the absence of Security Council ratification, it is ironic that the Russian Federation displayed little concern over such niceties in its peace operations in the former Soviet space. No international mandate was sought for intervention in Moldova and South Ossetia, despite the fact that both operations contained elements of peace enforcement in their early stages. In the case of Abkhazia, Russian intervention (October–November 1993) preceded a cease-fire agreement (May 1994). The formal deployment of the peacekeeping force subsequent to the cease-fire agreement began in June 1994, a month before UN consideration of the role of CIS forces (July 1994). The UN's approval of CIS operations was granted prior to formal regional approval of the deployment of the CISPKF in Georgia in October 1994.[32] Russia attempted to deal with such issues in the 1996 CIS statutes on collective peacekeeping forces, claiming for the CIS the "responsibility and authority for maintaining peace on CIS territory".[33] However, as the statutes were not embraced by the full membership, their applicability to those who did not accept them is questionable. Moreover, there is no reason to believe that they enjoy priority over the provisions of Chapter VIII of the UN Charter. Chapter VIII recognizes the right of regional organizations to respond to threats to peace and security in their area. Indeed, it states a preference for regional action prior to a Security Council response. However, it also prohibits enforcement action without the authorization of the Security Council.

One might argue that this is irrelevant, since in each instance Russian and CIS intervention occurred on the basis of consent from the government of the state in question. However, the active engagement of Russian power on the secessionist side in Moldova and Georgia prior to the conferral of consent leaves one with the impression that consent was coerced. In the case of Tajikistan, the constitutional legitimacy of the authorities granting consent was, at the very least, questionable, given the circumstances in which they took power. These circumstances included Russian support for an extra-constitutional seizure of power.

Operational norms

Operational norms regarding peacekeeping focus on minimal use of force in self-defence and on the principle of discrimination in warfare, that is to say that civilian persons and property are not, *ceteris paribus*, legitimate targets of military action. The norms are embraced in the 1992 CIS protocols on peacekeeping and the subsequent 1996 statutes on CIS collective peacekeeping forces. It is reasonably clear that Russian peacekeeping forces violated these norms in their interventions in Moldova, Georgia, and Tajikistan during the early phases of operations. Indeed, there was little evidence that Russian military personnel were conscious that the rules of engagement in such operations were any different from those applicable in war.[34] That said, it is also the case that (with the exception of Tajikistan) with the passage of time the forces comprised growing numbers of personnel trained and with experience in peacekeeping operations. This development, and also the stabilization of front lines and termination of hostilities in the cases other than Tajikistan, moderated the forceful behaviour of Russian forces. The effect was strengthened to some extent by the presence of and exchanges with international observers.

Effectiveness

One can assess effectiveness in various ways. One is to examine it in terms of Russian foreign policy objectives. This issue is peripheral to this chapter and will therefore not be dealt with in detail. The other concerns the extent to which Russian peacekeeping has furthered the normative objectives of the United Nations and the international community. Was intervention effective in terms of ending hostilities and promoting a durable political settlement? To what extent did intervention facilitate humanitarian action? To what extent did it contribute to the consolidation of the sovereignty and stability of the host state?

With regard to the first set of issues, conclusions on the role of Russian forces in limiting or ending open hostilities are difficult to draw, since we do not know what would have happened in their absence. In the cases of Moldova and Abkhazia, for example, secessionist forces had achieved their strategic and territorial objectives by the time Russian troops were deployed, and their opponents were not in a position to challenge their victory. In other words, the material preconditions for cease-fire already existed. Along the same lines, the May 1994 cease-fire has endured in and around Karabakh in the absence of any peacekeeping force because a durable military balance had been achieved. On the other hand, it is probably the case that the Russian presence in Georgia and in Moldova reduced the possibility of inadvertent resumption of hostilities. In the case of Tajikistan, most observers agree that the Russian peacekeeping presence has had some effect in reducing the level of conflict.[35]

Turning to political settlement, Russian peacekeeping efforts have on the whole had marginal confidence-building effects which, all other things being equal, contributed to the process of settlement. However, Russia's perceived lack of impartiality, growing incapacity to play the "powerful mediator", and inconsistency in policy handicapped efforts to reach settlements to these conflicts, with the important but qualified exception of Tajikistan. The Tajik case suggests a further observation – the settlement there is shaky and in danger of unravelling despite Russian support because of asymmetries of motivation between the parties to the conflict and the intervening power. Given the intensity of local interests (power, resources, survival) engaged in these situations of conflict, the capacity of external actors to determine peace is limited. Ultimately the process of settlement depends on the mutual decisions of indigenous parties over which the Russian Federation lacks control.

A number of other normative objectives are also in play, notably those related to the mitigation of human suffering. Both dimensions of humanitarian action – relief and protection – are relevant to these cases. In the first instance, most students of the subject would agree that although Russian peacekeeping forces have not been particularly helpful in the delivery of relief, nor have they been particularly obstructive. And it is probably true that at various stages, and to varying degrees, the mere presence of peacekeepers has provided a degree of security for humanitarian actors that has facilitated their efforts to service vulnerable populations.

In the second instance, for the most part Russian peacekeepers have resisted the function of protection, despite the implicit inclusion of it in some of the force mandates,[36] and in interviews have denied any responsibility for it. The humanitarian consequences were most evident in Georgia. In 1995, Russian forces failed to intervene during a substantial Abkhaz sweep through the security zone on the grounds that those involved had police documents and that the Russian force had no mandate to interfere with their internal security activities. Many Georgian civilians were brutally murdered in this instance. In 1998, the Russians also failed to intervene when the Abkhaz decided to evict several tens of thousands of spontaneous returnees, with substantial civilian casualties. In a way the Russian force has paid a price for this, since their indifference to the plight of Georgian civilians was one factor contributing to the increasing attacks on Russian patrols in which many Russian soldiers, in turn, have perished.

Likewise, although it may be true that the interposition of Russian forces had a stabilizing role in the domestic politics of some of the cases (for example Tajikistan), in some other instances their apparently permanent presence has become a destabilizing factor in domestic politics. In the case of Georgia, for example, the continuing Russian presence when there is so little progress towards a political settlement has become a lightning rod for criticism of the Shevardnadze government by nationalists who claim that he has sold out Georgia (and the displaced persons). This is related to another obvious point. With the exception of Tajikistan, the Russian presence, far from contributing to the strengthening and consolidation of sovereign statehood, has frozen the *de facto* dismemberment of the states in question, giving secessionist groups the time and space to consolidate their statehood.

Conclusion

In conclusion, and broadly speaking, Russian and CIS peacekeeping is consistent with the deductive propositions pertaining to regional-power peacekeeping discussed above. It has evinced serious problems relating to impartiality, it has reflected strongly the perceived self-interest of the regionally dominant power, and it has been less constrained by international norms regarding peacekeeping. The Russian case also appears to confirm the proposition that international observer groups can moderate the behaviour of regional peacekeepers by enhancing transparency and through the transfer of norms and expertise.

None the less, the experience of Russian peacekeeping does pose the obvious question of whether the United Nations should approve of and cooperate with Russian peacekeeping when it has departed so clearly from the organization's own norms. Here it is useful to stress that in the first place, in a number of instances Russian peacekeeping plausibly conduced to a level of stability that would not have been obtained in its absence, and it appears to have contributed to the emergence of conditions in which international humanitarian actors found it possible to pursue their mission. Moreover, there were no other volunteers. This was not merely a matter of sensitivity to Russian prerogatives in their "backyard". It also reflected the unwillingness of Western states to take on active peacekeeping roles in situations where they failed to perceive a strong interest. The probable alternative scenario would have not only been one of no Russian response, but of no response whatsoever to the region's civil wars.

Indeed, we may have the opportunity to observe this alternative in the not-too-distant future. There is good reason to believe that the Russian Federation will in future be less willing and able to respond militarily to crises outside its borders. It is true that no new conflicts have emerged in the non-Russian republics since the early 1990s. However, this lull may not last. There are numerous societal early-warning signals already evident. There has been little recovery in income for the great bulk of the region's population. Income differentials are growing as a small minority enrich themselves while the vast majority languish in poverty. Many are growing increasingly frustrated with the absence of any substantial payoff from economic transition. This may delegitimize not only serving leaderships but also the very process of political transformation itself.

At the political level, stability has been enhanced by the presence of strong leaders. A number of these are growing old (for example, Geidar Aliev and Eduard Shevardnadze), while facing the very real threat of assassination. If they disappear from the scene, it is an open question as to whether there are replacements with a similar capacity to hold things together. In the economy, although energy sector development may contribute to regional peace and stability in the Caspian Basin, it could just as well go the other way if differential benefits from this development destabilize subregional balances of power, or if particular countries (such as Armenia) are excluded from the process and have incentives to act as spoilers.

Finally, it bears mention that the region's past conflicts remain unresolved and the possibility of regression is strong, while the evolution of events in southern Kyrgyzstan and the Ferghana valley, and in the Javakheti region of Georgia, remind us that there is some potential for new conflicts to emerge. The worsening situation in the northern Caucasian jurisdictions of the Russian Federation may play a catalytic role in this regard through spillover into Georgia and Azerbaijan from Chechnya. If this reading of regional conflict potential is correct, then we may look back with slight nostalgia on the days when Russia could and would police the region.

Notes

1. Article 52(2) states that "the Members of the United Nations entering into such arrangements or constituting such agencies shall make every effort to achieve pacific settlement of local disputes through such regional arrangements or by such regional agencies before referring them to the Security Council". Article 52(3) notes that "the Security Council shall encourage the development of pacific settlement of local disputes through such regional arrangements or by such regional agencies either on the initiative of the states concerned or by reference to the Security Council".
2. Boutros Boutros-Ghali, *An Agenda for Peace*, New York: United Nations, 1992, paragraph 64.
3. For general treatments of peacekeeping in the former Soviet Union, see Roy Allison, *Peacekeeping in the Soviet Successor States*, Chaillot Paper No. 14, Paris: Institute for Security Studies of the WEU, 1994; Lena Jonson and Clive Archer, *Peacekeeping and the Role of Russia in Eurasia*, Boulder, CO: Westview, 1996; Lena Jonson, *Keeping the Peace in the CIS: The Evolution of Russian Policy*, London: Royal Institute of International Affairs, 1999; Dov Lynch, *Peacekeeping Strategies in the CIS, 1992–1996: The Cases of Moldova, Georgia, and Tajikistan*, London: Macmillan/RIIA, 1999; S. Neil MacFarlane and Albrecht Schnabel, "Russia's approach to peacekeeping", *International Journal*, Vol. 50, No. 2, 1995.
4. The CIS emerged as a successor organization to the USSR in December 1991. As originally envisaged, it included political, military, economic, and technical dimensions of cooperation. For a discussion of its distinctly mixed record since then in the republics of the southern rim of the former USSR, see Mark Webber, *CIS Integration Trends: Russia and the Former Soviet South*, London: Royal Institute of International Affairs, 1997.
5. For analysis of the Moldovan conflict, see Charles King, "Moldova with a Russian face", *Foreign Policy*, No. 97, Winter 1994–1995; and Jeff Chinn, "The case of Transdniestr (Moldova)", in Jonson and Archer, note 3. For analysis of peacekeeping in Georgia, see S. Neil MacFarlane, Larry Minear, and Stephen Shenfield, *Armed Conflict in Georgia: A Case Study in Humanitarian Action and Peacekeeping*, Providence, RI: Watson Institute, 1996. On Nagorno-Karabakh, see S. Neil MacFarlane and Larry Minear, *Humanitarian Action and Politics: The Case of Nagorno-Karabakh*, Providence, RI: Watson Institute, 1997. On Tajikistan, see Lena Jonson, *The Tajik War: A Challenge to Russian Policy*, London: Royal Institute of International Affairs, 1998.

6. For an assessment of these relationships with specific reference to Georgia, see S. Neil MacFarlane, "On the front lines in the near abroad: The CIS and the OSCE in Georgia's civil wars", in Thomas G. Weiss (ed.) *Beyond UN Subcontracting: Task-Sharing with Regional Security Arrangements and Service-Providing NGOs*, Basingstoke: Macmillan, 1998, pp. 115–138; and MacFarlane, Minear, and Shenfield, note 5. See also Ettore Greco, *Delegating Peace Operations: Improvisation and Innovation in Georgia and Albania*, New York: United Nations Association, 1998.

7. For a more complete treatment of these issues, see S. Neil MacFarlane and Thomas G. Weiss, "Regional organizations and regional security", *Security Studies*, Vol. 2, No. 1, Autumn, 1992.

8. For a general discussion of UN task-sharing with regional organizations, see Thomas Weiss (ed.), *Beyond UN Subcontracting: Task-Sharing with Regional Security Arrangements and Service-Providing NGOs*, Basingstoke: Macmillan, 1998.

9. For detailed discussion of the contending positions in Russian foreign policy debates in the first years after independence, see Alexei Arbatov, "Russia's foreign policy alternatives", *International Security*, XVIII, No. 2, Fall, 1993, pp. 5–43; and S. Neil MacFarlane, "Russian conceptions of Europe", *Post-Soviet Affairs*, Vol. 10, No. 3, July–September, 1994, pp. 234–269.

10. There was, however, a division of opinion within this group as to whether all or only some of the other newly independent states should be recovered. For some the former USSR as a whole was the target. Others argued that Russia should limit the recovery of territory to areas populated by Slavic groups (Belarus, Ukraine, and northern Kazakhstan).

11. Sovet po Vneshnei I Oboronnoi Politiki [Council on Foreign and Defence Policy], "Vozroditsya li Soyuz? Budushchee Postsovetskogo Prostranstva" [Will the union be reborn? The future of the post-Soviet space], *Nezavisimaya Gazeta*, 23 May 1996.

12. For official expression of this set of concerns and interests, see MID [Ministerstvo Innostranykh Del], "Konsteptsia Vneshnei Politiki Rossiiskoi Federatsii" [Concept of foreign policy of the Russian Federation], Document No. 1615/IS, 25 January 1993. Translated in *FBIS-USR-93-037*, pp. 1–20. For a more recent iteration, see "The foreign policy concept of the Russian Federation," 28 June 2000, http://www.mid.ru/mid/eng/concept.htm, pp. 7, 10.

13. For more substantial analysis of the Moldovan case, see King, note 5; and Chinn, note 5.

14. Population figures are from Chinn, note 5, p. 105.

15. For example, then Russian vice-president Aleksandr Rutskoi visited Tiraspol in the spring of 1992 and publicly supported the effort to secede.

16. Lena Jonson, note 3, p. 19.

17. The force initially comprised 1,800 Russians in 1992. This had dropped to 1,200 in 1994–1995, and fell further to 600 in 1994–1996. It currently stands at 500. (IISS, 1992–1999.)

18. Jonson, note 3, p. 19.

19. IISS, 1993–1999.

20. The stability of the situation on the ground has permitted a drawing down of the Russian force from 3,000 in 1994–1995 to some 1,500 in 1998–1999.

21. Iver Neumann and Sergei Solodovnik, "The case of Tajikistan", in Jonson and Archer, note 3, pp. 85–86.

22. Anna Kreikemeyer and Andrei Zagorsky, "The CIS", in Jonson and Archer, note 3, p. 159.

23. Neumann and Solodovnik, note 21, p. 89; Jonson, note 5, p. 9.

24. Indeed, originally the agreement was to be for a collective defence operation rather than peacekeeping. The terminology was changed at the behest of Kazakhstan's President Nursultan Nazarbayev. Kreikemeyer and Zagorsky, note 22, p. 158.

25. Jonson, note 5, p. 9.
26. Jonson, note 3, p. 11.
27. IISS, 1992–1999. Indeed, in early 2000 there were reports that the Russian Federation intended to increase its deployment in Tajikistan with paratroopers, in order to deal with the growing threat from Islamic militants.
28. Jonson, note 5.
29. For a similar discussion with a somewhat different periodization, see Jonson, note 3.
30. *Ibid.*, p. 11.
31. William Zartmann and Saadia Touval, "International mediation in the post-Cold War era", in Chester A. Crocker, Fen Osler Hampson, and Pamela Aall (eds) *Managing Global Chaos: Sources of and Responses to International Conflict*, Washington, DC: US Institute of Peace Press, 1996, p. 451.
32. See the discussion on Abkhazia in Kreikemeyer and Zagorsky, note 22, pp. 161–162.
33. Jonson, note 3, p. 30.
34. At a 1995 conference on CIS peacekeeping operations in Moscow, a deputy minister of defence stated flatly: "Peacekeeping, peacemaking, peace enforcement ... These distinctions do not matter. It's all local war." Personal notes.
35. Neumann and Solodovnik, note 21.
36. In the case of the CISPKF in Georgia, one of the roles mentioned is the fostering of conditions conducive to the return of refugees and displaced persons. See MacFarlane, Minear, and Shenfield, note 5, p. 52.

6

Towards more effective peace operations: Learning from the African "laboratory"?

Mark Malan

African countries have historically played an important role in international peacekeeping. Like other poor nations, they have been willing and able to provide sizeable contingents for UN peacekeeping operations, thus increasing the geographical spread of troop contributors and enhancing the representative nature, perceived impartiality, and legitimacy of such missions. However, African states are now more likely to be called upon to organize and sustain their own peace support operations for dealing with regional conflicts in Africa, or to contribute the bulk of formed military units where the United Nations launches such missions.

There are thus two basic issues at stake when analysing African peacekeeping capacity:

- African participation in and leadership of international peacekeeping operations under the auspices of the United Nations;
- African efforts to launch, lead, and sustain their own peacekeeping interventions under the auspices of the Organization of African Unity or one of the "subordinate" subregional organisations (with varying degrees of direct or indirect assistance from and cooperation with the United Nations and other elements of the "international community").

The first issue is complex enough, and is inextricably linked to current trends and developments affecting the concept and conduct of UN operations. It is also of critical importance to African countries, which represent 25 out of 89 UN member states that are currently contributing military and police personnel and assets to UN peace operations. Indeed, Nigeria was the top contributor of personnel at the end of 2000, with Ghana and Kenya also making a strong showing in the top 10 contributors worldwide.

The second issue is more difficult to address, as much of the thought on the roles of regional organizations in maintaining international peace and security is (wrongly) informed by the multinational peace support interventions of the North Atlantic Treaty Organization in the Balkans. The experiences of the OAU, ECOWAS, and the SADC (Southern African Development Community) in Africa have not impacted heavily on Western-dominated thinking about the "division of labour" between the United Nations and regional arrangements for the maintenance of regional peace and security.

The fact that the ability of African countries to meet the demands of contemporary peace support is severely limited also seems to be ignored by an increasingly vocal chorus of "African solutions to African problems". Such solutions, in the realm of peace support, amount to what Hutchful has described as "lean peacekeeping" – missions which operate under suboptimal conditions that would not normally support military operations.[1]

The advent of lean peacekeeping in Africa is often ascribed to the "Somalia" effect, or Western disenchantment with the failure of new-generation peace operations in Africa. However, it began under regional auspices with the Economic Community of West African States (ECOWAS) Monitoring Group (ECOMOG) intervention in Liberia in 1990.[2] The "Africanization" of peacekeeping continued under UN auspices in Angola, where the UN Angola Verification Mission III (UNAVEM III, February 1995–June 1997) was comprised mainly of troops from African nations and other developing countries. However, the precedent for stretching Chapter VIII of the UN Charter to its limits was firmly set in the Central African Republic (CAR), when on 6 August 1997 the Security Council retrospectively authorized the 800-member Inter-African Mission to Monitor the Implementation of the Bangui Agreements (MISAB) under a Chapter VII mandate.[3]

The results of these operations vary from fairly successful (in the CAR), to inconclusive (Liberia), and outright failure (Angola). However, it is the regional and international peace support process in Sierra Leone, as pursued from 1996 to the present, that illustrates the full absurdity of applying the lean peacekeeping recipe to ruinous civil wars in Africa. Much has been said and written on the dramatic events in that country since the first UN peacekeepers were taken hostage on 1 May 2000. The "I-told-you-so" brigade has included both interventionists and non-interventionists. But beyond all the hype (which includes suggestions of sending in mercenaries to fix the mess), the UN debacle provides an opportunity for serious reflection on some key unresolved doctrinal issues of peace support.

However, most innovations in doctrinal thinking have come from within the NATO alliance and are both Euro-centric and "Yugo"-centric. Moreover, it has been said that the evolution of NATO's intervention doctrine represents not so much an attempt to convert principles into practice, but rather to convert past practice into principles. The relevance for Africa of NATO experience with peace support in the Balkans can only be partial, and lessons learned in this arena must at least be complemented by a hard look at the more problematic operations in Africa if they are to have any meaning for the continent.

The aim of this chapter is therefore to sketch briefly some of the key operational and doctrinal dilemmas that have emerged from the UN mission in Sierra Leone, before outlining the progress (or lack thereof) in addressing such challenges at the international and African levels. Finally, the concept of "conflict-termination operations" is introduced as stimulant to further debate and ideas on a workable doctrine and viable agent for future African interventions.

The failure of UN peace support in Sierra Leone

Sierra Leone's eight-year civil war supposedly ended with a peace agreement signed in Lomé on 7 July 1999. After a decade of providing the backbone of ECOMOG forces in Liberia and then Sierra Leone, the democratically elected government of Nigeria could no longer sustain its ECOMOG commitments and informed the world that it would be pulling its troops out of Sierra Leone. Although Foday Sankoh's Revolutionary United Front (RUF) had been driven out of Freetown, they still controlled the countryside and the diamond-mining areas that create most of the country's wealth. No peace deal was possible without Sankoh and the RUF. Corporal Sankoh was in jail, awaiting execution for terrible crimes of which he is widely believed to be guilty.

The tense security environment and impending Nigerian withdrawal led to a frantic scramble among West African states, as well as Britain and the USA, to broker a peace agreement. The UN special representative initiated a series of diplomatic efforts aimed at opening up dialogue with the rebels. Negotiations between the government and the rebels began in May 1999. With coaxing from the UK and USA, a controversial peace agreement was signed by President Ahmad Tejan Kabbah and Corporal Sankoh in Lomé, Togo on 7 July 1999. The Lomé accord granted total amnesty to Foday Sankoh and members of the RUF, promised reintegration of the RUF into the Sierra Leonean army, assured the RUF several cabinet seats in the transitional government, left the RUF in control of the diamond mines, and invited Sankoh to participate in UN-sponsored elections.

In exchange for senior government positions for its commanders and a blanket amnesty for atrocities committed during the war, the RUF pledged to disarm, along with pro-government civil defence forces and other paramilitary units. Despite its obvious flaws, the United Nations was obliged to back the agreement with a peacekeeping mission. The Lomé accord requires that:

A neutral peacekeeping force comprising UNOMSIL [the United Nations Observer Mission to Sierra Leone][4] and ECOMOG shall disarm all combatants of the RUF/SL, CDF, SLA and paramilitary groups. The encampment, disarmament and demobilisation process shall commence within six weeks of signing of the present Agreement in line with the deployment of the neutral peacekeeping force.[5]

This process was to be completed within 60 days, according to the draft implementation schedule.[6] The Lomé signatories specifically requested the UN Security Council urgently to "amend the mandate of UNOMSIL to enable it to undertake the tasks provided for it in the present Agreement; [and] to authorise the deployment of a peacekeeping force in Sierra Leone".[7]

UNAMSIL

On 22 October 1999 the Security Council authorized the establishment of the UN Assistance Mission to Sierra Leone (UNAMSIL), with a maximum authorized strength of 6,000 military personnel, including 260 military observers, to assist the government and the parties in carrying out provisions of the Lomé peace agreement. At the same time, the Council decided to terminate UNOMSIL.

According to Security Council Resolution 1270, UNAMSIL had the mandate *inter alia*:
- to assist the government of Sierra Leone in the implementation of the disarmament, demobilization, and reintegration plan;
- to that end, to establish a presence at key locations throughout the territory of Sierra Leone, including at disarmament/reception centres and demobilization centres;
- to ensure the security and freedom of movement of UN personnel;
- to monitor adherence to the cease-fire in accordance with the cease-fire agreement of 18 May 1999 (S/1999/585, annex) through the structures provided for therein;
- to provide support to the elections, which were to be held in accordance with the present constitution of Sierra Leone (in early 2001).

In early December 1999, the first company of 133 Kenyan soldiers flew into Lungi international airport as the advance unit of the first new UN-

AMSIL battalion to join some 223 UN military observers from 30 countries already on the ground. Four ECOMOG battalions already in Sierra Leone (composed of troops from Ghana, Guinea, and Nigeria) were "rehatted" as UN peacekeepers. In the tradition of lean peacekeeping in Africa, the rest of the formed units were to come from India, Jordan, Bangladesh, and Zambia – with only a few military observers being volunteered by the developed world.

Deployment of the remaining units, as is customary for UN operations, was painfully slow. At the beginning of April 2000 (more than five months after Resolution 1270), UNAMSIL force commander Major General Vijay Jetley complained that he did not have sufficient troops to deploy into the diamond-rich Kono district because he was still waiting for the Jordanian and Zambian peacekeeping contingents to arrive.[8]

Although the Lomé agreement guaranteed the United Nations unhindered and safe access to all areas of the country, the UN peacekeepers were often denied freedom of movement, amidst frequent cease-fire violations that included ambushes against civilians and UN personnel, the maintenance of illegal roadblocks, and RUF troop movements.[9] It was also not entirely clear who was doing the disarming – UNAMSIL or the belligerents. In January, peacekeepers from Kenya and Guinea surrendered at least 110 assault rifles, several rocket-propelled grenade launchers, four armoured personnel carriers, communications equipment, and other military gear in at least three ambushes by elements of the RUF. In each incident, the troops put up no resistance.

The peacekeepers' failure to respond with force caused US, British, and some UN officials to worry that the rebels would step up their armed challenges to the UN forces as they assumed greater responsibility for security from the departing Nigerian-led West African force. On 3 February, Central Intelligence Agency (CIA) director George Tenet told Congress the rebels were "poised to break a tenuous cease-fire and resume a campaign of terror".[10]

In response to these and other incidents and concerns, the Security Council voted unanimously, on 7 February 2000, to approve the Secretary-General's plans for strengthening the UNAMSIL mission in Sierra Leone. This not only raised the maximum authorized strength from 6,000 to 11,000, but also granted the mission an expanded mandate under Chapter VII of the Charter.[11] In particular, the Security Council authorized "UNAMSIL to take the necessary action to fulfil ... [its] tasks ... and *affirms* that, in the discharge of its mandate, UNAMSIL may take the necessary action to ensure the security and freedom of movement of its personnel and ... to afford protection to civilians under imminent threat of physical violence ..." (Security Council Resolution 1289).

Resolution 1289 thus provided the legal framework for coercive action by UNAMSIL in pursuit of its disarmament mandate, but this could not be translated into assertive and credible action on the ground. Despite the more robust mandate, General Jetley continued to defend the peace-keepers' "soft" approach, saying that while the RUF is "not as fully committed to disarmament as it would like people to believe", patience was necessary. Jetley stressed that "[UNAMSIL is] a peacekeeping force, not a combat force", and that "peace is already here; we don't want to shred it ... a peacekeeper's role is very delicate ... restraint and neutrality are the watchwords".[12]

The RUF did not appear to be impressed by the concepts of restraint and neutrality. Human Rights Watch reported in March 2000 that the RUF was regularly committing atrocities, including rapes, abductions, and looting, near where UN forces were stationed in Port Loko. Intelligence sources also warned that, despite Sankoh's public pledges to disarm, he had told his commanders that there would be no disarmament until after the election was held and the RUF won.[13]

Although the total number of disarmed combatants passing through five UNAMSIL-supervised camps stood at around 23,000 by mid-April 2000, the United Nations was concerned over the low quality of surrendered weapons and the ratio of collected arms to the number of ex-combatants. Many fighters reported for demobilization only with ammunition or hand grenades.[14] As of 15 April, according to the National Committee for Disarmament, Demobilization, and Reintegration, only some 5,000 weapons had been handed in by Sierra Leonean belligerents, who reportedly number about 45,000.[15] Most of these weapons appear to have been surrendered by former members of the Sierra Leone army, rather than by RUF fighters.

Sankoh was obviously playing a double game: participating in the transitional government while keeping his war options open. The cash from illegal diamond sales would clearly enable him, if he saw his ambitions for power frustrated, to go back to the bush. The United Nations therefore came under increasing pressure (*inter alia* from the UK and USA) to end the RUF game. On 17 April 2000 the United Nations attempted to correct matters by opening four new camps – two of which were in the central RUF-held towns of Makeni and Magburaka. On 29 April, General Jetley declared that his forces expected to take over all diamond areas under RUF control by the end of June, and he informed reporters in Freetown that a Zambian contingent would deploy to Koidu (the seat of the RUF diamond-mining centre in the Kono district).[16]

This obviously amounted to a direct challenge to Foday Sankoh. On several occasions before the announcement, rebels had prevented UN troops from conducting reconnaissance missions to Koidu. Moreover, as the UN presence intensified in rebel territory, the newly established demobilization camps in Makeni and Magburaka became the flashpoint for the present emergency, with the first RUF abductions happening here on 1 and 2 May 2000 respectively. Significantly, these incidents coincided with the final departure of the last of four battalions of Nigerian ECOMOG troops.

With the Lomé accord in tatters, there are numerous lessons for the international community and Africans to learn from the recent UN experience in Sierra Leone – from the political issue of striking Faustian bargains with the likes of Sankoh and the RUF to the operational problems of cobbling together a "third world" UN force to implement the deal. But such lessons are often noted but seldom learned. A 1996 UNIDIR (UN Institute for Disarmament Research) study warned, for example, that any sources of UN leverage amount to naught unless the peacekeepers are adequately supported and the mission properly executed. This implies that the following four basic rules must be applied:

- peacekeepers must have the resources and determination to do the job and must ensure that the parties understand this;
- UN forces should absolutely minimize the amount of time it takes to deploy an effective monitoring and reporting capability;
- peacekeepers must act decisively immediately upon arrival and respond firmly to challenges;
- peacekeepers must act uniformly and respond uniformly to challenges.[17]

UNAMSIL missed the boat on all four of these points. Moreover, the notion of UN peacekeepers providing security through coercive disarmament and mandate enforcement defies the lessons of historical experience. For example, the UN seminar on lessons learned from the operations in Somalia concluded *inter alia* that a UN force is unsuited for non-voluntary disarmament and demobilization.[18]

The UN approach of minimizing risks though incremental military deployment also flies in the face of just about every recommendation of a series of "lessons learned" seminars that were conducted in the wake of the failed UN missions in Somalia and Rwanda. The most fundamental lesson to emerge from these endeavours is that there must be a clear and achievable mandate backed by sufficient means for its execution. If a peace operation is to be effective, it must be credible and perceived as such. The credibility of the operation is, in turn, a reflection of the parties' assessment of the force's capability to accomplish the mission.[19]

Yet the Security Council is increasingly invoking Chapter VII powers for the protection of civilians and the disarmament of combatants without a clear notion of how this is to be done in practice.[20] As David Cox has noted, "Until the UN finds a way between the hollow invocations of Chapter VII to which the Security Council is now prone, and acceptance that any recalcitrant party can sabotage a mission by withdrawing its consent, the frustration of complex UN peacekeeping operations, especially in regard to disarmament, is likely to continue."[21]

International efforts to enhance peace operations

The immediate response of the UN Security Council to the hostage-taking and RUF aggression was one of shock and outrage, even though they had ample warning that things were going very wrong with the UNAMSIL mission. As David Rieff puts it, "Only in the Alice-in-Wonderland atmosphere of the UN, where officials can simply deny realities everyone else sees plainly, could the RUF's defiance and the deaths of the peacekeepers have come as a surprise."[22]

Concerned about the safety of the UN hostages, the only plan that UN Headquarters could come up with was to speed up the deployment of the outstanding national contingents earmarked for UNAMSIL. The idea was to increase the number of peacekeepers from 8,700 to the full authorized strength of over 11,000 as soon as possible. Bemoaning the poor state of training and equipment of the existing UNAMSIL force, Kofi Annan was also quick to call for a "rapid-reaction force" to be deployed immediately, to stabilize the precarious situation and bolster the UNAMSIL forces.

To be fair, the UN Secretary-General has been pushing harder than any of his predecessors for doctrinal clarity on what can and cannot be done within the broad rubric of peace support. Following up on his September 1999 report to the Council on the protection of civilians in armed conflict,[23] Annan announced on 7 March 2000 that he was appointing an international panel to look at every aspect of UN peacekeeping, and to make recommendations on how missions can be more effective.

At the news conference where the appointment of the panel was announced, the Secretary-General outlined its brief as follows:

Partly it is a question of being clearer about what we are trying to do, and partly it is a question of getting the nuts and bolts right ... I hope that in the next six months or a year we would have enough ideas on when and how we intervene. Under our charter, we are allowed to use force in the common interest. But there are questions that we will have to answer. What is the common interest? Who defines it? Who defends it? And under what authority and under what circumstances?[24]

This panel was obviously hard pressed to come up with viable answers to the "million-dollar" questions posed by Annan – questions that have defied the best efforts of the peace research community for the past decade. The *Report of the Panel on United Nations Peace Operations*, or the "Brahimi Report", released on 21 August 2000, articulates some 20 recommendations that will require a great deal of support by UN member states for implementation. These represent a good blend of principle and pragmatism, and deserved the widespread support they received at the UN Millennium Summit. However, they are aimed mainly at the organization and mechanics of UN peacekeeping, including the issue of more rapid deployment, and do little to address some of the more fundamental questions posed by Annan. The single recommendation on "Peace-keeping doctrine and strategy" states simply that:

Once deployed, United Nations peacekeepers must be able to carry out their mandates professionally and successfully and be capable of defending themselves, other mission components and the mission's mandate, with robust rules of engagement, against those who renege on their commitments to a peace accord or otherwise seek to undermine it by violence.[25]

Canada was quick to respond to the higher-order deficit. During his address to the UN General Assembly on 7 September 2000 (during the Millennium Summit), Prime Minister Chrétien announced that his country would establish an independent International Commission on Intervention and State Sovereignty (ICISS).[26] The mandate of the ICISS is to promote a comprehensive debate and forge consensus around the vexing issues surrounding intervention and state sovereignty. The commission will have a year to complete its work before Canada reports its findings and recommendations for action to the 56th General Assembly.

The ICISS will be challenged to address the concerns of developing countries, which have hitherto been marginalized in the intervention debate and therefore have strong reservations (along with countries such as China and Russia) about the legitimacy of the concept of humanitarian intervention. For example, Chinese President Jiang Zemin emphasized in his address to the Millennium Summit that "respect for each other's independence and sovereignty is vital to the maintenance of world peace", and that "Dialogue and co-operation in the field of human rights must be conducted on the basis of respect for state sovereignty. Without sovereignty, there will be no human rights to speak of."[27] The massive investment in the Balkans and the refusal of the West to do something significant in Rwanda, and more recently in Sierra Leone, have also led to strong accusations by Africans of inconsistency in the application of formally universal humanitarian standards.[28]

While the jury is still out on the issue of intervention versus state sovereignty, the focus remains on addressing armed conflicts and threats to peace and security in Africa through the medium of externally sponsored programmes aimed at "enhancing African peacekeeping capacity".

The "P3" initiative

In adopting the 1993 Cairo Declaration on the establishment of a Mechanism for Conflict Prevention, Management, and Resolution, the OAU Assembly of heads of state and government decided that "the Mechanism will have as primary objective the anticipation and prevention of conflicts". Indeed, the Cairo Declaration stressed that the "emphasis on anticipatory and preventive measures and concerted action in peace-making and peace-building will obviate the need to resort to the complex and resource demanding peacekeeping operations which our countries will find difficult to finance". At the Cairo summit, the African heads of state and government emphasized that the United Nations, with its cumulative experience, expertise, and greater resources than the OAU, should clearly remain the pre-eminent international authority with the responsibility for dealing with international peace and security – including internal crises which threaten regional stability in Africa.

However, Western disengagement from African interventions was soon to be accompanied by attempts to devolve responsibility for peacekeeping to Africans themselves through a process of "peacekeeping capacity-building". At its 11th Ordinary Session on 10 January 1995, the central organ of the OAU Mechanism, meeting at the ambassadorial level, sought clarification on the various initiatives coming from outside Africa, all with the aim of supporting OAU efforts in the area of peacekeeping. In particular, reference was made to the British-sponsored peacekeeping seminar that was under way in Cairo at the time.

A French proposal for an African intervention force had also emerged from the Biarritz francophone summit of 1994. In essence, the French proposal aimed at the creation of a modest standing force, with possible contributions from African countries, which could be utilized during times of crisis. It was further proposed that this force would be mobilized under the auspices of the OAU and its member states. The French initiative included plans for an assessment of the capacity of member states in a particular subregion to intervene during crisis situations, the training of contingents in peace maintenance, and the training of a high-command staff.[29]

The main thrust of both the British and French initiatives related to the setting up of a multinational African rapid-deployment peace force. These initiatives, which enjoyed European and American support, further envisaged the pre-positioning of equipment at logistics bases in strategic points in Africa, with Europe, the USA, and others providing logistics while Africa would supply the personnel.[30]

In October 1996, former US Secretary of State Warren Christopher travelled to Africa to promote a proposal to set up an all-African military force. The African Crisis Response Force (ACRF), as it was then known, was to be used to deal with African crises where insurrections, civil war, or genocide threaten mass civilian casualties. The intermediate objective of the ACRF was to develop a rapid-reaction capability for such contingencies. It was hoped that the ACRF would be used for humanitarian intervention in Burundi. However, this "quick-fix" solution was met with widespread scepticism, and the USA transformed the idea of an African intervention force into a longer-term capacity-building initiative. By mid-1997, the original ACRF idea had evolved into the African Crisis Response Initiative, or ACRI.

According to the State Department, "The African Crisis Response Initiative (ACRI) is a training program which envisions a partnership with African and other interested nations to enhance African peacekeeping capacities, particularly the capacity to mount an effective, collective response to humanitarian and other crises."[31] The transformation of the US initiative caused confusion and some annoyance in Africa, and exposed the lack of donor coordination in the realm of African capacity-building.

Nevertheless, the USA went ahead with the ACRI programme. By the end of 1997, infantry battalions in Senegal, Uganda, and Malawi had participated in two-month ACRI training sessions presented by the US Third Special Forces Group under the command of Colonel David McCracken. On 7 February 1998, an ACRI team began the fourth round of two-month interventions when it started training an 837-strong battalion in Mali.[32]

Such sensitivities to the lack of coordination in the realm of external capacity-building initiatives moved the major players to announce, in late 1997, the launching of a "P3" initiative. This presents the ACRI as the US component of a joint initiative by the UK, the USA, and France. The French element of the P3 initiative is known as RECAMP (Reinforcement of African Military Peacekeeping Capacity), while the British element is known as the UK African Peacekeeping Training Support Programme.

In October 1997 the OAU Secretary-General Salim Ahmed Salim reiterated in his report to the central organ of the OAU Mechanism that "... the need for Africa to be prepared to take some degree of responsibility in peacekeeping is even greater today than ever before". Importantly, he went on to add that, "This feeling is primarily based on initiatives that have continued to emerge, all aimed at assisting Africa in the area of peacekeeping."[33]

In his concluding remarks to this report, the OAU Secretary-General noted that many OAU member states, while recognizing the necessity for a rapid-response capability for complex emergencies, contested some of the key assumptions and principles underpinning the P3 initiative. Special mention was made of unexplained and unresolved issues relating to:

- command, control, and doctrine;
- logistics;
- eligibility for participation by specific African states;
- operating procedures;
- the funding and sustainability of such training.

Secretary-General Salim also noted the emergent trend towards devolving responsibility for peacekeeping operations to organizations such as NATO in Europe and, by implication and in the absence of a similar military alliance, the OAU in Africa. The concern that many had expressed is that such arrangements had the potential of exonerating non-African players from involvement in resolving what some of them had described as intractable African conflicts.[34]

Finally, the Secretary-General recommended that the central organ of the OAU Mechanism could:

Entrust the forthcoming meeting of African Chiefs of Staff to deliberate on the [P3] Initiative, with a view to advising on the current evolution of the ACRI as sponsored by the US, French and UK Governments and to explore the possibility of adopting a common African position on the Initiative, after:
a) examining the issues of doctrine, logistics, participation, Command and Control, as well as financial sustainability of such an initiative;
b) determining allocation of various responsibilities to OAU member states;
c) determining issues of interoperability of equipment and forces; and
d) advising on what kind of situations such a force could be used for (peacekeeping, humanitarian assistance, observation, peace restoration) and the role of sub-regional organisations (ECOWAS, SADC, IGAD and ECCAS) in peace support operations.[35]

It is thus clear that the failure of the USA (or P3) to clarify how their peacekeeping capacity-building initiative would translate into actual utilization of such capacity (beyond vague references such as "under the auspices of the United Nations or the OAU") created a dilemma for the OAU. On the one hand, the organization did not want to be negative about outside assistance to enhance African peacekeeping capacity. On the other hand, the organization was being forced, through such initiatives, to deliberate prematurely on issues that were not envisaged to be pertinent at the time of the Cairo Declaration (such as the ability of the OAU to authorize, direct, and sustain large-scale multinational peace support operations on the continent).

African efforts to develop appropriate intervention doctrine

However, it was also realized that regional and subregional organizations on the one hand, and the UN system on the other hand, should endeavour to share proportionately the burden relating to the maintenance of worldwide peace, security, and stability. Moreover, the OAU realized the need to take primary ownership of its own problems, especially those relating to issues of peace, security, and stability. But the OAU Charter does not provide for a mechanism to control or enforce the implementation of the organization's decisions. Rather, under the auspices of the Mechanism, the OAU is mandated to coordinate activities with African regional and subregional organizations and to cooperate as appropriate with neighbouring countries with respect to conflicts arising in the different parts of the continent. The OAU thus encourages subregional organizations to initiate preventive diplomacy and peacemaking efforts.

Given the trend towards regional coalition operations, and the fact that Africa is once again host to the vast majority of UN peacekeepers, Africans themselves also have a responsibility to contribute to the evolution of a viable doctrine for peace support. It serves little purpose to bemoan the lack of institutional capacity in the OAU Secretariat to direct and sustain peace operations if no one has a clear idea of what the concept of such operations should be.

The first real African attempt to address the doctrinal deficit for the conduct of peace support operations (PSOs) was made at the second meeting of the chiefs of defence staff of member states of the OAU's central organ, which was held in Harare on 24–25 October 1997. This meeting was specifically tasked to come up with concrete and workable recommendations relating to the logistics, finance, training, doctrine, structure, and operational planning needed for the conduct of African peace support operations. The mandate emanated from the previous year's meeting of the chiefs of staff, which had called for a working group of military experts to "come out with practical and realistic recommendations on the technical issues raised" at that meeting on the subject of peace operations under OAU auspices.[36]

The OAU Secretariat had decided that this expert meeting would be held just prior to the second meeting of the chiefs of staff, and that it would be divided into three subgroups dealing respectively with logistics and funding; doctrine, training, and liaison; and command, control, and communications. The subgroup on doctrine, training, and liaison was more specifically requested to develop "guidelines which should inform doctrine and training" for the conduct of peace operations.[37]

The political sensitivities of African military officers soon became apparent, with one member objecting at the outset to the group's intent to discuss "doctrine". The objection was based on the grounds that the matters under discussion had no approval at the policy level, and that doctrine was a political and strategic concept. This, it was felt, implied abrogating the OAU principle of non-interference in the internal affairs of member states, and could not be discussed by a group of military experts. After lengthy deliberation, it was decided to refer to the development of recommendations on "guidelines" or "concepts" for the conduct of peace operations, rather than "doctrine".

Nevertheless, after two days of deliberation the group could only reach consensus on the notion that the OAU should adopt and adapt the concepts, principles, and practices of UN peacekeeping, and that member states should only engage in peace operations mandated by the United Nations. The latter point, namely that all operations involving OAU member states be conducted under a UN mandate, was challenged by the question: "What happens when there is a crisis or impending crisis, and there is no UN mandate?" This was followed by the more pertinent question: "Why would the United Nations not react to a crisis?" The answers included lack of finances and other resources – including political will.

It was felt that this problem may best be addressed by OAU efforts to strengthen the UN capacity for peace operations, by placing African crises on the UN agenda, and by providing the bulk of a ready-force package for utilization by the United Nations. However, it was noted that the OAU or subregional organizations may first have to take action in order to place matters on the UN agenda, as illustrated by the ECOMOG decision to impose sanctions on the military rulers of Sierra Leone, which was later endorsed by the Security Council.[38]

Given the reality of a number of existing crises on the continent, the need was expressed for a clear vision of what the OAU can realistically be expected to do to ameliorate conflict where the United Nations is unable, unwilling, or slow to act. The concept that eventually emerged for the conduct of OAU peace operations included the use of subregional organizations as a possible first line of reaction where the OAU is unable to act.[39]

The working group also reasoned that if the concept of peace operations under the auspices of the OAU is accepted, then the OAU's central organ needs to have some type of military instrument at hand for preliminary interventions. It was felt that this may be provided by a workable system of African standby arrangements, and that such a system would enjoy more support if contributors had an idea of the overall requirements of the end-user (the OAU). In this regard, the chiefs of defence staff recommended that "The OAU could earmark a brigade-sized contribution to standby arrangements from each of the five African sub-regions as a starting point, which could then be adjusted upwards or downwards according to evolving circumstances." They added that: "While the OAU should adopt standard UN staff procedures for training and operations, it must also develop its own Standard Operating Procedures" and that "these must be disseminated to Member States for use in training and preparation for peace operations".[40]

Significantly, the notion of brigade-sized standby forces was echoed some three years later in the Brahimi Report, in which Recommendation 9(a) states that:

Member States should be encouraged, where appropriate, to enter into partnerships with one another, within the context of the United Nations Standby Arrangements System (UNSAS), to form several coherent brigade-size forces, with necessary enabling forces, ready for effective deployment within 30 days of the adoption of a Security Council resolution establishing a traditional peacekeeping operation and within 90 days for complex peacekeeping operations.[41]

Unfortunately, there has been absolutely no progress on the implementation of any of these recommendations at the level of the OAU. Nor has a third meeting of the chiefs of staff been convened which might trigger some urgent action in this regard. Not that this makes much difference from the perspective of doctrinal development. The recommendations that emerged on "the concept of African peace support operations" were a compromise that amounts to little more than a confirmation of the move towards the "Africanization" of UN peacekeeping. However, the chiefs of staff did provide recognition for the concept of subregional engagement in peace operations, and this is perhaps where more significant progress can be made in the realm of future doctrinal development.

Progress at the subregional level: SADC

The Southern African Development Community (SADC), as an intergovernmental entity, has not succeeded in progressing much further than the OAU in the articulation of a common doctrine for peace support operations that includes peace enforcement. Indeed, while the southern region has over the past few years witnessed two extremely forceful "multilateral" military interventions under the auspices of the SADC (Lesotho and the Democratic Republic of Congo), the organization's military leaders have clung to the notion of embracing a "universal UN doctrine" for the conduct of PSOs. Doctrinal development has therefore been informed less by regional multinational operational experience than by "mainstream" UN-type training and capacity-building initiatives.

For example, the 1999 meeting of the Operations Sub-Sub Committee of the (Southern African) Inter-State Defence and Security Committee (ISDSC) did not address the issue of doctrine for PSOs, but chose to focus rather on training and capacity-building issues.[42] The debate on the latter has largely been shaped by the Harare-based SADC Regional Peacekeeping Training Centre (RPTC), which specializes in the presentation of a variety of UN peacekeeping courses for select members of the armed forces of the SADC countries. This role and focus have been embraced by the ISDSC, with the Operations Sub-Sub Committee recommending that the "ISDSC Defence Sub-Committee officially endorses Zimbabwe as the Regional Peacekeeping Training Centre". The March 1999 meeting of this committee was also presented with a report by the RPTC on a seminar that it had convened to consider the future of peacekeeping training in the SADC region.

Importantly, the deliberations of this seminar were guided by the assumption that any peacekeeping "capacity building within SADC should occur within the UN framework and comply with UN doctrine, procedures, guidelines, etc.".[43] The only decision taken at this seminar which is vaguely related to doctrinal development is recorded as follows: "Drawing from the direction of the ISDSC, the RPTC would provide guidance on peacekeeping concepts and serve as a repository for regional peacekeeping Standing Operating Procedures (SOPs) and policy documents."[44] Thus at the official regional level there is a strict adherence to "UN doctrine", with any further debate on doctrine for peace enforcement remaining taboo.

Learning from West African experiences

Although not articulated or presented as such, some basic tenets of African doctrine for PSOs are emerging from the West African region. This has not been a deliberate construct of ECOWAS – it is rather a by-product of the involvement of members of this organization in regional peace operations over the past nine years.

The ECOWAS Monitoring Group (ECOMOG) was formed spontaneously in August 1990 as a direct reaction to the carnage caused by the civil war in Liberia.[45] Armed with a peacekeeping mandate, ECOMOG forces landed in Monrovia on 24 August 1990, only to be met by fierce gunfire from the forces of Charles Taylor's National Patriotic Front of Liberia. No cease-fire was in place, and the refusal of a major party to the conflict to accept the impartiality of ECOMOG meant that the force found it extremely difficult to execute its peacekeeping mandate. Indeed, within its relatively short lifespan ECOMOG was forced to go through the full cycle of peace support operations – from peacekeeping and peace enforcement in Liberia to "restorative intervention" in Sierra Leone and Guinea Bissau.[46]

Former ECOMOG force commander Brigadier General Mitikishe Khobe categorized the type of peace operations conducted under the auspices of ECOWAS as intervention missions, peace enforcement missions, and peacekeeping missions.[47] This description of ECOMOG operations roughly parallels (or indeed precedes) developments in NATO doctrinal thinking. In fact, it goes quite a bit further than extant NATO doctrine in that it provides for "intervention operations".

Once the ECOMOG task metamorphosed into hybrid operations involving peacekeeping, counter-insurgence, and peace enforcement, the principles of internal security operations were applied in varying degrees according to their relevance to particular phases of operations.[48] The inclusion of aspects of "internal security operations" as part of the concept of peace support operations echoes, in some respects, Russian thinking on peace operations. Whether or not such principles will or should find their way into an African doctrine for PSOs remains a matter for debate and consultation. The important thing is not to discard such "doctrinal statements" as being extraneous to the "peacekeeping debate". Observations and statements by former ECOMOG commanders obviously do not constitute an eloquent and integrated doctrine for African peace support operations. There is room for much refinement and adjustment, and, importantly, a need for broader acceptance of such principles in Africa and abroad.

Progress in the evolution of West African doctrine for peace support has, as in the case of NATO in the Balkans, evolved less from academic reflection and the deliberations of "experts" than from the harsh experiences of force commanders and peacekeepers on the ground. The difference is that the "lessons learned" from the ECOMOG operations have not been as widely analysed, and they are certainly not as well packaged as those that have emerged from the Balkans. However, they do provide a far more robust and practical articulation of principles and guidelines for the conduct of PSOs in Africa than that which has hitherto been produced by either the OAU or the SADC.

Consulting with the colonels: A "bottom-up" approach

At the unofficial level some modest but promising progress has been made in advancing a more practical and pragmatic approach to the issue of doctrinal development for PSOs in Africa. From 24 to 26 August 1999, the SADC RPTC agreed to host an unofficial regional workshop of "military experts" (of the rank of lieutenant-colonel/colonel) on "Integrated Principles for Peace Support Operations".[49] Mindful of the objections raised to the term "doctrine" at the second OAU chiefs of defence staff meeting, the stated aim of this workshop was to "[e]nhance mutual understanding of the principles and guidelines for the conduct of PSOs at the operational and tactical levels, through the proposal of workable solutions to existing problems and the recommendation of research projects to address those key problems/issues that could not be adequately addressed by the participants".

A draft working paper was provided to orient participants and to guide discussions. The idea was to initiate a deliberate process which examines the best evidence of past conflicts, and draws on African opinions and African experiences to bring together a considered, robust set of statements that will inform the evolution of doctrine for peace support. It was agreed that the workshop should focus on doctrine (the operational level and the tactical levels) rather than political, legal, or strategic matters. These higher levels normally result in nebulous discussions without form or conclusion. The working document contained some forthright questions, such as:

- is there such thing as "UN doctrine for PSOs"?
- if so, what are its strengths and limitations?
- if Western doctrinal publications are not suitable for Africa, where are they deficient?
- how can we express the doctrine deficit as regards Africa's requirements?
- how can we best approach the deficit – by a series of statements relating to Africa or a whole new doctrine?

Participants found that the much-vaunted UN doctrine on PSOs consists of some training notes, manuals, and videos covering tactical matters. There is also a 17-page document on the conduct of peacekeeping operations, but it is thin on detail. Similarly, peacekeeping manuals from the Nordic countries emphasize "peacekeeping" techniques at the tactical level, largely to the exclusion of operational concepts. These publications all emphasize techniques, drills, and procedures and do not really address key issues of doctrine at the operational level.

It was also felt that training exercises within the SADC, based on such tactical skills, have shown up doctrinal weaknesses, and that the need exists within the SADC to train to a common doctrine that embraces the types of PSOs which these countries are conducting or are most likely to conduct in the future. At the moment, SOPs are being developed to fill the doctrinal lacuna. However, these do not address critical facets such as multinational command arrangements and relations between the regional military and civilian structures.

Without the political baggage associated with "official status", participants readily agreed that the doctrinal deficit in Africa centres around the need to define circumstances which should trigger peace enforcement methods. They agreed that extant traditional peacekeeping doctrine is not sufficiently robust to confront the new challenges of conflict resolution in Africa, and that war-fighting doctrine is overly destructive. Furthermore, war-fighting doctrine is predicated upon the defeat of a designated enemy and does not address the peace-building and reconciliation challenges necessary to create a secure and self-sustaining society and environment.

Participants felt that there is a need for a more comprehensive doctrinal publication to address this issue coherently and provide *inter alia* operational concepts as well as tactical SOPs. While extant (NATO) PSO doctrine goes a long way to filling the doctrinal lacuna between traditional peacekeeping and war-fighting, it needs to be updated and modified to suit the realities of Africa.[50] In terms of immediate steps towards addressing the "doctrinal deficit", the preference was expressed for a comprehensive draft publication which could be circulated for comment as widely as possible in the form of a discussion document.

The author of the extant NATO PSO manual[51] was therefore asked to produce a draft PSO manual which takes account of the special needs of PSOs in the African context and incorporates the doctrinal ideas developed during the workshop. The product of this endeavour, entitled *Peace Support Operations: A Draft Working Manual for African Military Practitioners*, was published by the ISS in February 2000.[52] This document is presently being circulated to select African command and staff colleges (and other relevant institutions) with requests for comments.

This is seen as a first step in a process designed to develop a common approach among African national military contingents for the conduct of "grey-area operations". It is, in many ways, a "quick-fix" approach that has many weaknesses, as much of the NATO manual is probably too alliance-specific. But if certain fundamental concepts and points of departure can be accepted, then this is a good starting point. In particular, acceptance of military *credibility*, through the immediate deployment of robust forces into the area of operations, as a *sine qua non* for success in PSOs will go a long way towards encouraging sound mission planning.

The draft manual is not meant to be a perfect product, nor is it complete. The endorsement of African multilateral organizations, such as the OAU and SADC, has therefore not been sought. The idea was not to claim universal applicability, but to invite African senior command and staff colleges to use what they find useful for instructional purposes, and to discard/replace that which they do not find useful. The aspiration is to begin an interactive process of peer review and refinement that will lead to greater consensus on PSO doctrine in Africa and will eventually influence decision-making and training across the continent.

However, this approach is also based on incrementalism and the need to forge minimal consensus in the shadow of Western PSO doctrine, rather than a true appraisal of what needs to be done and can be done by Africans themselves.

Thinking "outside the box": Conflict-termination operations

The humanitarian intervention regime contemplated by Western thinkers is centred on the Security Council and the military involvement of rich developed countries. It is not necessarily applicable to Africa. Moreover, the current commitments of the developed countries in the Balkans are proving increasingly difficult to sustain, whilst they severely deplete the stock of resources and political will available for interventions on the African continent (Tables 6.1 and 6.2.)

Nevertheless, the example of Kosovo proves that the United Nations is capable of deploying the requisite peace-building architecture once a situation of internal armed conflict has been stabilized or terminated. According to Doyle, "one cannot define peace as nothing short of economic justice or social harmony without losing an understanding of peace as something different from and, possibly, less demanding than those other worthwhile goals".[53] He also sees a temporal dimension to the process of peace-building, recognizing the fact that a temporary peace can be achieved through coercion, but that more durable peace involves aspects

Table 6.1 Ten largest contributors to UN peacekeeping operations as of 30 September 2000

Country	Troops	Civilian police	Military observers	UN total
India	3,816	661	30	4,507
Nigeria	3,201	219	19	3,439
Jordan	2,531	850	19	3,400
Bangladesh	2,134	156	72	2,362
Ghana	1,572	301	33	1,906
Australia	1,580	99	31	1,710
Pakistan	774	367	68	1,209
Kenya	1,130	36	31	1,197
Poland	990	62	25	1,077
Nepal	890	124	23	1,037

Source: *The Preparedness Gap: Making Peace Operations Work in the 21st Century*, policy report of United Nations Association of the USA, 2001, p. 27.

Table 6.2 Nine largest contributors to SFOR and KFOR peacekeeping compared
with UN peacekeeping contributions as of 30 September 2000

Country	SFOR (Stabilization Force)	KFOR (Kosovo Force)	NATO-led total	UN troops	UN police	UN observers	UN total
USA	6,300	6,500	12,800	0	865	36	901
France	2,800	5,300	8,100	261	180	49	490
Italy	1,600	6,300	7,900	62	75	32	169
Germany	1,800	5,400	7,200	14	448	11	473
UK	2,500	4,000	6,500	315	206	40	561
Russia	1,200	3,200	4,400	110	124	68	302
Spain	1,300	1,700	3,000	0	195	3	198
Turkey	1,000	1,100	2,100	0	165	13	178
Canada	1,500	0	1,500	189	116	27	332

Source: *The Preparedness Gap: Making Peace Operations Work in the 21st Century*, policy report of United Nations Association of the USA, 2001, p. 27.

of legitimacy, political participation, social integration, and economic development. However, "it does appear difficult, if not impossible, to secure the higher, more dynamic aspects of peace before the lower aspects of law and order are met".[54]

The challenge for Africa, as far as military doctrine for peace support is concerned, is to come up with a viable substitute for NATO's use of overwhelming air power to create a sufficiently secure environment for the international humanitarian and peace-building machinery to engage. The obvious substitute would be well-trained and well-equipped ground forces who are capable of confronting rebel forces that challenge *de jure* government forces and target innocent civilians in their unconstitutional quest for political power. This may seem like an oversimplification of the intervention dilemma, but Sierra Leone has confirmed a glaring inability to secure even the basics of humanitarian space and law and order.

What Africans can and should develop is a workable concept for conflict-termination operations and a viable capacity to conduct such operations. The primary aim of conflict-termination operations would be to stabilize the ailing state in order to stop the killing and maiming of civilians in the shortest possible time. Given the resource constraints confronting all African interventionists, this could be achieved through multilateral military intervention for the purpose of altering the internal balance of power and assisting beleaguered government forces in establishing an army capable of overpowering the opposition or winning a sufficiently decisive military victory to force all parties to the negotiating table.

Of course, this implies a rejection of the notions of impartiality and consent as a basis for intervention. The precedent for breaking with such established principles was well established with the NATO intervention in Kosovo. However, African conflict-termination operations would and could not be premised on air power, but could involve the following activities:

- training and assisting the chosen force towards a credible military posture or sufficient military victory;
- law enforcement (according to the mandate, but likely to include coercive disarmament);
- protection for emergency humanitarian aid to save lives, where this does not exacerbate the aim of speedy conflict termination (humanitarian agencies must not be allowed to derail the immediate objective of the operation);
- inculcating new standards of proficiency, professionalism, and cohesion in the assisted force.

Such interventions should contribute to popular political (and not parochial economic) outcomes. They must be aimed at changing, rather than sustaining, the *status quo*, for it is the legitimacy of the *status quo* that is at issue in communal conflicts. For example, when a force intervenes on the side of a legal (although perhaps corrupt or repressive) regime, such intervention must be predicated on a pre-agreed and viable programme for establishing political accountability, with benchmarks that can be monitored by the authorizing body.

Conflict-termination operations would be concluded when a cease-fire agreement is signed between the warring parties and negotiations begin for a lasting settlement. However, the conflict-termination force should remain deployed until the signing of a comprehensive peace agreement that complies with minimum standards and guidelines provided by a legitimate multilateral body such as the United Nations, the OAU, or a subregional organization. Authorization for such an operation would obviously have to be granted by the UN Security Council, invoking the full powers of Chapter VII of the UN Charter. Such authorization may not be readily forthcoming.

The intervening agent is also problematic. While its legal status would depend on a Security Council mandate which allows for very robust rules of engagement, the suggested concept of operations has no precedent within the UN system, and it is doubtful whether there is sufficient political will to involve national troop contingents in such a multilateral force. The viability of the proposed concept for conflict-termination operations in Africa therefore rests also on the development of an appropriate intervening agent.

The "conventional" notion of a layered response to African crises envisages local and national organizations responding initially, followed by responses at the subregional and regional (OAU) levels, and finally by those of the broader international community. This concept is meant to overcome the widely acknowledged inertia at the level of the United Nations, and enable more rapid and appropriate responses at much lower levels of the international security framework. However, the concept is flawed in that where the use of military force is concerned, there is just as much inertia at these lower levels when clearly identified national interests are not directly threatened.

Moreover, no international organization has yet assumed a supranational position of authority over the military forces of its members, despite Article 43(1) of the UN Charter. Where individual national armies have had the capacity and will to intervene in African crises, it has been in pursuit of the real or perceived narrow national interests of the intervening country. Subregional responses (such as ECOMOG in Liberia) have not fared much better in Africa. They have been messy, drawn out, and, arguably, as ineffective as UN responses.

The OAU has made great progress since 1993 in establishing the Mechanism for Conflict Prevention, Management, and Resolution, but it is a long way from fielding an all-African force for effective military intervention. African subregional organizations, like the OAU, are underfinanced in the extreme. There is also a limit to what the donor community is willing to provide in terms of assistance to such organizations. Any capabilities for intervention that are created at these levels will therefore have to be both effective and cost-efficient.

A possible solution might be the establishment of a relatively small but professional standing African Legion as the first layer of response during the emergency (conflict-termination) phase of crises. Such a legion should have, at a minimum, the following attributes:

- clear political direction from the OAU;
- clear command and control via the force commander and normal military command structures, including a common language;
- high cohesion (well-trained, well-paid, and highly motivated personnel);
- strict recruitment and promotional criteria;
- standardized doctrine and training for joint operations;
- standard equipment tables;
- access to strategic airlift and tactical air power on inventory;
- a binding code of conduct;
- transparency through the co-deployment of UN/OAU observers.

The force would have to be premised on quality and cohesion, rather than quantity, and the imperative of broad geographic representation. Recruiting according to a pan-African all-volunteer force recipe should ensure a fair geographical spread, but the selection criteria should be devoid of political imperatives. The force would recruit individuals, rather than units of national armies, so that it would be unconstrained by the domestic political imperatives of the countries from which the recruits are drawn. Standards for selection and promotion must be based strictly on operational proficiency. Soldiers would swear allegiance to Africa and the legion, rather than to any single nation. While there would have to be a single language of command and control (bound to be a thorny issue), members of the force should be encouraged to remain conversant in major African languages, such as Swahili.

With a permanent force commander and headquarters staff, the total size of the standing force need not exceed 1,000 personnel. This small size would be compensated by the élite nature of the force, and would keep personnel costs within reasonable limits. Even so, the annual salary bill of such a force would amount to at least $24m (based on an average individual salary of US$2,000 per month, or about twice the UN scale of reimbursement). However, recruitment would be based on a renewable contract system, allowing the force to expand and contract as the situation demands. Service in the legion should be recognized as honourable military service in an élite unit by all African military organizations for purposes of re-employment and seniority.

An African Legion would bridge the gap between legitimate but ineffective international responses and the recent trend towards "illegitimate" but seemingly effective responses by security entrepreneurs. It should have the longer-term effect of deterring future acts of armed rebellion and genocide and allowing people to rethink the political futures of their countries from a regional rather than a national perspective.

While the African Legion would be a professional standing force, it should be relatively inexpensive to maintain – especially when compared to some of the larger operations financed by the United Nations in Africa during recent years. Basic personnel expenses could be covered by an annual UN/OAU assessment. Its initial start-up costs could be financed within the limits of current donor-driven peacekeeping capacity-building schemes, such as the US-backed African Crisis Response Initiative. Weapons, equipment, and maintenance could be supplied by donor countries within and outside of Africa.

Conclusion

Peacekeeping in general, and in Africa in particular, is in a state of fundamental flux. In fact, it is in a process of reinvention. The United Nations has already apologized for its peacekeepers' failure to prevent the genocide in Rwanda and the massacre of the inhabitants of the Bosnian safe haven at Srebrenica. The virtual disintegration of UNAMSIL in Sierra Leone during May 2000 is perceived as the latest in a string of peacekeeping failures on the African continent, as a result of which few lessons have been learned and little doctrinal revision has occurred.

However, UNAMSIL may signal the turning point for peacekeeping in Africa. It went wrong in a very public way, with nearly 9,000 UN troops on the ground. The mission did not disintegrate, as UNAMIR did in Rwanda, with only a handful of UN troops in place and the world ignorant of the tragedy until it was half over. Moreover, this time the UN Secretary-General clearly challenged member states, particularly permanent members of the Security Council, to become part of the solution. Combined with the fact that public understanding of the politics of intervention has deepened, this has lent significant impetus and urgency to the intervention debate.

The challenge of reconciling the duty to intervene with the perceived sanctity of state sovereignty remains a daunting one, but it is time to end the preoccupation with questions of consent, impartiality, and the non-use of force. This is essentially a non-issue. Everyone knows how to do Chapter VI peacekeeping (within a benign security environment, of course). Everyone wants to do this kind of peacekeeping, even with its new-found "multifunctionality". Indeed, a whole industry has developed around new-generation (Chapter VI) peacekeeping with its attendant "civilian component" and notions of "new peacekeeping partnerships".

On the other hand, nobody really knows how to do peace enforcement operations. And no one really wants to do these operations – unless, of course, there are very strongly perceived national interests at stake. Hence the concept of peace enforcement remains an extremely under-developed area of military doctrine – even though it is perhaps the most needed. The progress made by NATO in developing a doctrine for peace enforcement is encouraging, and there is no doubt much to be learned from this by African countries. However, doctrine is informed by military capabilities and structures, and there are limits to the applicability of NATO's high-tech approach to intervention.

The notion of developing a concept for "conflict-termination operations" in Africa may not seem politically feasible at present, but this belies the fact that there has been considerable movement in this direction. The NATO air action against Kosovo and Belgrade is obviously a case in point. But in Africa this type of operation has been approximated by executive outcomes in Angola and Sierra Leone, by SADC forces in Lesotho and the Democratic Republic of Congo, and more recently by the British Army in Sierra Leone – specifically, its efforts at training and preparing the Sierra Leonean Army to take the offensive against the RUF so that the United Nations can get on with more "traditional" peacekeeping. If these practices are converted into theory, this would indeed approximate to a doctrine for conflict-termination operations. In each case, however, the legitimacy of the intervening agent has been dubious, at best. Hence the idea of an African Legion.

The proposed African Legion is also not seen as a "cure-all" for communal conflicts in Africa. The strength, composition, and orientation of the legion would make it a highly specialized force for the conduct of narrowly defined conflict-termination operations. It would therefore have to be supplemented and complemented by a much larger force for the conduct of multifunctional peacekeeping tasks once there are sufficient security guarantees. The latter type of force may well benefit from present initiatives to create a more "conventional" African peacekeeping capacity; but the real need is for a realistic concept of operations and assistance with modalities for extremely rapid deployment to halt the killing and maiming of civilians. This is what was needed in Rwanda in April 1994, and it remains a quintessential doctrinal challenge that, if not met, will make a mockery of all efforts to build "African peacekeeping capacity".

Notes

1. E. Hutchful, "Peacekeeping under conditions of resource stringency: The Ghana Army in Liberia", paper presented at a SAIIA/ISS conference, From Peacekeeping to Complex Emergencies? Peace Support Missions in Africa, Johannesburg, 25 March 1999.
2. ECOWAS membership comprises Benin, Burkina Faso, Cape Verde, Côte d'Ivoire, the Gambia, Guinea, Guinea-Bissau, Liberia, Mali, Mauritania, Niger, Nigeria, Senegal, Sierra Leone, and Togo.
3. The force, which had been operating without international approval since early 1997, consisted of voluntary troop contributions by Burkina Faso, Chad, Gabon, Kenya, Senegal, and Togo. Under Chapter VII of the UN Charter, MISAB was entitled to use force in order to implement its mandate, which included the disarmament of rebellious factions of the CAR military. UN member states were not assessed for any portion of the mission costs, which had to be borne by participating countries. In effect, France carried much of the burden of sustaining the African contingents in the field. The Security Council finally succumbed to French pressure for the United Nations to take over responsibility for the CAR peace process from the hard-pressed MISAB contributors with effect from 15 April 1998. The role of the UN Mission in the Central African Republic (MINURCA) was to provide security long enough for the government of the CAR to undertake the reforms it had promised and to provide for its own security.
4. In June 1998, the UN Security Council decided to establish UNOMSIL for an initial period of six months. By the end of August 1998, UNOMSIL had completed the first phase of the deployment of its military component, consisting of 40 military observers, a chief military observer, and a medical team of 15 personnel. The mission was supposed to help with national reconciliation and with the demobilization of former soldiers. However, it was never more than a "lame duck" UN presence, of minor significance next to the regional ECOMOG force, whose total strength varied between 12,000 and 15,000 men. Nigeria was providing between 10,000 and 11,000 of these troops.
5. Peace Agreement between the Government of Sierra Leone and the Revolutionary United Front of Sierra Leone, Lomé, 7 July 1999.
6. *Ibid.*

7. *Ibid.*

8. Interview with Reuters, 7 April 2000.

9. *Third Report of the Secretary-General on the UN Mission in Sierra Leone*, S/2000/186, UN Security Council, 7 March 2000, paragraph 10.

10. Colum Lynch, "UN troops disarmed in Sierra Leone, US worried about peacekeeping ability", *Washington Post*, 6 February 2000.

11. Reuters, 7 February 2000.

12. Douglas Farah, "Diamonds help fill rebel group's arsenal", *Washington Post*, 17 April 2000.

13. *Ibid.*

14. S/2000/186, note 9, paragraphs 23–24.

15. According to the draft military reintegration plan (Iteration dated 31 January 2000), the 45,000 "ex"-combatants are from the following groupings: CDF – 15,000; RUF – 15,000; "paramilitaries"/mercenaries – 2,000; SLA – 6,000; ex-SLA/AFRC – 7,000.

16. Robert Block, "Diamonds appear to fuel the fires in Sierra Leone", *Wall Street Journal*, 12 May 2000.

17. Donald C. F. Daniel, "Is there a middle option in peace support operations? Implications for crisis containment and disarmament", in *Managing Arms in Peace Processes: The Issues*, New York and Geneva: United Nations (UNIDIR Disarmament and Conflict Resolution Project), 1996, pp. 81–82.

18. Friedrich Ebert Stiftung, Life and Peace Institute, Sweden, and Norwegian Institute for International Affairs, in cooperation with the UN DPKO, *Comprehensive Report on Lessons Learned in Somalia, April 1992–March 1995*, Sweden 1995, pp. 75–78.

19. Examining several peace support operations over the past nine years that "exemplify success", Daniel and Hayes conclude that "[t]he common thread throughout these examples is the quick deployment of robust forces which, possibly through shock effect, implicitly if not explicitly deliver the message that they mean business". D. C. F. Daniel and B. C. Hayes, *Securing Observance of UN Mandates through the Employment of Military Forces*, Newport, RI: US Naval War College, 1995. UNITAF and Operations Turquoise, Provide Comfort, and Uphold Democracy are cited as operations that succeeded in inducing cooperation from belligerents.

20. For example, operative paragraph 8 of Resolution 1291 (25 February 2000), authorizing the expanded MONUC mission to the Democratic Republic of Congo, states that the Council, "Acting under Chapter VII of the Charter of the United Nations, *decides* that MONUC may take the necessary action, in the areas of deployment of its infantry battalions and as it deems it within its capabilities, to protect United Nations and co-located JMC personnel, facilities, installations and equipment, ensure the security and freedom of movement of its personnel, and protect civilians under imminent threat of physical violence."

21. David Cox, "Peacekeeping and disarmament: Peace agreements, Security Council mandates, and the disarmament experience", in *Managing Arms in Peace Processes*, note 17, p. 133.

22. David Rieff, "In Sierra Leone, the UN had no peace to keep", *Wall Street Journal*, 8 May 2000.

23. *Report of the Secretary-General on the Protection of Civilians in Armed Conflict*, S/1999/957, UN Security Council, 8 September 1999.

24. Barbara Crossette, "Annan sets up panel to study UN's peacekeeping predicament", *New York Times*, 8 March 2000.

25. *Report of the Panel on United Nations Peace Operations*, A/55/305-S/2000/809, UN General Assembly/Security Council, 21 August 2000.

26. One of the co-editors of and contributors to this volume, Ramesh Thakur, is a member of the ICISS.

27. David E. Sanger, "Clinton warns UN of a new age of civil wars", *New York Times*, 6 September 2000.

28. For a recent account of the international community's reactions to the Kosovo conflict, see Albrecht Schnabel and Ramesh Thakur (eds), *Kosovo and the Challenge of Humanitarian Intervention: Selective Indignation, Collective Action, and International Citizenship*, Tokyo: United Nations University Press, 2000.

29. *Report on the OAU's Position Towards the Various Initiatives on Conflict Management: Enhancing OAU's Capacity in Preventive Diplomacy, Conflict Resolution and Peace-keeping*, OAU Secretariat, Central Organ/MEC/MIN/3 (IV), Addis Ababa, July 1995.

30. *Ibid.*

31. Texts of a briefing by Ambassador Marshall McCallie on the African Crisis Response Initiative (ACRI), US Department of State, Office of the Spokesman, Washington, DC, 29 July 1997.

32. Jim Fisher-Thompson, *Joint US-African Peacekeeper Training Kicks Off in Mali*, USIA, 26 February 1998.

33. *Report of the Secretary-General on the African Crisis Response Initiative (ACRI)*, OAU Secretariat, Central Organ/MEC/AMB/3 (XXXVIII), 9 October 1997, p. 4.

34. *Ibid.*, p. 28.

35. *Ibid.*, pp. 12–13.

36. The first chiefs of defence staff meeting of the central organ of the OAU was held in Addis Ababa, Ethiopia, on 3–6 June 1996.

37. *Report of the Military Experts Subgroup on Concepts, Training, and Liaison*, compiled by Mark Malan, Harare, 22 October 1997.

38. On 25 May 1997, President Kabbah was violently overthrown by Major Johnny Paul Koromah in a typical palace *coup d'état*. On 26 May 1997, the OAU condemned the coup and called for an immediate restoration of the constitutional order, urging the leaders of ECOWAS to take immediate action against the coup makers. In view of the intransigence of the *junta*, on 28 and 29 August 1997, the ECOWAS authority of heads of state and government decided to adopt a package of sanctions and establish a blockade against the regime as a further measure to force the early restoration of the democratically elected president.

39. *Draft Report of the Second Meeting of the Chiefs of Defence Staff of the Central Organ of the OAU Mechanism for Conflict Prevention, Management and Resolution*, Harare: OAU Secretariat, 25 October 1999.

40. *Ibid.*

41. *Report of the Panel on United Nations Peace Operations*, note 25, paragraph 91.

42. During the meeting of the 20th Session of the ISDSC, held in Swaziland in March 1999.

43. *Report of the SADC Seminar on Peacekeeping Training*, Harare: SADC Regional Peacekeeping Training Centre, 27–31 July 1998.

44. *Ibid.*

45. S. V. L Malu, "Political control and guidance of peace support operations in Africa: An ECOMOG perspective," paper presented at an international workshop, "Towards a Global Consensus on Peace Support Operations: The African Dimension", hosted by the ISS and the Institute for International Relations (Prague), Pretoria, 21–23 October 1999. Major-General Malu is a former ECOMOG force commander and is presently chief of army staff, Nigerian Army.

46. E. T. Dowyaro, "ECOMOG operations in West Africa: Principles and praxis", paper presented at an international workshop, "Towards a Global Consensus on Peace Sup-

port Operations: The African Dimension", hosted by the ISS and the Institute for International Relations (Prague), Pretoria, 21–23 October 1999. Brigadier-General Dowyaro is currently serving at Nigeria Army headquarters as commandant of NACAS.

47. M. M. Khobe, "The evolution and conduct of ECOMOG operations in West Africa", paper presented at an international workshop, "Towards a Global Consensus on Peace Support Operations: The African Dimension", hosted by the ISS and the Institute for International Relations (Prague), Pretoria, 21–23 October 1999. Subsequent to his ECOMOG command, Brigadier-General Khobe was appointed chief of defence staff, Sierra Leone Military Forces, a position which he occupied until his death on 19 April 2000.

48. Dowyaro, note 46.

49. The workshop was organized and facilitated by the Pretoria-based Institute for Security Studies (ISS) in partnership with the Prague-based Institute for International Relations (IIR). It was funded by the government of Norway as part of the "Training for Peace in Southern Africa" project, and is seen as part of a process of building consensus around real regional capacity-building for peace support operations. However, participation was not based upon any regional grouping or mandate. Rather, the group was constituted through personal networks that enabled the identification of a number of experienced military officers and civilian experts who were willing and able to contribute to a candid debate in pursuit of the aim and objectives of the workshop. The group that finally assembled in Harare included military officers from Botswana, Britain, Kenya, South Africa, and Zimbabwe, as well as a few civilian scholars and experts.

50. For a detailed exposition of the discussions and recommendations, see M. Malan, *Integrated Principles for Peace Support Operations*, ad hoc ISS report, September 1999.

51. Colonel Philip Wilkinson, British Army, who was a participant at the Harare workshop.

52. *Peace Support Operations: A Working Draft Manual for African Military Practitioners* (DWM 1-2000), Pretoria: Institute for Security Studies, February 2000.

53. Michael W. Doyle, *Peacebuilding in Cambodia*, IPA Policy Briefing Series, December 1996, p. 3.

54. *Ibid.*

7

Establishing the credibility of a regional peacekeeping capability

Vere Hayes

Recent events have again highlighted the difficulties the United Nations experiences in establishing "peacekeeping" missions where there is no true peace to keep. The insertion of a force under a Chapter VI self-defence mandate in such circumstances has been acknowledged as both unsuccessful and damaging to the credibility of the United Nations. Despite this it is sometimes hoped that providing more soldiers or "toughening" the mandate for the troops already in theatre will rescue a mission perceptibly failing in circumstances such as Sierra Leone. Neither is viable in an environment where there is less than total commitment by some factions to a peace agreement. An increase in UN forces merely offers a wider range of potential hostages; a change in mandate without the commensurate upgrading of weaponry, training, and command and control to act upon it raises false expectations and heightens the likelihood of a humiliation akin to Srebrenica or Rwanda.

In response to the events in Sierra Leone and the impact of the arrival of a small British contingent, UN Secretary-General Kofi Annan reportedly noted the need to rethink how troops are equipped and prepared for such operations, which also drawing a comparison with the UN deployment to eastern Slavonia in 1997. A UN assessment team was charged with the task to come to Freetown and uncover what had gone wrong with the peacekeeping mission.

The keyword that explains British success and UN difficulties in Sierra Leone is "credibility". The British force was trained, equipped, commanded, and sustained in a way that gave it credible combat power. There was the political will to employ that combat power as necessary under robust rules of engagement, and confidence that the professionalism and discipline of the troops would prevent an excessive use of force. In contrast, the UN force was lightly equipped and had little combat power; command and control was hampered by the lack of common doctrine and poor communications; collective political will amongst the troop-contributing nations, notoriously difficult to achieve in UN operations, was lacking; and standards of professionalism and discipline varied widely. The rebels perceived the United Nations Assistance Mission in Sierra Leone (UNAMSIL) to lack cohesion and be incapable of operating against them. When the credibility of the force was tested, as inevitably it was, they were proven right. The remainder of this chapter offers an examination of the issue of credibility in peace support operations.[1]

The case for regional forces

Classic peacekeeping missions, relying on consent and with a mandate under Chapter VI, are usually undertaken in the wake of interstate conflict. They are increasingly unlikely to occur. Intrastate conflict, in which not all parties accept an accord or can be guaranteed to abide by it, requires a coercive but impartial approach to the establishment of peace and thus a Chapter VII, or peace enforcement, mandate. Peace enforcement missions are increasingly common and, since their complexity is beyond the ability of the limited command and control resources of the United Nations, they are usually delegated to a coalition of the willing, an alliance or a regional military body authorized to act on behalf of the United Nations under Chapter VIII of the UN Charter. The Brahimi Report recognizes this, but advises caution "because military resources and capability are unevenly distributed around the world, and troops in the most crisis-prone areas are often less prepared for the demands of modern peacekeeping than is the case elsewhere". The report notes that: "Providing training, equipment, logistical support and other resources to regional ... organizations could enable peacekeepers from all regions to participate in a UN peacekeeping operation or to set up regional peacekeeping operations on the basis of a Security Council resolution."[2]

The spectrum of peace support operations

Although peace support operations (PSOs) include conflict prevention, peacemaking, peace-building, and humanitarian operations, only military

Table 7.1 An abbreviated spectrum of peace support operations

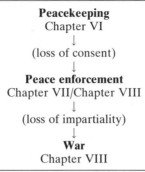

Table 7.2 Complexity of peace support operations

	Peacekeeping	Peace enforcement	War
In theatre	Consent (all levels)	Partial consent (some levels)	No consent (any level)
Casualties	Rare	Questioned	Expected
Home front	Acceptance	Ambivalence	Support

peacekeeping and peace enforcement are addressed specifically in this chapter. In simple terms the abbreviated spectrum being considered can be portrayed as a logical progression from peace to war (Table 7.1).

However, in terms of the complexity of the operating environment the spectrum is changed. Peace enforcement operations, where troops are deployed without an agreed settlement to police, slip down the line. "Consent" to the operation in theatre is ill-defined whilst public and political support for the operation "at home" can be fragile and largely dependent on the level of casualties (Table 7.2).

Avoidance of combat, and thus casualties, is a *sine qua non* for peace support operations. Success in PSOs is therefore largely dependent on a credible combat capability that is commensurate with the level of consent pertaining to the operation. This is illustrated in the British military publication JWP 3-50. Paragraph 312 is reproduced below.

Decisions concerning the profile and deployment of a peace support operations force should be based broadly on the model [Figure 7.1]. The horizontal line indicates the minimum level of consent necessary for the conduct of peacekeeping – "you cannot PK unless there is a peace to keep" – and the vertical line indicates the minimum force level below which peace enforcement is not feasible – "you cannot fight wars from white-painted vehicles". In the top left quadrant consent is

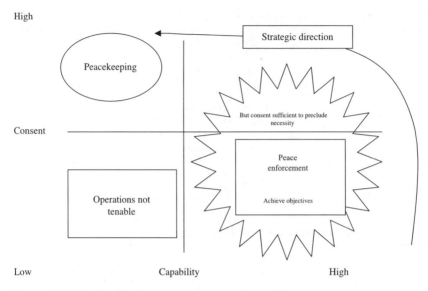

Figure 7.1 Relationship between consent and capability

high, thus a peacekeeping operation can be successfully conducted by a force with low combat capability. This is traditional, classic peacekeeping. In the top right quadrant consent would appear to be high but is assessed as uncertain or fragile and there is the expectation that it might be withdrawn. In such circumstances the judicious action will be to deploy prepared for peace enforcement with the expectation that the deployment of such force will ensure compliance from the outset … In the bottom right quadrant a peace enforcement force has deployed, consent for the operation is not forthcoming and it is necessary to use force to ensure compliance with the mandate. In the bottom left quadrant consent for the operation is below the critical level necessary to conduct peacekeeping but the force does not have the capability to operate against concerted opposition and achieve its objectives. In this quadrant a peacekeeping force will lose credibility and the operation becomes untenable. This quadrant should be avoided.[3]

Another way to illustrate this relationship can be seen in Figure 7.2.[4] As consent lessens, so capability must increase if the mission is to succeed.

Consent

Whilst Figure 7.2 suggests that peace enforcement does not necessarily require "consent", it does not differentiate between the strategic, operational, and tactical levels of command in this regard. At the strategic level

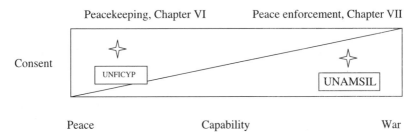

Figure 7.2 Consent and capability

there are two perspectives to be considered: that of the "interveners" and that of the "intervened-in state".[5] Countries contributing to the forces deployed need to secure the backing of both their own publics and the wider diplomatic community if the political will to intervene is to be sustained. The cost of the intervention, especially in terms of casualties, is a key factor governing public support for the operation, and thus political will to sustain it. There is therefore a need for "acceptance" of the mission within the United Nations, by the parties to the conflict at the highest levels, and amongst the general population of the country to which it is to deploy.

Recent deployments to Kosovo and East Timor were not authorized until strategic or governmental agreement had been reached on them, and they were "accepted" by Serbia and Indonesia, respectively, as well as in the Security Council. Without strategic-level consent, peace enforcement borders on war and the expectation of casualties will be high.

At the operational level consent is again a necessity if a slide into full combat is to be avoided. Those contributing resources will have a greater chance of success if there is a coherent and coordinated campaign plan. This requires common operating procedures and "consent" to a unified command and control structure, including logistic sustainability. From the perspective of the "intervened-in state", and turning again to recent operations, no ground troops were committed to Kosovo or East Timor until the indigenous armed forces of the countries had "consented" to the intervention in as far as they agreed not to oppose the incoming forces. Without operational-level consent there may be the expectation of an unacceptable level of casualties.

At the tactical level it is accepted that consent may be patchy, but this is not critical provided that the force deployed is credible. However, even if the appearance is of a combat-capable force, the cohesion between the various contingents (operational) and their will to act (strategic) is likely to be "tested". A robust, proportionate, and consistent response at the

Table 7.3 Credibility in peace support operations

Strategic	Operational	Tactical
political will (cost/time)	campaign plan (accepted/ understood/executed)	resources (trained/equipped/ directed)

tactical level will reinforce cohesion at the operational level and sustain political will for the mission at the strategic level. It is essential, therefore, that at the tactical level any force is credible.

Credibility

Whilst the key to success is credibility, at the tactical level this cannot be achieved in isolation. Credibility is essential at the strategic and operational levels as well in order to achieve success in any mission (Table 7.3).

Tactical-level credibility

At the tactical level of operations three factors reflect on the credibility of the force deployed. These are interrelated, and directly influence the higher-level sustainability of the operation and thus the achievement of the mission (Figure 7.3).

However, the credibility of a regional peacekeeping/peace enforcement force cannot rely solely on the effectiveness of the armed forces assigned to it, whether at the tactical or the operational level; simply overmatching the opposition will not work alone (for example, the USA in Somalia) and is but one facet of credibility. There must be political commitment to establishing both the force and a political-military decision-making mechanism to direct it. This control and direction body will need to be in existence and functioning regularly if it is to be credible and act efficiently in a time of crisis. There are therefore four areas that together make a credible regional peacekeeping/peace enforcement force: preliminary requirements and then, in time of crisis when operations are undertaken, the strategic, operational, and tactical levels of command. The needs in each of these areas are outlined in the following sections.

Preliminary requirements

Agreement to commit national resources to a regional peace support operations force

Although extremely difficult to achieve, if this is to be a firm commitment it will require the contributing nation to accept that the units assigned to

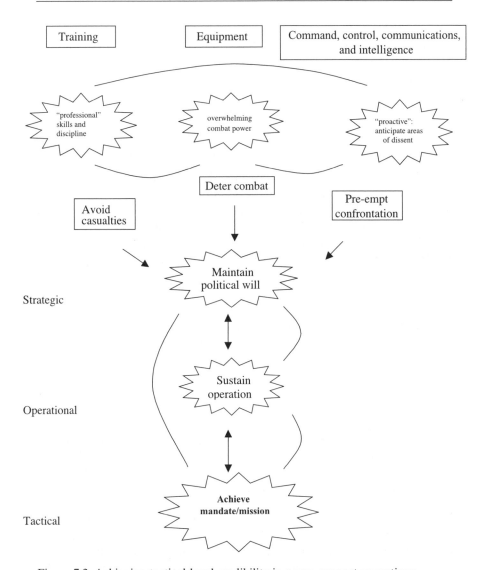

Figure 7.3 Achieving tactical-level credibility in peace support operations

the force are no longer under full national control. The practice on current UN missions is that the national contingent commander maintains a separate link and national chain of command to his capital city in order to verify that the direction he is receiving from the force commander is acceptable; this practice should end. It is vital for operational effectiveness that the force commander can be assured that the troops under his command will comply with his orders, not question, verify, or amend them to accord with a separate national agenda. This will necessitate the surrender of an element of "sovereignty" by troop-contributing nations and the use of clearly defined lines of command. It is perhaps the hardest requirement to meet, and realistically it may be impossible to achieve until the concept of the force has been proved and "matured". Nevertheless, it is an area that must be explored and discussed between nations.

Identification of framework nation for C3I (command, control, communications, and intelligence) and logistics "backbone"

For the exercise of effective command and control there will be the need for uniformity within the headquarters staff system, communications, and operating procedures. This is best achieved by nominating a "framework nation" to provide the bulk of the C3I and logistics infrastructure. A model for this can be seen in the NATO Allied Rapid Reaction Corps, where the UK has taken on this role.

Effective politico/military regional crisis response body, making timely decisions

This may be obvious, perhaps, but essential nevertheless and worthy of highlighting. A standing body in permanent session may not be necessary, but the procedures to assemble and inform the decision-makers must be in place. These must be tested regularly if the ability to act swiftly in a crisis is to exist.

Training of political and military elements at all levels to agreed standards

As in all matters there is no substitute for practice. For the politico/military decision-making machinery, "crisis management" exercises are the ideal way to ensure that structures and procedures will operate efficiently in times of need. Regular joint training is the military equivalent of the "crisis management" exercise. However, agreeing standards of training and readiness, then assessing and testing them, are resource-dependent and will not be easily achieved. This is an area in which donor countries can collaborate to sponsor and facilitate training, but it will be essential that "ownership" of the training remains firmly with the countries of the region.

Identified areas requiring external support

There are few nations that have the equipment and expertise to launch and sustain an operation outside their own country or the immediate adjacent states. The strategic lift, strategic communications, and third-line logistics essential to the projection of a force are areas in which Western nations might provide material assistance to a regional force.

They are not "front-line" functions, and as such the risk of casualties is very low.

In crisis – strategic-level "consent" (needed)

Unanimity from the regional body

Those nations intending to deploy troops must be in agreement over the action proposed, and there should be public support within them for the commitment of troops on the ground.

UN-endorsed mandate

Unanimous international support from the UN General Assembly may not be attained, but the authorization of the Security Council – in other words no veto from any of the permanent members – is essential. In line with the recommendations of the Brahimi Report on UN peace operations, any mandate given to a regional body should be clear, credible, and achievable, and preferably discussed with the relevant regional military authorities in advance.[6]

Identified and resourced end state recognizing the long-term nature of peace support operations

There are few "quick fixes" in any peace support operations, and the military often find themselves holding the ring for many years whilst others seek solutions to the underlying problems that are stalling a universally accepted peace; an example is Cyprus, where UNFICYP has been deployed for over 20 years. Flowing on from the need for clear, credible, and achievable mandates is the necessity to plan realistically rather than "apply best-case planning assumptions to situations where the local actors have historically displayed worst-case behaviour".[7]

Acceptance by the nation/government receiving the force

If there is not agreement to the deployment, the arrival of the force may be opposed physically as well as diplomatically. Such an eventuality runs the risk of a slide into serious combat. Even quite simple non-cooperation by the local population can be extremely disruptive in the early stages of a mission.

Sustainable external support requirement; public support and defensible "motive" in contributing nations

Public opinion will be influenced by the media view of the arguments put forward, and national governments must be ready to defend their decisions in the face of criticism. Given the likely length of an operation there will be an ongoing need for troop-contributing nations to be fully committed to, and ready to articulate their reasons for, supporting it. Swift and accurate information through the chain of command is essential in the age of real-time reporting by the international media.

Rapid deployment elements for assisted "force projection"

Within the overall contingency force element table drawn up by the military, certain high-readiness units must be identified to ensure that an immediate response to a crisis is possible when ordered. The cost of maintaining these high-readiness elements must be balanced against the impact and benefits of swift deployment in the face of a deteriorating situation. Ideally the financial burden of equipping and training high-readiness units should be shared across the regional organization. In practice they are likely to fall to the framework nation or nations.

Concomitant and coordinated political/diplomatic activity

The threat or use of force does not settle a dispute or bring a lasting peace. Deploying the military can only set the conditions in which others can work to attain a solution to the underlying disagreements. Failure to act politically and diplomatically in concert with a military deployment will lengthen the operation.

In crisis – operational-level "consent" (needed)

Acceptance by and cooperation (or at a minimum non-hindrance) from the armed forces of the nation/government receiving the force

As in the case of the civilian authorities and general public, failure to secure acceptance from the indigenous military may lead to confrontation and combat. It is also important to confirm that the chain of command of these forces is active and respected, and that units will obey the orders passed down from their commanders.

Common doctrine and a viable campaign plan

The exercise of command and control is facilitated and speeded up by the use of a common doctrine understood and applied at all levels. The operational-level commander will develop his campaign plan in accordance with it, balancing the resources at his disposal and the dictates of the mandate. Provided the latter has been carefully considered at the strategic level, the tasks for the military should be within the art of the possible.

Effective C3I with accepted chain of command

Trained and efficient staff officers, properly directed and with robust communications, are needed. There must be confidence that there will be no use of the "national red card", and that the orders given will be acted upon without referral to national capitals.

Robust and universally enforced rules of engagement

The requirements of the mandate will dictate the rules of engagement to be used. These must be robust enough to allow the use of force in more than self-defence, and thereafter must be applied consistently across the operational area. In past UN operations, complying with the dictates of the rules of engagement has been beyond the professional ability of some national contingents; differences have been exploited by dissenting groups to the detriment of the credibility of the mission. Agreeing and adhering to training standards for a regional force should ensure this does not occur.

Visible ability to match or overface non-compliant forces

This is important not just in regard to equipment but also in terms of the professional bearing and conduct of the troops. It can be enhanced by in-theatre training exercises and live-firing demonstrations to reinforce, overtly, the capability of the force.

Logistic sustainability

A demonstrative ability to sustain the force affirms commitment to the operation and builds confidence that there will be a continuing presence while a "peace" is sought by politicians and diplomats.

Clearly defined civil/military cooperation (CIMIC) plan

Cooperation between the military and civilian agencies is essential in any reconstruction effort, delivery of humanitarian aid, return of refugees, or care for displaced persons. Relations are quite often difficult between civilian aid agencies and the military, but are greatly assisted by a clear definition of responsibilities and goals.

Effective media operations

The need to keep the international press informed of events and incidents is paramount. Briefings, well-informed spokespersons, and transparency are essential prerequisites for dealings with the media.

In crisis – tactical-level "consent" (not needed)

Common standard operating procedures (SOPs)

This is a natural progression from agreed standards of training for all troop contingents and use of a common doctrine. It speeds reaction times and, if operationally necessary, makes deployment of units across as-signed national tactical areas of operations feasible.

*Responsive chain of command capable of timely and
effective decision-making*

High standards of staff training at all levels, from formation to subunit,
will be of importance if the force is to be proactive and thus able to anticipate and pre-empt confrontations. Quick decision-making is a product
of doctrinal understanding of the commander's intent that gives subordinate commanders the confidence to act on their own initiative to exploit
opportunities as they arise.

Effective contingents – trained, disciplined, equipped, and sustained

Properly prepared and equipped soldiers will deter non-compliance or be
able to defeat any opposition if necessary. The need to be psychologically
as well as physically prepared for combat should be remembered.

*Common application of consent and compliance techniques
in accordance with international humanitarian law*

Consistent and legally defensible action should be evident throughout the
area of operations. All troops must be aware of and abide by the recognized conventions of international humanitarian law.

Effective military information operations

There are often considerable efforts made to discredit the force in the
eyes of the local population. If these are successful, consent to the presence of the troops may be lost. It becomes essential, therefore, to counter
misinformation and make the aims and objectives of operations clear to
all. This is especially important at ground level where troops and people
meet.

Training to deliver a credible peacekeeping/
peace enforcement regional force

It is impossible to provide a training programme that will, succinctly, describe the totality of the training needs in establishing a regional force that
is credible. However, based on the experience of a British military training
team in southern Africa, working with the SADC countries, an outline of a
three-year programme has been constructed. The aim of the programme is
to assist nations within the region in the military aspects of creating a
credible regional peace support operations force of brigade size; this
would be done by building a common basis of doctrine, staff work, and
training standards on which it can be established. Two types of training
are suggested: *staff training* to enable officers to fill appointments in a
headquarters either at sector/brigade and tactical level (junior officers) or
mission headquarters and operational level (senior officers); and *field*

training to improve basic military skills, primarily based on the "training the trainer" concept and aimed at company and platoon commanders.

Staff training courses

Regional junior officers command and staff course (RJOCSC)

The *aim* would be to train junior officers with no previous staff experience (ideally captain/major) to be junior staff officers (staff officer grade 3 – SO3) at unit and formation (brigade/sector on a mission) level. In units these officers would become adjutants and operations officers, the two key appointments assisting the unit commander in planning and conducting operations. The *duration* would be eight weeks. This would be the core of the staff training. It would concentrate on the staff duties of a junior officer and the coordination of operations at unit and brigade levels, based on British Army doctrine for both conventional and peace support operations. Finally, it would allow officers of those nations which do not have access to their own staff college (or enough places on other nations' staff training courses) to train a core of young officers to a high standard, capable of taking their place on peace support operations.

Regional senior officers doctrine update course (RSODUC)

The *aim* would be to update senior staff officers (lieutenant-colonel/ brigadier) on the instruction being given to their juniors, and introduce them to British Army doctrine. The *duration* would be two weeks. It would ensure that the majority of senior officers in each of the SADC armed forces are made aware of the common basis of doctrine being taught to their subordinates, and that their knowledge is expanded of the roles of a senior staff officer on both conventional and peace support operations.

Regional higher command PSO course (RHCPSOC)

The *aim* would be to introduce high-ranking officers (one- or two-star generals) and their police and civilian equivalents to the complexities and requirements peculiar to running a mission headquarters on peace support operations, not necessarily in Africa. The *duration* would be two weeks. It would draw heavily on outside speakers with direct experience of peace support operations. They would be able to pass on their invaluable experience to senior SADC officers who might be expected to participate in UN-authorized operations within Africa.

Field training courses

Regional company commanders PSO course (RCCPSOC)

The *aim* would be to develop the ability of company commanders (captain/ major) to command a company during conventional and peace support operations. The *duration* would be eight weeks. It would provide a vehicle to improve the leadership, command, and training skills required at sub-unit level to train for, deploy on, and conduct peace support operations. Tactical deployment on peace support operations is usually centred on company bases from which framework operations are conducted. Military experience has shown that subunit, or company, level is a vital level of command for success in peace support operations.

Regional platoon commanders PSO course (RPCPSOC)

The *aim* would be to develop the ability of junior officers (lieutenants) to command a platoon during conventional and peace support operations. The *duration* would be eight weeks. It would concentrate on providing the knowledge and skills required to command a platoon and supervise its training in basic field skills, including the safe handling of weapons particularly applicable to peace support operations. It would include "specialist" peace support operations techniques and tactics. It is at this level that troops come into contact with the local population; individual professional standards and discipline, so vital in peace support operations, are controlled at this level.

General training

All courses, whether staff or field, would include modules on ethics and the armed forces as well as instruction on rules of engagement, humanitarian issues, AIDS, dealing with the media, and the requirement to operate alongside NGOs and UN agencies. Methods of instruction techniques would also be included. Clearly the courses would not cover all the training needs identified in creating a credible regional force for peacekeeping and peace enforcement. One level not touched is that of staff officer grade 2 (SO2), or brigade-level "senior" staff. Training for officers to fill such appointments is intensive and undertaken over a period of one year in national staff colleges. The SO2 is the working-level desk officer and key to operational effectiveness (credibility) at brigade and mission levels. There is a strong case to be made for having a presence in these institutions to maintain common doctrinal instruction and currency throughout the regional staff training courses. Action would be required from others to develop, exercise, and advise a politico/military body to control and direct a regional force. There is also a need to liaise closely with the United Nations DPKO and UN-recognized establishments, such as the SADC Regional Peacekeeping Training Centre (RPTC) in Harare, to avoid duplication of efforts. While the courses proposed do not cut across the RPTC's activities directly, they would need to be tailored to dovetail into RPTC courses such as the UN staff officers, UN peacekeeping for company commanders, and conflict prevention courses.

There is also great scope for cooperation with the US Africa Crisis Response Initiative (ACRI), and the French Renforcement du Capabilité African pour Maintien la Paix (RECAMP) programmes, especially in such areas as crisis management exercises, military training exercises to validate progress, and field training.

It is envisaged that the three-year programme would be designed to conduct six courses per annum: junior staff training (two), senior officers update (one), higher commanders (one), company commanders (one), and platoon commanders (one). Over three years this would train 240 junior staff officers and 120 senior officers, all familiar with the same material; 120 one-star or two-star officers, brigadiers or major-generals (or their police/diplomatic peers) trained in higher-level UN command, plus 120 company and 120 platoon commanders trained as trainers in the military skills needed to prosecute peace support operations. The resources needed to complete this programme are not great. Based again on the experience of the British team in southern Africa, a permanent cadre of 14 officers is needed to set up and facilitate the courses. This would include an element to assist two staff colleges within the region in the training of SO2 grade officers, and would be supplemented by individuals attached on a short-term training team basis to be the instructors or directing staff on the regional courses. The cost of the programme is estimated to be in the order of US$12m over the three years. This would include the costs of the permanent team resident in Africa, the costs of deploying short-term training teams, and the training and travel costs for the students on regional courses. The costs of the students at regional staff colleges would be a national responsibility. Some expense would be incurred by regional nations hosting courses, but this would be minimal. If coordinated with ACRI/RECAMP to enhance unit skills, and diplomatic/political activity to create the organizations needed to underpin the credibility of the regional force, this training programme could provide a regionwide base for a comprehensive validation and assessment exercise, and it would create the basis of a usable force.

Conclusion

Experience has shown that peacekeeping in Africa involves entry into volatile, high-risk, anarchic environments where large quantities of arms are available. The destruction of social cohesion and state infrastructures can remove the support mechanisms needed to sustain life, thus often resulting in humanitarian crises. These are "complex emergencies", not the traditional image of peacekeeping intervention, demanding a well-trained, disciplined, militarily effective force if those intervening are not to become a part of the problem. Without the ability to use military force proactively, the ability of a peacekeeping force to maintain its freedom of action will be limited and depend to a large extent on the consent of the belligerent parties. Such consent may not be forthcoming, and troops involved in peace support operations must therefore have the ability to escalate their activities from those covered under Chapter VI of the UN Charter to those under Chapter VII. Whether this is in self-defence (a fundamental right enshrined in international law) in a peacekeeping mission, or in coercive operations in a peace enforcement mission, they are both combat actions which require the same training. The conclusion is that peacekeepers must be trained to be effective soldiers first. Failure to provide for and meet the full range of military functions will result in mission failure as peacekeepers.

However, there can be no credible military peace support operations force without the political backing of all the nations participating in it. High-level decision-making procedures must be agreed, national commitments made (and fulfilled), and the political/military decision-making machinery must be tested and be seen to be working. All this is necessary and most likely to be achieved on a regional basis, where shared interests should promote greater cooperation in setting up a force.

However, the creation of such forces will not be without cost. Undoubtedly assistance would be of value in refining and exercising politico/military decision-making bodies. Help in training and equipping contingents to agreed standards with a common doctrine would also be an area where involvement could be welcomed. The equipment needs of a framework nation to lead in C3I and sustainment are unlikely to be met without the help of the USA or Europe in strategic lift, communications, and third-line logistics. While there is an acknowledged reluctance from "the West" to become involved in African conflicts, these requirements do not entail the commitment of troops "on the ground" in the conflict zone and it should therefore be possible to meet them. Finally, however, it must be remembered that any involvement in the creation of credible peace support operations forces can only be at the invitation of the sovereign states that will resource and deploy them. Many African nations have considerable experience of UN missions; such experience should be tapped in dialogue, discussion, and decision-making on how best to establish credible peace support operations forces. The absence of such credibility is a UN, not solely African, problem; solutions will not be reached unilaterally.

Notes

1. The focus of the chapter's suggestions is on brigade-sized formations, in military terms the smallest viable formations capable of independent operations over a sustained period.

The Brahimi Report highlighted their suitability as follows: "If United Nations military planners assess that a brigade (approximately 5,000 troops) is what is required to effectively deter or deal with violent challenges to the implementation of an operation's mandate, then the military component of that United Nations operation ought to deploy as a brigade formation, not as a collection of battalions that are unfamiliar with one another's doctrine, leadership and operational practices. That brigade would have to come from a group of countries that have been working together ... to develop common training and equipment standards, common doctrine, and common arrangements for the operational control of the force. Ideally the United Nations Standby Arrangements System (UNSAS) should contain several such brigade-size forces, with the necessary enabling forces, available for a full deployment to an operation within 30 days in the case of traditional peacekeeping operations and within 90 days in the case of complex operations." *Report of the Panel on United Nations Peace Operations*, A/55/305-S/2000/809, New York: UN General Assembly/Security Council, 21 August 2000, paragraph 115.

2. *Ibid.*, paragraph 54.
3. UK Ministry of Defence Joint Warfare Publication 3-50. Crown copyright.
4. Developed from a model attributed to Mark Malan, senior researcher at the ISS.
5. Taken from "Developing mandates for potential intervenors", a paper presented by Christopher Clapham at Sopa Lodge, Tanzania, June 1999.
6. *Report of the Panel on UN Peace Operations*, note 2.
7. *Ibid.*, paragraph 51.

Part III

Experiences from Cambodia, former Yugoslavia, and East Timor

8

The politics of UN peacekeeping from Cambodia to Yugoslavia

Yasushi Akashi

"UN peacekeeping" is an all-embracing term covering a variety of peace-keeping activities, starting from the UN Truce Supervision Organization (UNTSO) established in 1948 right through to the present. The classical "first-generation" peacekeeping operations represent a UN "presence" on international borders or cease-fire lines, separating the contending parties from physical contact by the interpositioning of UN military observers or soldiers as the third party. Such a presence is intended to bring about cessation of hostilities and the reduction of tension, thus gaining time for the resumption of dialogue and, hopefully, the ultimate solution of the conflict.

In most cases, the United Nations dispatches a group of unarmed officers or lightly armed soldiers to the area concerned, with a view to separating the combatants from each other. It is essentially a holding operation to freeze a volatile situation and create room for peacemaking or diplomatic efforts. Unless accompanied by diplomatic action, classical peacekeeping tends to become an operation with limited significance, preserving the *status quo* at best, as shown in Kashmir and at times in the Middle East.

"First-generation" peacekeeping became a large-scale operation composed of organized troops in the Suez Canal area in 1956. At the request of the United Nations, thousands of troops from mostly non-aligned countries were sent to the area to provide a physical cushion between the Egyptian troops and the invading troops from the UK, France, and Israel, enabling the latter to withdraw from Egypt without losing face. Inter-

149

positioning by the United Nations can be very useful. However, the cooling down of diplomatic temperature through third-party interpositioning proved to be transitory when tension heightened again after President Gamel Abdul Nasser asked for the withdrawal of international troops in 1967, leading to the resumption of hostilities. Thus one cannot emphasize too much the importance of a comprehensive, coordinated approach by the international community in which peacekeeping becomes one component in an overall political strategy, and is combined with diplomatic efforts aimed at the political change of a situation.

The end of the Cold War around 1990 led to the upsurge of ambitious "second-generation" peacekeeping, in which the United Nations became a vital link from war to peace. The organization established a transitional authority to fill a vacuum of political power in Cambodia as well as in Namibia and Mozambique. Major peacekeeping operations with multifaceted activities, such as the supervision of administration, the maintenance of law and order, the reform of the judiciary, the relief and reintegration of refugees, the protection of human rights, the organization of democratic elections, and the recovery of the war-torn economy, were combined together under a civilian head, with the military providing physical support to several other components.

The UN Operation in Congo (ONUC) from 1960 to 1964 was a precursor to "second-generation" peacekeeping, but most such operations took place in the early 1990s. The United Nations is at present playing such a role in East Timor after the departure of the multinational force led by Australia. The organization participates in a similar operation in Kosovo, but it shares responsibilities with other bodies such as NATO, which is responsible for the military component, the OSCE, charged with the observance of human rights and justice, and the European Union (EU), responsible for the restoration of the economy.

In the euphoria after the end of the Cold War, as reflected in *An Agenda for Peace* issued by Secretary-General Boutros Boutros-Ghali in 1992,[1] the United Nations embarked on limited peace enforcement in Somalia in 1993. This phase may be called "third-generation" peacekeeping. However, the Second UN Operation in Somalia (UNOSOM II) ended in a tragic debacle due to the lack of coordination in the multinational force, insufficient intelligence, and inadequate equipment and training of its troops. It became clear that a real fighting force under Chapter VII of the UN Charter could not be organized by the United Nations in the present circumstances, and that such a task could best be entrusted to a multinational force sanctioned by the Security Council but organized and financed by a group of countries with political will and military competence and with a unified command structure outside the UN Secretariat.

The UN operation in the former Yugoslavia was an extremely complex operation, comprising a more classical peacekeeping operation in Croatia, a precedent-setting preventive deployment in Macedonia, and an operation in Bosnia whose mandate evolved from humanitarian protection to something bordering on peace enforcement. In the end, the UN Protection Force (UNPROFOR) in Bosnia had to cede its place to NATO after air attacks and the Dayton peace agreement. NATO sent to the area the Implementation Force (IFOR), which had much more muscle to undertake peace enforcement but was in practice notable for caution similar to UNPROFOR.

The United Nations was largely successful in attaining its ambitious objectives in Cambodia relating to the implementation of the 1991 Paris peace agreements to restore peace and democracy in the country, although the disarmament and demilitarization aspect of the accord was not attained due to the intransigence of the Khmer Rouge. The UN's success in Cambodia derived partly from the international situation, in which all major powers were ready to dissociate themselves from the Cold War entanglement, and partly from the prevailing desire for peace by the Cambodian parties, exhausted after the prolonged 20 years of war. They were ready to lay down their arms (with the exception of the Khmer Rouge, which dropped out of the peace process in the second part of 1992 and more decisively in 1993). One should also not forget the diplomatic skill and political determination of those involved. Broad consensus by the internal parties, by the regional powers, and by the five permanent members of the Security Council had been crystallized in the Paris peace agreements reached in October 1991. Such a political framework was essential, but did not provide sufficient guarantees for eventual success. It had to be interpreted and implemented with imagination, flexibility, and wisdom, and had to be blessed by some luck. The establishment of a "core group" of 10 ambassadors in Phnom Penh who frequently met with the special representative of the Secretary-General, the clarity and skill of the two co-chairmen, France and Indonesia, the behind-the-scenes diplomacy of Japan and Thailand, and the close collaboration between Prince Norodom Sihanouk and the special representative of the Secretary-General all played their part in weathering several crises during the process.

The setbacks experienced by the United Nations in former Yugoslavia, particularly in Croatia and Bosnia, were due to the almost complete lack of unity of outlook among the major powers, namely the USA, Russia, France, the UK, and Germany, the lack of readiness by the internal parties in conflict to replace arms with diplomacy, and the lack of coordination within the United Nations between the executive body in New York (that is, the Security Council) and the operation in the field.

The special representative of the Secretary-General tried to create a small group of ambassadors from key countries and resident in the former Yugoslavia – a device so successful in Phnom Penh in bridging the gap between the United Nations and major member states. But this was not possible for reasons beyond his control.

The ambiguity, imprecision, and lack of consistency in the relevant Security Council resolutions, particularly the tragic lack of correspondence between the mandate proclaimed in New York and the resources given to the field, were among the main reasons for the Yugoslav consequences. It has to be added, however, that under difficult and even dangerous conditions the UN force did help in limiting the scope of conflict and was able to achieve a measure of stabilization through a series of cease-fires and weapons-withdrawal agreements concluded and monitored under its auspices, and through substantial humanitarian relief operations which enabled internally displaced and encircled civilian populations to survive four winters and summers.

Lessons

Numerous lessons can be learned from the Cambodian and Yugoslav operations, which are among the two largest peacekeeping operations in UN history.

First of all, it is vital that the Security Council adopts a clear and realistic mandate for peacekeeping operations, with well-defined objectives, taking fully into account the means to be made available to the operations concerned. This requirement was met in Cambodia, but unfortunately not in the former Yugoslavia.

Second, the Security Council should carefully heed the recommendations by the Secretary-General, which were followed by the Council in the case of Cambodia but were mostly ignored in the case of Yugoslavia, where the Council members were more sensitive to newspaper headlines, the television coverage of the events, and the public emotions aroused by the tragedy taking place in Bosnia. The result was the adoption of numerous high-sounding resolutions and presidential statements which did not correspond to the reality unfolding on the ground but merely heightened the level of public expectations, which were subsequently disappointed.

Third, there should be close coordination and interaction between UN Headquarters and the field. Field operations should always include experienced UN staff who are able to communicate the needs and requirements of the field to New York so as to ensure adequate logistical and manpower support from UN Headquarters.

Fourth, it is vital to have ample financial resources to assure post-conflict reconstruction and recovery. The combatants should be informed of how the lives of the people could be improved after the war if they gave up arms. Post-conflict peace-building can thus be a big incentive for peace. The Cambodian parties were made aware that Japan, the USA, and others were ready to provide generous economic assistance to back up their own efforts. In the Yugoslav conflict, however, the special representative of the Secretary-General found that the Bosnian Serb leadership, obsessed with ongoing fighting, did not show much interest in the post-war conditions.

Fifth, unity of outlook among the major powers, including the permanent members of the Security Council, is highly desirable and necessary. This was clearly missing in the Yugoslav case, but was available in Cambodia.

Sixth, in a peacekeeping operation the principle of civilian supremacy and solid teamwork has to be observed, while it is also vital to have well-qualified military commanders who are motivated and attuned to the political situation. The author was fortunate to have them in Cambodia as well as in the former Yugoslavia. It is also important that peacekeeping and diplomatic negotiations be well coordinated and synchronized. In Cambodia this was achieved, but in the Yugoslav case there were too many actors and mediators in New York, Geneva, and elsewhere, although personal efforts overcame some of the difficulties.

Seventh, at a time of diminishing resources, the United Nations should not embark on an open-ended large operation. The Security Council should have the clarity and courage to know what tasks should be given to a UN peacekeeping operation, what kind of tasks are more suitable for a multinational force or a regional organization, and what tasks are better performed by other types of activities involving sanctions under Article 41 of the Charter – diplomatic, communication, or economic pressures to be mobilized by the international community. We should by all means avoid the slippery road of the creeping expansion of mandates, which happened in the case of the ill-fated UN operation in the former Yugoslavia.

Conclusion

In the author's view, the United Nations is groping today for the "fourth-generation" peacekeeping operation, which lies somewhere between the "second-generation" and "third-generation" peacekeeping operations. Thought is being given to the nature of the "consent of the parties" required as well as to the realistic "rules of engagement". For example, the UN peacekeeping operation in East Timor has robust rules of engagement. The distinction and elaboration between "strategic" and "tactical" consent of the parties is also important. Furthermore, the "minimum use of force for self-defence" may have to be prudently expanded to include the "defence of missions". In a massive humanitarian tragedy and a large-scale violation of human rights, the principle of impartiality of the United Nations may have to be somewhat modified. These thoughts are well reflected in the report of the Brahimi Panel, issued in August 2000.[2]

The Japanese are now thinking hard about the so-called five conditions for their participation in UN peacekeeping. While Japan must adhere to its constitution, it should not define too narrowly the conditions under which its troops join a UN operation. Japan has to be conscious of the fact that peacekeeping operations are constantly undergoing an evolution in accordance with the changing nature of conflicts and wars in the world. Since the end of the Cold War, the United Nations has been compelled to cope with internal conflicts that do not have fixed confrontation lines or a fixed number of parties. It has to deal with militias, irregular forces, even criminal elements and child soldiers who possess only scant or no knowledge of and regard for international humanitarian law. In short, we live in a new environment for "fourth-generation" peacekeeping. It would be unfair to national contingents in UN peacekeeping if they are subjected to legal strait-jackets dictated by domestic considerations rather than by the practical necessity on the ground. The time has come for Japan to reflect upon the evolving situation in the world so that it may not find itself left behind the trail-blazing frontiers of UN efforts to maintain peace, represented by a peacekeeping operation which is an essential building block of international peace and security.

Notes

1. Boutros Boutros-Ghali, *An Agenda for Peace: Preventive Diplomacy, Peace-making and Peacekeeping*, New York: UN Department of Public Information, 1992.
2. *Report of the Panel on United Nations Peace Operations*, A/55/305-S/2000/809, New York: UN General Assembly/Security Council, 21 August 2000.

9

The Cambodian experience: A success story still?

John Sanderson

So much was promised to the Cambodian people by the United Nations in its role as the Transitional Authority from 1992 to 1993 that it is all the more poignant they find themselves in a state which remains largely lawless some nine years after the Paris peace agreements were signed in October 1991. While the tragic country has a long history of extra-judicial killings carried out with impunity by those in power, the opportunity to make the responsible authorities at least answerable to the people through the ballot box seems to have been less than successful in producing a form of properly consensual government.

Some people might find this judgement too harsh, given that the Cambodian government has shape and form, the country has membership in most international organizations, has undisputed representation in many capitals, is a member of the Association of South-East Asian Nations (ASEAN), and the former opposing factions have, in theory, surrendered their authority over sections of the Cambodian countryside to the coalition in Phnom Penh. All these things are true enough, and this may be a reflection of the world at large, but laws in Cambodia continue to be made at the whim of the controlling élite rather than the legislature, and justice does not exist for the large majority of Cambodians. The opposition exercises its privileges at the discretion of the executive rather than by law, as it does in liberal democracies, and there is a distinct sense of foreboding and awe associated with anyone or anything that confronts this reality. At the risk of banishment or death, some very brave Cambodians continue to speak out in support of justice and the rule of law, but their courage is not matched by support from the international community.

The changes in Phnom Penh itself belie the state of the remainder of the country. A new-found modernity and feeling of being part of a world in which things are happening can be sensed in the hustle and bustle of a busy and developing city. This is a remarkable contrast with the atmosphere that prevailed when the UN Advance Mission in Cambodia (UNAMIC) first entered the city in 1991. But the disparity in living conditions between the city and the countryside has always been Cambodia's problem. The history of sucking wealth out of the rural communities in the form of its youth, natural resources, and produce, while putting very little back, has been the source of division and revolution for many centuries. It made possible the Khmer Rouge mobilization of the peasants into a revolutionary force, and explains in part the ferocity with which the rank and file of that movement approached the task of tearing down the pre-revolutionary society.

The commitment of the international community to overcome this tendency through development aid has been frustrated to a great extent by the relatively lawless pursuit of the quick dollar by the Cambodian leadership and those associated with them, in the form of criminal business arrangements linking timber and mineral concessions with drugs and illicit forms of property and commercial development. A direct consequence of this is an underlying criminality that also embraces and exploits the large number of demobilized and serving armed forces personnel, who are both underpaid and underemployed. Life remains insecure and tenuous for most Cambodians.

UNTAC in context

How did things get this way? Why, after spending US$2bn on the UN Transitional Authority in Cambodia (UNTAC), did the international community fail to set Cambodia on a more constructive course?

The paradigm of UNTAC and the extent of its success have been the subject of much conjecture since 1993. The author has long been a proponent of the view that UNTAC was a success insofar that it fulfilled its mandate on time and under budget, no mean achievement given the complexity of the undertaking and its precedent-setting nature. Very few UN missions could make similar claims. If, as suggested, UNTAC was successful, then what has been the reason for the disappointing turn of Cambodian governance since 1993? It is the contention of this chapter that shortfalls in the United Nations itself, as given expression in the UNTAC mandate, are the source of this failure and many others that have occurred during the last decade of the twentieth century.

The differences between the Cold War and post-Cold War demands on the United Nations have been analysed in great depth. It is not simply the demise of the bipolar world order brought about by the collapse of the former Soviet Union which has changed the texture and complexity of the UN's role. The fact that both technology and environmental pressures have sparked a surge in global concern with what goes on *inside* sovereign boundaries, and the unprecedented and consequent growth of international law, have fundamentally changed the nature of international intervention, making enforcement both necessary and more likely. Because there has been a concerted attempt within the United Nations to retain the sanctity of state sovereignty which underlies the international order proposed in the Charter, there has been a marked reluctance to take up the challenge entailed in reaching into failing or failed states.

For this reason the international community has gone to great lengths where it could to ensure that a high level of agreement exists as to its role before it engages inside national boundaries, even in those cases where the state has collapsed or is patently abusing the rights of its citizens. There have been many salutary experiences where this has not occurred, with disastrous effect. Somalia, Rwanda, Bosnia, Kosovo, and East Timor are vivid examples. At the same time, the United Nations has received much criticism for procrastinating while it seeks to achieve the objective circumstances that will allow peacekeeping rather than enforcement. Rwanda, Bosnia, Kosovo, and East Timor come into the category of countries where large numbers of civilians had to die before the United Nations was moved to endorse an enforcement operation.

Cambodia preceded these activities, and was the outcome of nearly 20 years of war and two solid years of negotiation at the Paris peace conference. The negotiations only had real form and substance once the Vietnamese withdrew from Cambodia in 1989, the same year the Berlin Wall came down. The negotiations themselves were a substantial part of the reconciliation process as the Cambodian factions came to terms with the fact that their sponsors were more interested in solving their own problems than in continuing to support the deepening of a conflict which no longer made sense in strategic terms. No one seriously contemplated an enforcement operation in Cambodia, even though there was a strongly held view in the West that some Khmers were guilty of gross crimes against humanity. The memory of Viet Nam was so strong in the American psyche that the mere suggestion of an enforcement operation in the former Indochina would have been sufficient to throw the Cambodia question out of the Security Council, particularly in a presidential election year.

Much effort was therefore given to negotiating a carrot-and-stick form of agreement whereby the factions understood that their own influence in the transition and future government of Cambodia was dependent on their compliance with a very detailed process embracing cease-fire and disarming/demobilization, repatriation, human rights, universal enfranchisement, and elections. All of this was to be assisted and supervised by the most intrusive UN presence attempted up to that time. Achieving an agreement to such a presence was widely regarded as a triumph for the international community, but was treated with a degree of wariness by the Cambodian factions and the surrounding countries. The creation of a Supreme National Council to represent Cambodian sovereignty throughout the agreed process was therefore an essential element, bringing the leadership of all factions together under the head of the resistance, Prince Norodom Sihanouk.

Like all such agreements, those concluded in Paris in October 1991 depended on a balance of good faith and coercion. Most of this resided in the United Nations itself. The nature of the issues that were stumbling blocks in the closing stages of the negotiations, such as those of genocide and the existence of the political police, made clear that there was very little trust between the Cambodian factions, particularly the Phnom Penh government and the Khmer Rouge. Each side was persuaded that the UN's presence would act in their favour by moderating the power of the other, and allowing the weaknesses that they were convinced existed in the position of their opposition to bear fruit. What none of the four factions fully appreciated was the extent to which the war- and crime-weary Cambodian people were alienated from all of them. This alienation cast the United Nations into the role of the "fifth faction", riding a wave of moral authority which should have allowed it to build a solid foundation of law for the future Cambodian society. That it was unable to seize full advantage of this favourable position is a matter that deserves detailed analysis to determine the extent to which it was due to failings in the United Nations itself, as opposed to the intransigence and recalcitrance of the players.

Can the United Nations govern? UNTAC as a case study

UNTAC's legacy can help us define more effective missions in the future. UN Security Council Resolution 1272 established the mandate for the UN Transition Administration in East Timor (UNTAET). In it, the Security Council gives the special representative of the Secretary-General powers that equate to those of a Roman provincial governor of 2,000 years ago, primarily those of being able to make and enforce laws. Because of its unprecedented boldness, one assumes that significant consultation with the members of the Security Council and other interested nations has occurred in the preparation of this resolution. Unlike Bosnia and Kosovo, where the troops of NATO and Russia, forming SFOR (Stabilization Force) and KFOR (Kosovo Force), enforce a peace, UNTAET is intended to "keep the peace" from within its own organic structure.

For the United Nations, UNTAET, as mandated by the Security Council, is a step forward of millennial proportions. The United Nations has not "occupied" a country before, depending on all previous occasions on some other body to perform the enforcement functions while it goes about the business of helping to build new foundations for governance. What are the factors that have caused the United Nations to be that emboldened, and can we draw confidence from its earlier performances that the organization will be able to deliver on the mandate that is proposed?

The answer to the first part of this question must owe something to the fact that East Timor is a small and relatively isolated country. With a population of less than one million, and very little in the way of administrative infrastructure, the situation in East Timor lends itself to political experimentation in a way that would be very difficult and costly in most other places. With the departure of the Indonesians, there was no pre-existing government. The ambiguity of East Timor's status as a former Portuguese colony in a suspended state of transition makes the people very dependent on the goodwill of the international community. Their suffering since the UN-supervised "consultation" (the referendum) has induced a very high level of sympathy worldwide, which permitted consideration of a sustained, high-quality intervention.

The second part of the question requires some analysis of the level of success achieved in governance by the United Nations in other missions, and the reasons for its failures. In terms of international intervention and governance, UNTAC is regarded as a paradigm, and in this respect provides a useful case study of the UN's capabilities. As has already been suggested, UNTAC was a peacekeeping mission which achieved its objectives but failed to leave the country in the progressive democratic state intended by those who set up the peace process. This failure has been ascribed to many reasons, including:

- the United Nations arrived too late to take advantage of the dynamics created by consummation of the negotiations, namely the Paris agreements;
- the mission did not have sufficient safeguards built in to ensure that the countryside was disarmed;
- too much reliance was placed on the ability of Prince Sihanouk to achieve a consensus in the Supreme National Council;

- insufficient emphasis was given to the building of an effective rule of law and justice system;
- the United Nations should have been prepared to play a stronger hand in the development of the constitution of Cambodia;
- the United Nations should have stayed longer.

Why did the United Nations arrive too late?

Few people comprehend the full bureaucratic nature of the United Nations, and the significant difference between the impressive rhetoric of the organization and its ability to mobilize the resources of its membership. This is not meant as criticism of the hard-working officials who represent member nations and those who make up the higher levels of the Secretariat staff. It is simply the way things are at this stage of the UN's role in the complex web of global governance.

- There is no UN army or police force to respond to crises.
- There is a deep concern to ensure that the interests of the rich and powerful nations do not override those of the less well off.
- There is a system of patron and client relationships which must be exercised to gain decisions.
- There is a concern among those who make the greatest financial contributions to operations about being able to assure their constituents that the money is not wasted.
- The United Nations continues to be dependent on member states to provide talented people to carry out the complex functions in the field that the Security Council deems necessary, at a time when most countries are rationalizing their own administrative structures to cut costs.
- There is no effective civil-military planning at UN Headquarters to plan and oversee operations of increasing complexity and magnitude, and the organization is therefore forced into a template approach to what are always unique missions, thereby creating an inevitable impasse between the needs of the mission and the bureaucracy.

All of these factors came into play in delaying the UNTAC mission from reaching what could be considered an effective status until some nine to 12 months after the Paris accords were signed. The shortfalls in the capacity of the Secretariat were compounded by the parallel demands of equally complex situations in Somalia, Angola, and the former Yugoslavia. Traditional peacekeeping nations which had considered contributing to the Cambodian operation found that their strategic interests directed their resources elsewhere. New players in the business of international intervention, such as Japan, Germany, and several former Eastern bloc countries, were constrained by domestic political processes that inhibited them from making firm commitments.

Why the cease-fire and disarming provisions did not work

While the United Nations was diverted by its own politics and logistic problems, the leadership of the Cambodian factions reverted to characteristic mischief as they manoeuvred for power in the vacuum created by the expectation of a strong UN presence. In theory this vacuum was filled by UNAMIC, a Secretary-General's "good offices" mission that was supposed to help the factions maintain the agreed cease-fire. In practice UNAMIC was a confused and weak presence with a creeping mandate, which it was never able to fulfil. It both inflamed and emboldened the factions in the belief that the United Nations was being or could be manipulated to achieve outcomes either contrary to, or in favour of, their interests. The consequent mischief began from the moment that Prince Sihanouk arrived back in Phnom Penh in early November 1991 and announced that he was proposing an alliance between his "two sons", Prince Ranariddh and Hun Sen, which appeared to exclude the Son Sann faction (the Khmer People's National Liberation Front – KPNLF) and the Khmer Rouge. It gathered momentum when Khmer Rouge members of the Supreme National Council were the subject of violent demonstrations (state sponsored, but clumsily disguised as spontaneous) and forced from the city back into Thailand on 27 November 1991.

Four months later, when UNTAC began to build a presence, the country was in a state of turmoil and the chances of generating a sufficient level of trust to enable a sustained cease-fire and demobilization process were gone. In the intervening period much valuable diplomatic work was done to keep the factions engaged, both with each other and with the international community, but diplomacy is a poor substitute for substance when in comes to building trust in a lawless country. The cautionary interventions of the United Nations and the major powers failed to divert the criminal elements that had taken hold within the major factions, all of which were now dependent on maintaining an armed presence in the countryside.

Sustained attempts by UNTAC to draw all the factions into a disarming and demobilization process continued throughout the remainder of 1992, but the damage was done. It only required one faction to refuse cooperation for the entire plan of disarming the countryside to fail. The three alternatives that then confronted the international community were either to withdraw, to move to an enforcement mandate, or to ignore the armed factions and get on with the task of enfranchising the Cambodian people in the hope that sufficient momentum could be built up in the democratic process to overcome the criminal interests of the leadership. This last course of action emerged out of the debate as the only real alternative once the United Nations was committed.

The question remains, could the negotiators have built more safe-guards into the Paris accords to ensure that disarming actually occurred? The answer is probably no, given that enforcement was out of the question in a war-torn, mine-infested country in a region with which the West associated grim memories of division and dissent within their own societies. Even if the idea of punitive action against a recalcitrant faction was conceivable, there were no sides to the Cambodian conflict which were decidedly right, and therefore nothing short of the United Nations taking over the whole country would have allowed for successful enforcement. There should be little doubt that there never would have been any Paris accords had negotiations contained even a hint of such a proposition.

Why the Supreme National Council failed

Was the Supreme National Council (SNC) ever intended to work? It was clearly a requirement that was at one with the UN commitment to the idea of sovereign states being the foundation of its dealings with people. If the United Nations did not deal with a representative body while it controlled the transition, then how could it be said to be fulfilling the wishes of the Cambodian people? And if it was not seen to be responding to the dictate of the people, could its status be said to be any better than that of the colonial powers it had done so much to wrest power from over the past half century?

There seems to be little question that if the SNC under Prince Siha-nouk's leadership was ever able to generate a consensus on any issue, and provided it met the test of the human rights dimensions of the Paris accords, UNTAC would have been required to comply with the SNC's decisions. The fact that such a consensus was never achieved on any matter of significance meant that the special representative of the Secretary-General had to proceed on the basis of the international community's assessment of the best interests of the Cambodian people, sometimes in direct opposition to the stated position of the Prince. Whether this opposition and frequent accompanying withdrawals were of substance, or were theatre in aid of the longer-term interests of the SNC's chairman, is a moot point.

What can be said is that the SNC was never set up to manage the development of the complex agenda that a full process of national reconciliation demands. Its secretariat was weak and unrepresentative, and the discursive character of its chair inhibited its proceedings. While its members claimed to represent the Cambodian people, it was clear that, with few exceptions, their primary motivation was to promote the interests of individuals or party leadership. As a consequence, there was dissent in the SNC on almost every issue placed before it, causing a rapidly developing sense of futility on the part of the Cambodians, and almost a feeling of relief among the UNTAC leadership when the Prince's frequent absences caused the postponement of meetings.

Can you have a neutral political environment without law and order?

The Paris accords demanded of UNTAC the development of five fundamental building blocks to deliver effective governance to Cambodia:
- establishment of a secure environment through the cessation of hostilities and the disarming/demobilization of forces;
- establishment of a neutral political environment through the supervision/control of the most significant areas of national and local government, namely foreign affairs, defence, finance, internal security, and public information;
- promotion of the political process through the registration of voters, and aiding the development of multiple parties;
- conduct of the election of a constituent assembly;
- overseeing the development of a constitution in accordance with the spirit of the Paris accords.

The cornerstone of this was the establishment of a neutral political environment, through which it was intended that individuals and political parties would have the right to freedom of assembly, freedom of speech, and equal opportunity to communicate their ideas to the Cambodian electorate. The principal obstacle was the now familiar characteristic of former one-party states where both the internal security system and the justice system exist to secure the interests of the party rather than the people. While the pretence that the party represents the people ceases to have credibility, the security apparatus remains linked to the leadership by a network of loyalties and dependencies, often seeing no other alternative for gainful employment. When the party leadership divides along the lines of those who offer a weak and fractured ideology, and those who use the old instruments of power for criminal gain, then political terrorism and crime become one.

Against these inevitable developments in Cambodia the United Nations established a human rights component with the intention of fostering a momentum within Cambodian society which would act as a cautionary brake on criminal behaviour and promote a system of justice. This was supported by a large civil police component that was intended to supervise the party police and ensure that all crimes were properly investigated and criminals brought to justice. Unfortunately, the civil police were never able to come to terms with the complexity of their role. The police force lacked the quality and the structure to bring the political pursuits of the Cambodian police under control, and quickly reverted to the veneer tasks of regimentation, traffic management, and process. The civil police were not to blame for this deficiency. Little attention was given in the agreements and the mandate to the critical role the Cambodian police would play in countrywide security. There was no plan to disarm them, and yet they were as armed and potent as most of the forces of the other factions. After the Phnom Penh riots of November 1991 it must have been very clear to the Khmer Rouge that to disarm while the Cambodian police remained armed and engaged in both political and criminal pursuits would have been suicidal.

The human-rights-driven initiative to establish a criminal code through the SNC and create the Office of the Special Prosecutor to investigate crimes and raise warrants for the arrest of criminals did little to attenuate the political violence, although it may have had some deterrent effect. It did, however, set a precedent and highlight the need for such initiatives to embrace the totality of a justice system if they are to be successful.

It would have been necessary that a new police force and a new judiciary, free from the taint of the former communist parties and independent of the political parties, could emerge from the process. This may or may not have demanded enforcement, but what it would have definitely required was a commitment to training a replacement force and an independent international judiciary in transition until Cambodians could be trained and equipped for this role. Strangely, while the United Nations cannot fund such initiatives, there is good reason to believe that this more enduring solution to Cambodia's problems would have cost less than the largely nugatory work of the UNTAC civpol component.

At the closing stages of the political campaign the special representative of the Secretary-General was moved to admit that UNTAC had failed to create a neutral political environment. It settled instead for an environment of equal opportunity whereby UN assistance was given to those political parties that were deprived of opportunity by the criminal activities of the Phnom Penh faction. Smarting from his defeat at the polls, Hun Sen has continued to claim to this day that this was unfair, and that UNTAC was the worst thing that ever happened to Cambodia.

The United Nations and the constitutional process

Violence and invective clouded the post-electoral environment in Cambodia. Everyone except FUNCINPEC (the National United Front for an Independent, Neutral, Peaceful, and Cooperative Cambodia) realized that they had made fundamental mistakes. In a fit of panic some elements in Cambodia declared an autonomous zone east of the Mekong. The Khmer Rouge, utterly confused by the fact that the so-called resistance forces had gained the majority vote, found that they were unable to rally forces in their own autonomous zones.

In this confusion UNTAC seemed to lose its focus on the principal objective of its mandate, which was to leave Cambodia with an effective democratic government firmly in place. It was slow to inject itself into the constitutional process, and relatively weak in its advocacy when it did. The fear engendered by the violent response of the Phnom Penh faction, and lack of leadership on the side of the successful parties, forced constitutional compromises which were inherently unstable and set the course for the inevitable overthrow of the democratic process four years later.

The attitude that the outcome was acceptable, given the reality of where power actually lay in Cambodia, was widespread in UNTAC and the international community as a whole. This comforting thought overlooks the fact that the United Nations itself did much to contribute to that power imbalance by allowing the state of Cambodia to retain its security forces while doing everything to strip the other parties of the power to resist. At the very least, the United Nations could have insisted that the constitution was a better reflection of the wishes of the Cambodian people. The extent to which this neglect reflects the UN's traditional commitment to minimal interference in the internal affairs of nations deserves further analysis.

Should UNTAC have stayed longer?

The United Nations continued to maintain a presence in Cambodia after its role as the transitional authority was concluded with the establishment of the constitutional monarchy and the national legislature. This presence was of a minor nature, and was designed to inform the international community of compliance or otherwise with the fundamental tenets of the Paris agreements, including the commitment of surrounding nations to stay out of Cambodian affairs. This was much less than many Cambodians desired, fearing as they did the potential for political terror on the part of those elements of the security forces that continued their allegiance to the party. While this fear turned out to be warranted, there was little the United Nations could do once it had accepted the constitutional construct devised by the Constitutional Assembly.

There could not be two authorities in one country and, like it or not, the United Nations had to let the Cambodians work out their own relationships from that point onwards. There was no will in the international community to continue the engagement, and extensive problems called for expensive solutions in the rest of the world.

Summary

The Paris agreements were the result of thoughtful and deliberately time-consuming negotiations. They did result in an improvement in the Cambodian situation, in that they allowed the international community to engage in a constructive way in the entire region of Indochina. In this sense UNTAC was a success, but there is substantial evidence that a vastly better set of dynamics could have emerged from the experience if the mission had been better planned.

Of all the failures, the most costly in terms of long-term outcomes was the inability to deploy both military and civilian capability at short notice. This failure confronted the factions with a vacuum, making it impossible for them to control the destructive elements within their ranks. The moral authority that was lost by this delay was partly recovered by the response of the Cambodian people to the electoral process, when 97 per cent of the population registered and, of these, 90 per cent voted. But much of this was lost again by the lack of preparedness of the United Nations to seize the initiative in the constitutional process that followed. The question remains, is the United Nations better prepared for governance in the twenty-first century than it was in 1991?

Conclusion

Many UN missions have been conducted since UNTAC, some successfully and some with disastrous consequences for the peoples involved. Back in 1991 the United Nations could not be blamed for lacking experience in the multifaceted operations which became possible and necessary after the limited opportunities of the Cold War period. It was found wanting in its ability to plan and rapidly deploy forces and to field high-quality administrators in sufficient numbers to provide effective supervision and governance in disrupted states.

From time to time Secretaries-General have called for greater commitments from the international community: rapid-response forces in the case of Boutros Boutros-Ghali, and regional leadership in enforcement operations in the case of Kofi Annan. Both of these initiatives admit a certain planning and controlling incapacity on the part of the Secretariat, which has both built up and lost military capability during this period, primarily through the enforcement of strict organizational ceilings on the part of the General Assembly, and partly because of protests from some members about the fact that volunteered staffs favoured the richer nations.

The truth of the matter is that the Secretariat is no better placed to plan and control operations than it was in 1991, and remains dependent on outside help when complex missions are to be organized. Where it might be better served is that there are now many experienced peacekeepers worldwide who can be called on to assist in missions. What is lacking, however, is the capacity to occupy and run countries. Once a highly developed art in colonial nations, this bold form of administration is now a thing of the past, and will be difficult to recover.

10

UN peacekeeping operations in the former Yugoslavia – from UNPROFOR to Kosovo

Satish Nambiar

As it evolved over the years, peacekeeping has become an extraordinary art that calls for the use of military personnel not to wage war, but to prevent fighting between belligerents, to ensure the maintenance of cease-fires, and to provide a measure of stability in an area of conflict while negotiations are conducted. It is therefore important to distinguish between the concepts of "collective enforcement" and peacekeeping in the international environment. Whereas the former is a punitive process designed to be carried out with some degree of discrimination, but not necessarily impartially, the latter is politically impartial and essentially non-coercive. Hence peacekeeping has always been based on a triad of principles that give it legitimacy as well as credibility; namely, consent of the parties to the conflict, impartiality of the peacekeepers, and the use of force by lightly armed peacekeepers only in self-defence.

The premise on which international peacekeeping is based is that violence in interstate and intrastate conflict can be controlled without resort to the use of force or enforcement measures. Needless to say, there are many theorists and, no doubt, a few practitioners who believe that force needs to be met with force. An objective analysis of the history of conflicts would make it evident that the use of force and enforcement measures, particularly in internal conflicts, tends to prolong the conflict rather than resolve it speedily. This is not, however, to suggest that the use of force is to be ruled out altogether; in certain circumstances, use of force may well be essential as a catalyst for peaceful resolution.

Enforcement actions, by their very nature, are subjective and biased towards one side or another; and that is why if prolonged, which they invariably will be, particularly in intrastate or internal conflicts, they tend to be counterproductive. Peacekeeping initiatives, on the other hand, will also only too often ensure the *status quo* and are thus equally counterproductive, unless complemented by associated initiatives such as peacemaking (working towards a negotiated political solution) and peacebuilding (working towards the restoration of an equitable economic and social order, among other nation-building activities). Peacekeeping operations, being more objective and non-partisan, lay a stable base for the pursuit of peacemaking and peace-building. Quite often, however, a measure of stability brought about by the cessation of hostilities is not exploited speedily to progress peacemaking activity and there is a reversion to conflict, for which ironically the peacekeepers are blamed rather than those who should have exploited the advantage. Sadly, this was the experience of those of us who served with UNPROFOR in the early period.

The immediate backdrop to the deployment of UNPROFOR

With the end of the Cold War and the relatively successful conduct of the Gulf War, there was a great sense of euphoria of the emergence of a new world order regulated by the international community led by the Western powers. UN activities in the maintenance of international peace and security increased enormously, the impact being both quantitative and qualitative. In the first 43 years of its existence, namely from 1945 to 1988, the United Nations had mounted 15 peacekeeping operations. In the five years following the end of the Cold War, that is between 1989 and 1993, 16 missions were mounted in Europe, Asia, Africa, and South America.

The qualitative change was even more important, in that most of the recent conflicts have taken place, or are taking place, within states or between units that were part of unitary states until they began to fall apart. They are not being fought by national armies, but by paramilitaries and irregulars; in many cases led by warlords without any principles or scruples. In the process, civilians have been the main victims (90 per cent today against 10 per cent a decade or so back). In many cases, state institutions have collapsed; in a few cases, there are no governments. As a result, humanitarian emergencies have forced the international community to intervene. This is why the demands on UN peacekeeping have gone well beyond traditional peacekeeping and encompassed activities like demobilization of troops and armed paramilitaries or irregulars, promotion of national reconciliation, restoration of effective governments, the organization and monitoring of elections, provision of broader support to humanitarian aid missions, including protection of "safe areas" and escort of relief convoys, and so on. UN peacekeeping operations have therefore become more expensive, more complex, and more dangerous.

The UNPROFOR experience

At the outset, it needs to be stressed that for the author the command of this mission was a tremendous challenge, a great honour, and a privilege; it was a unique and unforgettable experience. It became the high point of a service career which had in any case been something to look back on with a great sense of pride and satisfaction. The significance of the challenge of the mission was that it not only drew on all the professional ability acquired in the Indian Army over three-and-a-half decades, but that it also demanded a display of diplomatic and political negotiating skills, which were refined as the mission progressed. The sense of achievement on return to the rolls of the Indian Army arose from the fact that the pioneers in UNPROFOR had successfully set up from scratch what turned out to be the largest UN peacekeeping operation ever. This was achieved despite some very serious handicaps in terms of organizational, administrative, and political back-up, and under the fierce glare of the sophisticated media of Europe and America. A striking feature of the operation was the tremendous sense of dedication and selflessness displayed by all who served with UNPROFOR; particularly gratifying was the unreserved response from all segments of the mission to the heavy demands placed on them.

One cannot do complete and objective justice to the developments in that unfortunate region of the world in a brief chapter such as this. Hence, while refraining from any detailed comment on aspects that are in any case now only a matter of interest to historians, it is intended to try and dwell on those aspects from which we can draw lessons for future operations, or even possibly apply mid-course corrections to the ongoing operations in Bosnia-Herzegovina and Kosovo.

A brief historical background to the region

To understand the nuances of the Yugoslav situation, it is useful to have some insight of the history of the Balkans and how various European powers and Turkey have influenced events there over the last 500 years or so. Since this chapter cannot take that path, however, it will focus briefly on more recent events. The collapse of communism in the erstwhile Soviet Union and Eastern Europe, and the emergence of a united Germany as an overwhelming influence in West European politics and its economy, are important factors. The potential threat posed by a strong, united Yugoslavia in the volatile backyard of Europe was possibly the catalyst for some of the moves that were initiated in the region in 1990–1991. Germany, Austria, and Hungary, with their historical links with the region, together with Italy (and, some say, even the Vatican) without doubt encouraged nationalistic and secessionist elements in Slovenia and Croatia; the developments that followed were inevitable. Equally inevitable was the Serb view that what they were being subjected to was a German plot to subjugate them.

When the problems assumed an overt form in 1990–1991, the European Community (as it was then called) initiated some tentative processes to contain the situation. One of the moves initiated was to set up the Badinter Commission, whose task it was to establish whether or not the newly emerging states fulfilled the primary requirements for recognition by the Community. These included, among others, provision for the protection of minority rights. The Commission came to the conclusion that Slovenia (with a 98 per cent Slovene population) fulfilled the requirements for recognition; however, it ruled that Croatia and Bosnia-Herzegovina did not. It is a cruel irony therefore that, even so, under sustained and unrelenting German pressure the European Community and the USA recognized the latter two countries prematurely, thus setting alight the flames of conflict. Hence, if one were to try objectively to pinpoint responsibility for the carnage in the former Yugoslavia purely in terms of the immediate root cause, the onus is on the European Community and the USA. It is an even further irony that this possible guilt complex has led the governments of these countries to deflect total blame on the Serbs as the villains of the peace throughout the last seven years, including the recent developments in Kosovo. That the Serbs had a case in Croatia was recognized in the Security Council resolution setting up UNPROFOR, which among other things stated that "the United Nations troops and police would be deployed in certain areas of Croatia, designated as United Nations Protected Areas (UNPAs); the UNPAs would be areas in which the Secretary-General judged that special arrangements were required during an interim period ... they would be areas in which Serbs constitute the majority or a substantial minority of the population ...". The Serbs in Bosnia-Herzegovina also had a case, considering that they then constituted about 34 per cent of the population. All this was, however, submerged in the symbolism and rhetoric indulged in by some members of the international community, and by the Serbs' stubbornness and heavy-handed responses to developments.

Political aspects

One of the major shortcomings of the UN operation in the former Yugo-slavia was that it was launched much too hurriedly, without the degree of preparation essential for a venture so complex and demanding. During the preliminary negotiations and discussions conducted by the Secretary-General's special envoy, Cyrus Vance, and senior staff of the UN Secretariat with the political and military leadership of the parties to the conflict prior to the submission of a report to the Security Council, it was evident that there were a number of contentious issues on which there were significant variations of interpretation. While these were apparently taken note of, they were glossed over in the hope that they may get resolved or disappear as the operation got going. In the event, these issues assumed serious proportions and continued to plague the operation. It would be useful to recall what turned out to be prophetic remarks made by the Secretary-General in his report of 15 February 1992 to the Security Council:

[I]mmediate UN deployment is the only remaining hope for avoiding an even more destructive civil war than that which prevailed during the second half of 1991. Many member states [obviously the West Europeans] also have urged me not to delay in recommending the deployment of a UN Force in accordance with the Plan [the Vance Plan] ... If it is only now that I am proposing such a force, it has been because of the complexities and dangers of the Yugoslav situation ... As will be evident from Section 1 of the present report, there remain a number of *unanswered questions* about the extent to which the Force will, in practice, receive the necessary cooperation. But after careful deliberation, I have come to the conclusion, that the danger that a UN peacekeeping operation will fail because of lack of cooperation from the parties, is less grievous than the danger that delay in its dispatch will lead to a breakdown of the cease-fire, and to a new conflagration in Yugoslavia.[1]

In the intervening period between the approval of the Vance Plan by the Security Council in December 1991 and the Secretary-General's report on the setting up of the mission in February 1992, many developments had taken place which had substantially altered certain basic features on which the plan was premised. However, the original plan was not modified to allow for the new realities. Mission headquarters did not have anyone on its staff who had been associated with the negotiating process and the positions taken by the belligerents. In the initial stages, therefore, the UNPROFOR hierarchy was unable to interpret and respond effectively to the positions taken by the parties to the conflict.

Serb ground positions had changed and were well beyond the boundaries of the *opstine* (municipalities) listed in the Vance Plan. These areas became very contentious as UNPROFOR deployed and began to deal with the belligerents; at a certain stage they came to be designated as "pink zones" remaining under Serb control, much to the chagrin of the Croatian authorities. Croatia and Slovenia had since been recognized as independent nations by the European Community members and others; in due course, they were also recognized by the United Nations. Such recognition carried with it the aspect of sovereignty within existing borders. On this basis, the Croatian government took the view that the Krajina Serbs had no *locus standi* and therefore should not be a party to be dealt with by the UN force. While this position may have had some validity from their point of view, it was in conflict with the Vance Plan, which categorically set out that deployment in the areas designated as UN Protected Areas was to be an "interim arrangement" subject to a final political resolution, which was to be arrived at under the aegis of the European Conference on Yugoslavia.

The main lesson that emerges from this consideration is that of preparation, including the securing of firm agreements and commitments from the parties to the conflict. To the extent feasible, the prospective special representative of the Secretary-General and/or the force commander should be associated with the preliminary negotiations and discussions. The Namibia success story and the relative success of the Cambodia operation reinforce this recommendation; almost a decade of negotiations in the former case, and similarly exhaustive negotiations in the latter, with participation by some of those who subsequently had a hand in running the operations. Equally, to the extent possible, the special representative and/or the force commander should be associated with the drafting of the Secretary-General's report for the setting up of the mission, so that the mandate is achievable and the rules of engagement framed accordingly in the field.

With the changed political situation insofar as Croatia was concerned, and the outbreak of civil war in Bosnia-Herzegovina even before the allotted forces for the original mandate arrived in full, UNPROFOR was saddled with additional tasks. This came to be known in due course as "mission creep". Between June and December 1992, the Security Council in its immense wisdom conferred nine extensions to the original mandate. These were the reopening of Sarajevo airport for humanitarian purposes; establishment of a joint commission and functions in "pink zones" in Croatia; monitoring of heavy weapons around Sarajevo; immigration and customs functions on UNPA boundaries that run along state borders; deployment in Bosnia-Herzegovina for escort of humanitarian aid convoys; monitoring of demilitarization of the Prevlaka peninsula; deployment of observers at airfields and monitoring of the "no-fly zone" over

Bosnia-Herzegovina; control of the Peruca dam; and preventive deployment in Macedonia. It need hardly be mentioned that UNPROFOR never came close to having the resources for the execution of all these tasks before the author relinquished command and left the mission on 2 March 1993. What merits emphasis, however, because it is not often well understood, is that civil war broke out in Bosnia-Herzegovina while UNPROFOR was still in the process of setting up for the mission in Croatia. And even so, for at least the first couple of years UNPROFOR did not have a mandate for "peacekeeping" in Bosnia-Herzegovina. The various measures instituted from time to time were therefore symbolic responses to assuage political pressures and that of the media in the West. Well-drafted specimens of UN intentions remained pieces of paper, because the resources required to implement the resolutions either did not arrive at all or arrived well after the situation that they were meant to deal with had changed totally.

As UNPROFOR operations progressed, it soon became evident that shared responsibility between the United Nations and the European Community (with NATO preparing to make its presence felt in due course in Bosnia-Herzegovina) was an unsatisfactory arrangement, to put it very mildly. Regional organizations should either handle such operations on their own under the umbrella of a Security Council resolution, or the operation must be completely under the United Nations. UNPROFOR's experience showed that when situations emerged where positive results appeared likely, the European Community came on the scene in the hope of drawing credit, but the moment things went wrong, UNPROFOR was left to pick up the pieces; an art the force gradually came to master, insofar as weathering the flak directed at it was concerned. In due course, with the rather dubious arrangements that were put in place for Bosnia-Herzegovina, it was inevitable that copies of reports, analyses, and recommendations emanating from UNPROFOR headquarters began finding their way to Brussels, some national capitals, and the office of the European Community negotiator. The irritating and unacceptable part of this development was that, using such information, attempts were made to arrive at arrangements with the belligerents without consulting UNPROFOR; in most cases with disastrous results.

A vital requirement for any UN operation to be successful is that of continuous political support. Sacrificing this at the altar of political expediency is not only hypocritical, but also a source of danger to the personnel in the mission area, who continue to work in a dedicated manner under most trying conditions. Regrettably, the operations in the former Yugoslavia have been characterized by a degree of symbolism, rhetoric, and hypocrisy for which a heavy price has been paid in terms of human lives and suffering; posterity will no doubt judge the international community harshly for this. For future operations, as also for the pursuance of current operations, it is not only desirable but essential that some mechanism be put in place where either members of the Security Council and/or troop-contributing countries or a designated group of countries get together and identify specific areas of support for an operation. They can then direct their individual and collective political efforts accordingly, in close coordination with those in the field.

Military aspects

Besides the great challenge of dealing with the complexity of the situation in the former Yugoslavia, another immediate challenge in setting up the mission was that of moulding a large multinational force with military, civilian police, and international civilian staff from so many different regions, with different cultures and languages, different backgrounds and approaches to the problem, varying levels of training, varied types of equipment, and so on, into a single cohesive force. That this was largely achieved in a relatively short period of time was a tribute to the dedication, professionalism, understanding, and application displayed by all members of the mission collectively as contingents, as well as individually. This was in many ways the single most satisfying feature of the author's experience with UNPROFOR.

One of the major problems faced by UNPROFOR was the inordinately long time it took for the various contingents to arrive in the mission area. It took almost four months for the complete military components of the mission to be deployed for the initial mandate; by which time extensions to the mandate had already begun to be framed. This serious shortcoming has been addressed somewhat by the earmarking of "standby" forces by member countries; it is understood that this arrangement today provides for about 100,000 personnel pledged by 74 countries. However, it is a moot point whether such forces would, in fact, be available immediately on demand by the United Nations; the Rwandan experience indicates that political expediency and domestic compulsions will always influence the responses of member states. Therefore, while the earmarking of "standby" forces is an arrangement that should continue, the only real answer for meeting crisis situations that call for speedy deployment of military forces for the maintenance of international peace and security is to raise and maintain a "standing" UN force of a defined composition, properly organized, trained, and equipped, to be available for immediate deployment when authorized to do so by the Security Council. Reservations about costs, and possible biased utilization at the behest of the more powerful members of the Security Council, are aspects that need to be resolved in the context of the need to restructure the various organs of the United Nations. It is important to stress that utilization of such a force is premised on its early replacement by another force constituted under the authority of the United Nations in the normal course from the "standby" commitments made available by member countries.

Another serious problem was the time it took for mission headquarters and the four sector headquarters to become effective, given the fact that the commanders and staff were gathered together at short notice from various corners of the globe. Most of them had never even seen each other before. This type of arrangement may have worked in earlier years, when the pressures and dangers in the mission areas were not so serious as they are today. In the case of UNPROFOR, the solution resorted to when additional deployment for the execution of tasks in Bosnia-Herzegovina took place was to draw the core of the headquarters from NATO resources. Whereas this was no doubt effective from the operational point of view, it was an uncomfortable arrangement. While the professionalism of the staff assured that their unreserved focus would be channelled to the tasks in hand as members of UNPROFOR, they were often embarrassed by the demands placed on them by the parent organization as well as their national governments.

A possible solution to this problem may be found by setting up two or three regional UN "cells" in selected locations, comprising personnel drawn from as many countries as desire to participate. Such staffing should include military personnel, civilian police, civil affairs personnel, and some administrative staff. In the normal course, these "cells" could be tasked to monitor, analyse, and assess developments in designated regions, and provide input to the UN Headquarters in New York. They could also maintain liaison with governments in the region on aspects of peace operations, assist in training of contingents, and so on. They could then provide the nucleus for the constitution of a force headquarters in the field when required. What needs to be stressed is that they should be UN organizations functioning under the control of the Secretary-General, and not adjuncts to regional organizations.

A vital aspect that has surfaced from time to time is that of the command and control of a UN operation. In the case of UNPROFOR, notwithstanding the large number of contingents and the fact that these included contributions from permanent members of the Security Council and many developed countries of the Western world, there were no major problems in this regard in the first year of its operation. This was as much due to the fact that no compromises on the subject were allowed as due to the unqualified support the mission received from UN Headquarters in New York. This is, however, an aspect that needs particular attention in the context of situations that arose in the mission in subsequent years, and it has also apparently plagued some other UN missions. There can be only one option insofar as the operational command of a mission is concerned. All forces deployed in the mission area must take their orders from the head of mission or the force commander, and implement them in the right spirit. It is for the head of mission or the force commander to be careful and discreet in decisions that are sensitive. One must be realistic enough to recognize that no matter what the efforts put in, mutual interaction ensured, and understanding developed, national interests and national pride will always take precedence over any form of commitment to the UN flag. The experience of UNPROFOR was that in itself this is not a bad thing, provided that such national interests and the national pride of the contingents are effectively harnessed towards the common purpose of the mission.

Coordination with aid agencies

One of the major tasks that UNPROFOR had to undertake, particularly in Bosnia-Herzegovina, was to assist in the provision of humanitarian aid. In this context, the interaction between the UN forces and aid agencies like the UN High Commissioner for Refugees (UNHCR) and non-governmental organizations (NGOs) such as the International Committee of the Red Cross (ICRC) merits some reference. It took some time for an institutionalized arrangement to be set up, primarily because of the magnitude of the problem and the fact that all organizations were struggling to cope with their own internal dynamics in the early stages under fairly adverse conditions. In the process, some very serious reservations about one another developed, and it took a great deal of effort at various levels for it to dawn on all concerned that they were in fact working towards a common purpose.

Insofar as aid agencies are concerned, it is essential that their efforts are coordinated, in terms of both aid effort and the assistance desired from the military; the best arrangement would be for the UNHCR to be the lead agency. The problem remains that most NGOs have an agenda of their own and are reluctant to subordinate themselves to any other organization; their argument is that they have to show results to those who fund their activities, whose aims and purposes may not totally coincide with those of the international community. At a seminar the author attended at the University of Oxford in October 1995 on the subject of the role of the military in humanitarian emergencies, he was shocked to note the intense distrust of the military by most NGO personnel (and vice versa) as a result of their interaction in the field in various mission areas. Sadly, at the end of the three-day seminar the author's impression was that the gap between the military and the NGOs had not narrowed, but may well have widened. This is a factor that should be addressed by senior commanders and staff in the field, UN Headquarters, and other international organizations, to correct the wrong perceptions that seem to persist on all sides.

The media and the public information system

The importance of the media, both electronic and print, in whatever activity is undertaken cannot be overstated. There is possibly no other single factor that has a greater influence on the evolution, preparation, and conduct of a peace operation than the influence of the media. Some operations in the recent past were rushed into without adequate preparation and thought purely because of pressures generated by media reports; in other cases, conduct of operations in mission areas has been influenced by media coverage even to the extent that it was against the better judgement of commanders on the ground. It is therefore imperative that the international community recognizes the impact of this vital aspect and, while using it to good effect to further the cause of international peace and security, has the strength to resist pressures for deployment of forces short of having taken into account all implications and made full preparations.

A related aspect is the need to recognize the equally vital importance of providing qualified staff and essential equipment for running an effective public information system as part of any peace operation as it is being set up. Wherever this has been done well, the mission's success has been greatly assisted. And where it was conspicuous by its non-existence for many months, as was the case in the former Yugoslavia, the mission was seriously handicapped. This is because truth is invariably the first casualty, particularly in cases of ethnic intrastate conflict. In fact, in such operations this vital tool must be available from the very outset in order to deal with the propaganda put out by the parties to the conflict and by unscrupulous and irresponsible media persons.

The route to Kosovo

In the process of keeping in touch with events in the Balkans since 1993, it was disturbing to note that many of the fears about the command and control of the operations, and the direction they may be forced to take, began to come true. It is unfortunate that the UN presence was used as a facade for the machinations of some NATO members. Inevitably, the mission appeared to have become a tool of this regional alliance and, on other occasions, the "whipping boy". Even so, it was indeed tragic to note that the UN mission was forced to execute tasks that were not feasible without matching resources being made available. The most unfortunate was that of the establishment and security of what came to be called "safe havens" or "safe areas". The subject was first raised with UNPROFOR in about October 1992 in the context of pressures on the UN Secretariat to declare as "safe areas" certain places in Bosnia-Herzegovina such as Sarajevo, Bihac, Tuzla, Goradze, and Foca. It was then made quite clear to the Secretariat that the concept of a "safe area" had two major connotations: no weapons within, and no entry of weapons from without in each "safe area". It was also made clear that to ensure the implementation of this requirement, a "muscular" deployment of UN forces was essential. The requirement of troops that was then assessed as the minimum essential to meet the commitment was about four-and-a-half divisions; 60,000 troops (the size of NATO deployments after the bombing of the Serbs and the Dayton agreement). Needless to state, there was no further direction or reference on the subject to UNPROFOR before the author left the mission area on 2 March 1993. The disastrous results of the callousness displayed by the Security Council in subsequently endorsing inadequate deployment, leading to developments as in Srebrenica, are matters that merit more detailed and separate evaluation.

The much-acclaimed Dayton Accord is another reflection of the symbolism that has characterized most of the initiatives in the region. At Dayton, the Serbs of Bosnia-Herzegovina were given almost all they had asked for as early as the end of 1992; including recognition as a separate entity, control of Serb majority areas, and almost half the country. The Muslims and Croats of the republic have been grouped into a federation, which even to the casual observer of the scene is a superficial arrangement that will last only as long as NATO forces are present in some strength; the real fact is that these two communities are probably as antagonistic to each other as they are to the Serbs. Therefore, notwithstanding all the rhetoric, NATO is in for a long period of deployment in Bosnia-Herzegovina. The saving grace may be that as economic activity picks up and the quality of life improves, the people of the region may feel less inclined to respond spontaneously to the call of nationalism.

Even before the provisions of the Dayton Accord had begun to be properly implemented, Kosovo exploded. It is a matter of deep regret that the political leadership of the USA and the countries of Western Europe did not apply their efforts to a resolution of the Kosovo situation during the deliberations at Dayton in November 1995. It is inconceivable that anyone dealing with developments in the Balkans could have failed to recognize that Kosovo was a "tinder box". Since this is not the place to dissect the Kosovo situation, suffice it to state that the manner in which

NATO has blatantly violated all norms of international behaviour in dealing with the developments emerging from its own mishandling should be a matter of concern to the international community. NATO actions against Yugoslavia in Kosovo are in violation of the UN Charter. They are in violation of the charter of NATO itself. The attempts at coercing Yugoslavia to sign up to what was drafted at Rambouillet are in violation of the provisions of the Vienna Convention on the Law of International Treaties. All that has happened in recent times leads one to speculate on the bleak future of the United Nations as an organization.

The way ahead

There is apparently some considerable discussion, particularly in the Western world, which seeks to cloak NATO's actions in Kosovo under the mantle of humanitarian intervention. While there may be merit in such discussion from the moral point of view, the legal position cannot be ignored. The use of force is governed in international law by the provisions of the UN Charter, at the root of which is the principle of the sovereignty and integrity of the nation-state. The Charter clearly prohibits the threat or use of force against the territorial integrity or political independence of any state, with two exceptions. The first is individual or collective self-defence when a member state is the victim of aggression, and the second is when the Security Council acts under Chapter VII to deal with a threat to peace, breach of peace, or an act of aggression. Whereas there cannot be much disagreement that human rights violations and humanitarian catastrophes merit the attention of the international community, it is for consideration whether physical intervention to deal with such situations can be given primacy over the aspect of the sovereignty of states. This has been the subject of discussion at the United Nations in recent years, and it would appear that there is some consensus that the international community has a responsibility in this regard. In pursuance of this commitment, there have been occasions in the recent past where humanitarian intervention has been authorized by the Security Council. However, the apprehension of most of the member states is that the primacy of the UN Security Council in the maintenance of international peace and security is being compromised. The supreme irony in this context is that although the United Nations today is perceived as a tool of the world's pre-eminent superpower, the USA, in the case of NATO intervention in Kosovo the alliance led by the USA still found it expedient to bypass the Security Council. If humanitarian intervention is to be undertaken by some members of the international community on the basis of the perceptions of the leadership of one or two powers, the very foundations of the UN Charter stand eroded. This is a central issue that needs to be addressed.

The primary concern is whether the United Nations will recover from what is perceived to be a "knock-out" blow. There are enough indications that NATO appears to have arrogated to itself, on its own terms, the responsibility for the maintenance of international peace and security; which in fact is the primary role of the United Nations. Where will NATO interpose its forces next, now that it has been established that the application of brute force is the panacea for the problems in the world? Having shaken off the colonial regimes that exploited our countries and peoples, are we now witnessing a new regime of continuing Western domination by the induction of military forces, or those of their surrogates?

Such perceptions have already begun to generate initiatives to ensure that the international community does not become hostage to the machinations of a few powerful countries of the Western world. There is already a growing body of opinion in India that we should seek an arrangement with Russia, and in due course China, to dilute the domination of the Western alliance. Such initiatives do not, however, seem to take into account the realities of the situation that obtains today. Russia's economic situation makes it far too dependent on the West. Hence, notwithstanding the Russian leadership's resentment of the dominant role of NATO in the international arena, it would be too much to expect more than rhetoric and symbolism from Moscow for some time to come. That does not, however, preclude alignments with countries like India in articulating a perception of what should be the new world order. As things stand, for all the posturing on the international stage, China is too closely linked economically with the USA and Europe to indulge in more than symbolic positions; even more so because the leadership is fairly confident that there is unlikely to be any physical interference in what is conceded as China's area of interest. Significantly, India, Russia, and China arrived at similar positions on the Kosovo issue independently and without prior consultations. However, while there could be greater consultations between the three, there does not appear to be any move towards forming any new alliances or setting up new blocs in a post-Cold War era. Other countries, too, are concerned. The Japanese prime minister's statement on 19 June 1999 at the meeting of the G7 about the need for restructuring of the United Nations is a pointer. Many countries that could have reservations have remained muted in criticism, some because of their dependence on Western largesse, and others because of the Islamic factor, as the Muslim population in Kosovo was supported by NATO.

A likely fall-out of NATO's intervention in Kosovo and the perceptions it has generated is that many developing countries may feel compelled to move towards ensuring greater security for themselves and self-reliance through the acquisition of more weaponry. This is good news no doubt for the arms industries of the developed world.

The end of the Cold War and the relative success of Operation Desert Storm had induced a sense of euphoria that the international community was geared to deal with dangers to international peace and security in a more effective manner than hitherto. However, the experiences of Somalia, former Yugoslavia, Liberia, Angola, Rwanda, and those in some of the former republics of the erstwhile Soviet Union quickly dispelled these expectations and, in fact, may well have induced a sense of retrenchment in regard to peace operations. Even so, there can hardly be any doubt that as and when new conflict situations arise, the international community and the belligerents will turn to the United Nations for attempts at resolution. Hence operations for the maintenance of international peace and security will continue to be required and must therefore continue to receive the attention they deserve, in terms of both political support and military preparation.

International peace operations, whether under the aegis of the United Nations, regional organizations, or multinational groupings, are the only answer to conflict resolution when all else fails. But it must be emphasized that the root of most conflicts lies in deprivation in society and, to that extent, some early investment in potential conflict areas towards building society would be more cost-effective. In this context, maximum efforts need to be directed towards preventive action by the international community; in this effort, whether it should be the United Nations or regional organizations is a matter of statesmanship.

As we look into the twenty-first century, it is essential that we do not allow the perceived inadequacies of some recent operations to cloud our judgement and swing from one extreme of attempting to undertake too much to the other extreme of undertaking too little. There is so much the international community can do to ensure the maintenance of international peace and security, and there is no way it can absolve itself of that responsibility.

Notes

1. Security Council Document S/23592, 15 February 1992, p. 7.

11

Civilian police in UN peace operations: Some lessons from recent Australian experience

John McFarlane and William Maley

The demise of the Cold War, the onset of globalization, and massive developments in technology, communications, and international transportation have had a profound effect on the political, economic, military, environmental, and societal issues which previously contributed to security and stability in the Asia Pacific region. However, although the threat of nuclear war has diminished, at both international and regional levels the security environment is anything but stable. Issues such as the nuclear tests on the Indian subcontinent, serious tensions in the Taiwan Straits and South China Sea, the Asian financial crisis, the proliferation of weapons of mass destruction (including the use of sarin gas by a religious cult in Japan in 1995), the South-East Asian haze problems of 1997, the mass migration of people (internally and externally), the spread of AIDS (acquired immune deficiency syndrome) and other pandemics, and, closer to home, the violence associated with the demise of the Suharto regime in Indonesia, the tragedy of East Timor, the unresolved crisis on Bougainville, the Sandline crisis in 1997, major law and order problems in Papua New Guinea, interethnic violence in the Solomon Islands, and allegations of massive money laundering of Russian money through certain South Pacific island countries, all serve to demonstrate that our region is anything but stable and pacific.[1]

The situation in East Timor has dominated Australian foreign policy thinking over the last two years, and complicated Australia's relations with Indonesia for much longer than that.[2] It will take a considerable time for East Timor to stand on its own feet – long after the UN peace-keeping forces have been withdrawn. The East Timorese leadership has to establish the political, economic, and security measures to enable it to survive as an independent state, and it will be some time before the thousands of East Timorese who were forcibly removed to West Timor or other parts of Indonesia after the act of self-determination will be able to return home. The East Timorese infrastructure has to be rebuilt from scratch, and this will involve long-term commitments from the United Nations, the international aid agencies, non-governmental agencies, and others willing to support this fledgling nation. The process is already proving a complex and challenging one for the international community.[3] However, it is very unlikely that East Timor will be unique: the portents are not good in West Papua,[4] Ambon, the Moluccas, Papua New Guinea, and the Solomon Islands, all of which are very much within Australia's immediate neighbourhood. A serious breakdown in the stability of any of these countries could involve additional Australian military peacekeeping or police peace operations.

The aim in this chapter is a specific one: to explore the implications for UN civilian police (civpol) operations of state disruption, fragmentation, and breakdown, drawing on the lessons learned from the deployment of Australian Federal Police (AFP) to East Timor during the 1999 UN Assistance Mission in East Timor (UNAMET),[5] and on interviews conducted with police who served in the mission. This exercise is important for two reasons. First, civpol are separated from their personal support networks, and forced to cope with problems that may be unfamiliar and unpleasant. Any lessons which can minimize the dangers and discomforts associated with such deployments are therefore important to note.

Second, the *Report of the Panel on United Nations Peace Operations* chaired by Under-Secretary-General Lakhdar Brahimi (the Brahimi Report) has recently set out a series of important recommendations with respect to civilian police operations. The panel encourages member states to "establish a national pool of civilian police officers that would be ready for deployment to United Nations peace operations on short notice"; to "enter into regional training partnerships for civilian police in the respective national pools in order to promote a common level of preparedness"; and to create "a revolving on-call list of about 100 police officers and related experts ... to be available on seven days' notice with teams trained to create the civilian police component of a new peacekeeping operation".[6] The roles which civpol can and should play in peacekeeping are beginning to receive the attention they deserve, and the Australian experience can augment lessons learned from other UN operations.[7]

State fragmentation

In recent years the process of state fragmentation has been the subject of serious scholarly attention, driven by the sense that state sovereignty is eroding.[8] Other players – such as multinational corporations – are becoming more important, and these could erode the state's ability to serve and protect the public interest, thereby also hastening the demise of state power as we now know it. We cannot predict what governments will operate in future, nor what resources they will control.

The typical pattern of state disintegration involves several clearly identifiable steps. First is an increase in instability and in governance problems. Second are threats to state sovereignty and the state's monopoly over the legitimate exercise of force.[9] Third, the state is increasingly unable to perform the basic functions expected of a sovereign state. Fourth, threats surface to the control of the political élite, and in some circumstances to the advantages they have derived from corruption, nepotism, and crony capitalism. Fifth, this may lead to greater repression of the population by the political élite, exercised through the police, the military, other security forces (including government-controlled militia groups), the criminal justice system, and the manipulation of the media. Sixth, severe economic problems develop, leading to a serious increase in unemployment, poverty, hunger and malnutrition, criminality and public order incidents (including "scapegoating", interethnic violence, and ethnic cleansing), human rights violations, and the effective collapse of state authority, which may in turn result in international concern and pressures for intervention.

In a stable state, "state authority is acquired through a capacity to legitimize the exercise of power", with the police as "the conduit through which the exercise of coercive power and authority is channeled". Policing "is not only derived from state developments and processes, but ... also mirrors them". A police system is "an organization made up of groups and individuals, existing for a specific purpose, employing systems of structured activity with an identifiable boundary", designed to maintain civil order. Civil order is a key concept for all police studies.[10]

However, states face significant disruption when they can no longer discharge basic functions, whether through a loss of income or through a legitimacy crisis. Where authority, law, and political order have fragmented, diverse actors vie for power. From the policing perspective, this is likely to lead to an increase in repression, with the police and the military demonstrating the fears held by the regime. In comparison with the military, the police are regarded as "poor cousins". However, much policing in developing countries is paramilitary. The distinction between insurgency and riot control is blurred, especially in urban areas. A police force notorious for corruption, greed, weakness, or partiality is seen as part of the problem by most of the population. As a result, the police system may be bypassed, leading to vigilantism or the use of militia groups or foreign mercenaries. The proper role and functions of the police are largely ignored. Policing in many developing countries is characterized by low status, paramilitarism, and the propensity for violence.

Conflict is always present during state fragmentation, resulting in a blurring between political conflict and crime, and in alternative forms of power structures. The military tends to retain its cohesiveness, but the police may not, due to their close links with the regime. This can give rise to shadowy, nocturnal groups under the patronage of senior military or police officers filling the power vacuum. These groups may then be used to conduct extra-judicial killings, kidnappings, robberies, pay-back attacks, or other criminal activities generally beyond the capacity of the conventional police to deal with. The police organization, policies, and operational capabilities are related to the nature of the regime. The police "provide symbolic and actual evidence of the power and authority of a regime, as well as reflecting its concerns and weaknesses". Policing "mirrors governance, at the same time as governance reflects policing".[11]

Policing can affect the political process by determining who can participate in the political process via the decision as to whom to arrest or detain. The police perform a greater political role during periods of fragmentation. They can also regulate the competitive political process, defending (or abandoning) regimes from (or to) attack. Police can "covertly monitor or manipulate political groups", leading to the abuse of power and brutalization. Police violence probably exists in inverse proportion to the fragmentation of state structures. Police can also "advocate policy inside or outside government", and "provide material aid to regimes".[12] The police possess the force, local knowledge, intelligence, and communication networks which can be exploited as long as the regime is able to give directions. Yet it is also worth noting that, generally, police do not precipitate coups.

The United Nations or any other international body (such as NATO) which accepts the responsibility to intervene in a fragmented state to re-establish stability has a range of capabilities at its disposal, including military peacekeeping and police peace operations – supported by the political, electoral, and aid sectors, as well as by non-governmental organizations (NGOs).[13] The response to the problems of fragmented states may include bilateral expressions of concern at developments, offers of assistance, and mediation to support conflict resolution; multilateral concern, possibly leading to debate in regional fora or the United Nations; and consideration at the UN Security Council of options for intervention under powers conferred in Chapters VI or VII of the UN Charter.[14] The options available to the United Nations in such circumstances include economic sanctions, the provision of observers, peace monitors, and the like, and the introduction of peacekeeping forces (military and/or police),[15] as well as intervention by peacemaking forces (military). Normally, stability is established in disrupted states through military peacekeeping operations, supported as appropriate by civilian police. Once relative stability is re-established and the post-war reconstruction phase of civil order and institutional development has commenced, the importance of re-establishing the rule of law is paramount. This is where the civilian police role becomes so important.

Unfortunately, however, many people at the UN, international, and national levels confuse the roles of the military and civilian police because they do not understand – or have overlooked – the fundamental differences between the role of the police and that of the military, at least in democratic states. While each entails use of the powers of the state, the differences between the two are profound. It is to these distinctions that this chapter now turns. There are times when the military have the only role to play in an intervention: They neutralize armed conflict and provide a secure environment. Once the environment is stabilized, civpol can begin their part of the operation. Again, it must be stressed that police have no role in a war zone and have no particular role to play in settling armed conflict.

Police and military roles

Both the military and the civilian police have important roles to perform in peacekeeping, but it is important to understand that they are *different* and *complementary*, and that a stable and sustained resolution of the problems of a fragmented state will not be achieved unless there is an appropriate contribution by *both* the military and police, each operating in their specialist role. Table 11.1 may help to demonstrate the distinction between the two roles. It describes the difference in individual and organizational roles and responsibilities of a policeman/police force and a soldier/military formation.[16]

Policing is predicated on the attributes of non-negotiable force and discretion. The routines of all policing, especially at the operational level, are characterized by discretion – the use of discretion being an important key to policing. Discretion marks a very important difference between the police and military roles.[17]

Police peace operations

In brief, the civilian police role in a fragmented state includes the following:
- providing a stable and secure environment;
- assisting in dismantling the old instruments of repression;

Table 11.1 Roles of the military and the civilian police

Comparison	Police	Military
Activities		
Principal purpose	Law enforcement Crime prevention	Combat deterrence
Objective	Justice	Victory/political aim
Focus	Law and order – internal	Security – external
Activity	Constant	Preparatory and periodic
Relevant law	Domestic law	Law of armed conflict
Constitution	Instrument of law No political interference	Instrument of policy Political control
Accountability	Domestic courts Rule of law	Chain of command Executive government
Procedures	Gather evidence Need for proof	Limited information Decisions under uncertainty
Use of force	Minimum	Graduated
Individual		
Responsibility	Individual "office of constable"	Primarily a member of a unit
Duty	To the law/judiciary	To the state/monarch
Knowledge	Law	Lethal force
Unlawful orders	Uphold the law	Refuse unlawful order
Status	Citizen with special powers	Citizen with no special powers
Service	Voluntary	Voluntary or conscripted
Career	Starts "on the beat"	Soldier or officer entry
Organization		
Control	Local/central	Central
Structure	Hierarchical	Strongly hierarchical
Personnel	Uniformed/non-uniformed	Uniformed
Origins	Emerged in the nineteenth century	Seventeenth century and earlier
Public	Direct relationship Practical cooperation	Desire for general support Public esteem
Mobility	Limited	Part of core function

- establishing and maintaining a law enforcement and criminal investigation capability;
- selecting and training new members of an indigenous police force, which will ultimately take over the law enforcement role from UN civilian police;
- undertaking investigations and collecting evidence appropriate to the prosecution of alleged serious violations of human rights;[18]
- assisting in re-establishing the criminal justice system and civil administration, including the court system and jails;
- confidence-building with the civil community by operating impartially to enforce the law.

It is critical that civilian police should not be withdrawn before these objectives are largely achieved, or there is every chance that the state will again fragment, requiring further UN or international intervention. In addition to the above, as Caslen has cogently argued with respect to Haiti, police peace operations also contribute in the areas of justice, the economy, and politics.[19]

In the justice sector, the aim is "to treat citizens and institutions equally under the law",[20] and through the courts, police, and civil service to engender a respect for the rule of law. The reality for some time will be that there will be jail-breaks, officials will be bribed, and due process will be nearly non-existent. As Caslen notes, "judicial reform critically lags behind police and security reform".[21]

In the economic sector, the country must survive economically for democracy to succeed, but foreign capital may be needed to overcome a shortage of domestic savings. Massive poverty must often be addressed. Institutional reform is needed, not just aid. The Bretton Woods institutions (the International Monetary Fund and the World Bank) typically encourage private initiative, deregulation of the economy, and liberalization of trade. The key point from a police point of view is that such processes of economic change create both winners and losers, and for both there may be powerful temptations to engage in criminal activities.

In the political sector there will be international pressure for accountability, for freedom of speech and the press, for respect for minority rights and a culture of peaceful élite competition, for "the people" to become active players and leaders, for the development of a sound electoral process, for legitimate mechanisms for the voicing of opposition, for programme flexibility and integration, and for the dignity, sovereignty, and needs of the developing country to be respected. None of this is straightforward. At its most basic level, democracy requires that the ruled have the opportunity to change their rulers without bloodshed. This, however, requires the development and institutionalization of a complex set of rules and practices, often in the face of threats from those whose short-term interests would best be advanced by the unravelling of a democratization process. Time is vital to such processes; unfortunately, it is also the ultimate scarce commodity.[22]

Police-military relations

No matter how well trained and professional they may be, military police are not appropriate for a civpol role. The role of the military police – for which they are trained – is to enforce law and discipline within the military. Traditionally, police are intended to be used to intervene to prevent a breach of the law, whereas the military are designated not to be deployed but to be kept in reserve as a last resort to enforce national policy when all else fails. In a democratic society, the police "police" a community "by consent", not by force.[23] Many states will not accept a foreign military component on their own territory, even under a UN mandate, whereas they may well be prepared to accept an unarmed international police presence. This is an important reason for the international community to pay more attention to the roles of civilian police in peace-keeping and peace-building operations. However, police operate best in a peacekeeping context when there is a military security back-up, infrastructure, and logistics to rely on, and they do not take part in the conduct of hostilities.[24]

Although it is important for UN peacekeeping forces to operate under a unified command, it is equally vital to separate the military peace-keeping role from the civilian police peace operations role. At the practical level, police tend to live and work in urban environments and are generally not as familiar as the military with operating in non-urban conditions. On the other hand, at least as far as Australia is concerned, military personnel are more familiar with operating in remote or jungle environments than in urban areas.

Military deployments, planned by the Australian Department of Defence, are subject to extensive contingency planning based on long-standing intelligence assessments and specific training. They are also well equipped, employ excellent communications, and rely on good reconnaissance and advanced deployments. On the other hand, the experience in Australia so far is that an interdepartmental committee undertakes planning for the deployment of police on peace operations, chaired by the Department of the Prime Minister and Cabinet (DPMC) or the Department of Foreign Affairs and Trade (DFAT), in which the Australian Federal Police is just another member. Such arrangements are less well practised: there is less contingency-planning experience in this area; peace operations are only one of a range of police functions, therefore training in peace operations is limited; the equipment available may be limited to personal issue kit; and the day-to-day pressures on police services result in few people being available for immediate deployment. There is no fat in the police community, particularly at the federal level, so regardless of the importance of the peace operations role from a national perspective, this is yet another demanding task which has to be responded to. In spite of these considerations, Australia has participated in many of the 17 UN-sanctioned police peace operations that have been launched since 1960.

The Australian Federal Police and peace operations[25]

The most significant recent peace operation for the Australian Federal Police was the commitment to serve in East Timor. The decision to commit the AFP to East Timor was made during a meeting between the Australian prime minister and the Indonesian president in Bali on 27 April 1999. It appears that neither the minister for justice nor the commissioner of the Australian Federal Police was consulted prior to this commitment being made. Under the agreement of 5 May 1999 between the governments of Indonesia and Portugal, the responsibility for the security and safety of UN staff (including unarmed civilian police) in the period leading up to the act of self-determination remained with the Indonesian police (PolRI) and military (TNI, or Tentara National Indonesia). The roles of the civilian police in East Timor for the UNAMET period leading up to the act of self-determination (30 August 1999) were limited to advising the Indonesian police during the operational phase of the popular consultation, and supervising the escort of ballot boxes to and from the polling stations. In other words, prior to the act of self-determination, the civilian police had no law enforcement role.[26]

The role of civilian police in East Timor in the period following the act of self-determination (and the subsequent withdrawal of Indonesian forces) falls within the broader remit of the UN Transitional Administration in East Timor (UNTAET):[27]

- to provide security and maintain law and order throughout the territory of East Timor;
- to establish an effective administration;
- to assist in the development of civil and social services;
- to ensure the coordination and delivery of humanitarian assistance, rehabilitation, and development assistance;
- to support capacity-building for self-government;
- to assist in the establishment of conditions for sustainable development.

It is important to note that in performing these duties, Australian Federal Police personnel can draw on skills developed in operations elsewhere – in Cyprus (1964–present), Namibia (1989), Thailand (1988–1991), Cambodia (1992–1993), Somalia (1993–1995), Mozambique (1994), South Africa (1994), Haiti (1994), and Bougainville (1997–present).[28]

Selection of Australian Federal Police and other Australian police for civilian police operations

On 28 October 1998, the United Nations asked countries contributing to peacekeeping operations to send no civpol officers or military observers under the age of 25 years, and to send only troops over age 21, and never under 18. The objective was to ensure that only "experienced, mature, and well-trained" people would serve as peacekeepers.[29]

The current selection criteria for Australian Federal Police members (and other Australian police) serving on civilian police duties in East Timor go much further: the person concerned should currently be appointed as a police member under the Australian Federal Police Act 1979 and have a demonstrated capacity to perform the duties; have a knowledge of the UN's role in East Timor; have the demonstrated ability to exercise self-discipline, and a willingness to accept a military-style working and living environment; have knowledge of the ethnic culture relevant to East Timor and a sound knowledge of the history surrounding the UN commitment; have the demonstrated ability to be culturally aware and tolerant and sensitive in dealing with difference; and be aware of the requirement to adhere to, and implement, UNTAET directives, orders, and procedures. In addition, the following are mandatory:

- basic motor-vehicle maintenance skills;
- map-reading skills;
- a current driver's licence;
- four-wheel-drive skills;
- a firearms permit.

First-aid qualifications are desirable, as is demonstrated knowledge of occupational health and safety policy and procedures, and a demonstrated commitment to the principles of equity and diversity.

Why unarmed civilian police?

It is the view of both the United Nations and the Australian Federal Police that police on peace operations should be unarmed and independent when performing their role. While this view may lead to concern for the safety of members, the authors maintain that an unarmed presence has the greatest chance of success in gaining the respect of the local community.[30] The influence and effectiveness of civilian police is based on moral authority rather than the threat of force. This is even more important when the threat by the militias in East Timor to regard armed police officers as targets is taken into account. Would being armed enhance the performance of civilian police officers, or would it rather cause additional risks and only hinder them in the discharge of their duties?

An armed police presence in a fragmented state, such as East Timor, not only threatens the combatants in any conflict, but also serves to instill a belief in the general population that the use of firearms in a civilian police environment is a necessary law and order tool. This may serve to undermine confidence-building measures undertaken by civilian police. This, in turn, may run counter to the entire post-conflict rebuilding process for which the UN mission is responsible. The fact that the police (in blue) do not carry firearms, whereas the military (in green) do, also helps to underline the importance of the new civil structure that does not have to rely on military power to maintain itself in power. Civilian police should *not* be seen as a threat by the local community.

The use of force, and in particular firearms, presents difficult legal consequences which are not generally addressed in UN mandates or status of forces agreements. For example, if an armed civilian police officer discharged a firearm causing injury or death, what authority has jurisdiction? The international composition of civilian police leads to varying national standards and regulations in the use of firearms. Most contributing countries have adopted the UN covenant requiring the minimum use of force by police officers, which really amounts to the use of a firearm only to protect one's own life or that of another person in imminent danger. However, police from some countries have a much wider interpretation of the use of firearms, and this could have a serious impact on the overall objective of a mission.

It was the unanimous view of all the Australian Federal Police officers in the UNAMET detachment that the decision not to have firearms was the correct one. Australian Federal Police and state/territory police members were deployed unarmed to Haiti (which was not a UN operation), but the USA, which was in charge of the operation, authorized members to be armed and equipped members in the USA during predeployment training and briefings. Firearms were available to civpol in East Timor, although during UNAMET they were held in safe storage in Darwin. During the UNAMET period, the responsibility for law enforcement in East Timor was that of PolRI. After the Indonesian withdrawal and before an East Timor police service had taken over the responsibility of law enforcement, the UNTAET civpol officers, supported by a small but increasing number of local police officers, were responsible for law enforcement in East Timor. Members on current deployments to East Timor now carry firearms and have done so since the end of the second contingent.

Comments by AFP officers on peace operations[31]

I will never forget that without that group and their willingness, or rather determination, to hold on in a desperate and dangerous situation, the United Nations may have withdrawn and the popular consultation process been placed in jeopardy.[32]

To provide background for the preparation of this study, a number of AFP officers, including a police psychologist, were interviewed. These officers had served in a wide variety of Australian Federal Police peace operations overseas, including Cyprus, Cambodia, Somalia, Mozambique, Haiti, and Bougainville. Many of their comments could be regarded as anecdotal and subjective, but they are particularly pertinent to future UN civilian police deployments, which are very likely to involve the AFP and other Australian police. As a political satirist once observed, the plural of anecdote is data. Without necessarily endorsing all the comments, the authors offer a digest of them under various headings as a contribution to the lesson-learning process.

Planning for peace operations

The military often undertake contingency planning for peacekeeping operations six to nine months in advance, but civilians (including civpol) tend to be deployed in haste a few days after a Security Council resolution has been adopted. Civilian police deployment plans should be made well in advance of deployment, in anticipation of the requirement. Whilst unpredictable and sudden situations can arise, civpol deployment plans are made when there is a reasonable likelihood that a police commitment will be required. Using personnel previously experienced in peace operations to make up the first detachment buys time to train "fresh" members for future detachments.

Civpol deployments and strategies should be made with full understanding of the police role generally, and especially the civpol role in a fractured state. With the passage of time, policy-makers in this area are becoming more familiar with the complexities and unique challenges of police peace operations.

The roles of civilian police

Police are accustomed to operating in small numbers with very limited support. The police team structure is somewhat ad hoc, but police are used to working independently. A police officer is accustomed to using his/her discretion – such as whether or not to arrest – and then taking full personal responsibility for his or her actions, even if that action is contrary to the views of a more senior officer.

Civilian police officers are normally unarmed (as they should be), and in this way they contribute to confidence-building and trust. For example, in Cambodia during the UN Transitional Authority in Cambodia (UNTAC) mission, members of the Australian Federal Police detachment were never threatened by the Khmer Rouge soldiers amongst whom they lived and whom they later trained (along with members of the other two Cambodian factions) as local policemen. Male and female civilian police officers can be deployed on an equal footing in any situation. This sends a very positive message to the local population.

Police should not be used in enforcement operations sanctioned under Chapter VII of the UN Charter, except to assist in the investigation of human rights abuses. Civilian police work well with other civilian organizations, including the UN administration, aid agencies, and NGOs. The visibility of the civilian police role sends the correct message to the local people planning a future civilian administration.

Support from the parent police service

A number of questions were raised in this area. How well is the parent police service (PPS) equipped to provide infrastructure support for the civilian police deployment? Are police peace operations regarded as "core business" for the PPS? If so, are the organizational structure and doctrine to support such operations appropriately developed? Does the PPS have a peace operations doctrine? How do members of the PPS regard their colleagues carrying out peace operations – as mercenaries or missionaries? Are the conditions for peace operations service established and consistent? Are the officers representing the PPS at interdepartmental and international meetings concerning peace operations of sufficient experience and seniority to ensure that the civilian police "line" is properly presented?

Selection of civilian police officers

A range of factors should govern selection of personnel. These include good leadership; prior experience in similar operations overseas, if possible; high-order negotiation skills; "visionary" thinking, as there is little initiative displayed by the United Nations in its police peace operations role;[33] a capacity to work with officers with different professional backgrounds; and consciousness that in their civilian police role the personnel are working, in the first instance, for the United Nations rather than for Australia or their own police service.

Civilian police initiatives

Civilian police officers from all the various national detachments generally worked well together, even though there were significant cultural and professional differences between them. This was particularly the case in East Timor when there was a programme of extremely useful and relevant pre-deployment training in Darwin, based on the types of scenarios likely to be faced by civilian police officers immediately on their arrival in East Timor. This training, which was conducted by the AFP and an excellent team of consultants, was regarded by all who undertook it as invaluable.

As many police come into the profession after having already obtained some other technical or professional skills (such as electrician, plumber, soldier, or accountant), these skills could be very effectively harnessed in support of peace operations. For example, in Thmar Puok, Cambodia, the civilian police detachment (comprising Australian Federal Police plus police from Germany and Tunisia) supervised and assisted in building the police station, accommodation blocks, training classrooms, parade ground, and an obstacle course for the training of local police (from each of the three factions). Each officer donated US$1,000 of his salary for these projects, as well as purchasing sweets, paper, and pencils for the local schoolchildren (through whom they were eventually able to gain the trust and friendship of the parents). Australian Federal Police officers in Cambodia also gave English lessons to the local people in their own time, and this contributed substantially to building trust and friendship. In all, 480 local police were trained before the AFP withdrew, and the project appears to have been sustained to the present day.[34]

When the AFP were deployed to Thmar Puok there were no courts, no lawyers, and no prisons. In fact, there was no law to enforce, so the officer in charge wrote, and obtained approval for, a simple legal code based on that applied in the refugee camps on the Thai border, and this was applied and accepted by the local people, with the approval of the United Nations.[35] A basic AFP concept for rebuilding the rule of law and public confidence in fractured states (like Cambodia and East Timor) is to develop a small, well-policed area within a secure perimeter, and then gradually expand the perimeter. This approach works as well in an area subject to serious criminality as it does to a chaotic traffic situation, as was demonstrated in both Cambodia and East Timor.

When a civilian police deployment is made to a fractured state where there is no law, the United Nations should have on hand a simple "model law" which could be imposed (or adapted as appropriate) so that both civilian police and the local population understand what is expected of them. Even in the most disrupted state, the local people do not want lawlessness and would prefer to know "what the rules are". Eventually, the local people should be encouraged to take responsibility for their own law enforcement.

Civilian police always try to maintain their neutrality, and are usually seen as non-threatening by all sides. In Cambodia this enabled them to work effectively with all the political factions without any threats or violence, and in East Timor civilian police were able to go where the military would not have been able to go without substantial support, because in the main civilian police were trusted.

Civilian police problems

The infrastructure support that moves with 3,000 soldiers just is not there for police who serve in small teams all around the island, often in isolated circumstances. The conditions for each of our contingents have been rough to say the least.[36]

There needs to be greater quality control of the police selected for peace operations; international standards need to be set, and the performance of detachments deployed in such operations should be subject to efficiency audit.

Unlike in Cambodia and Haiti, in Mozambique and East Timor all national detachments were split up and mixed with other nationalities, although it was usual for at least two officers from each nationality to be deployed to a post. Sometimes this led to cultural and professional problems. For example, some officers from conservative backgrounds had difficulty working with female civpol officers. There is a need to spend some time briefing all civpol officers on the cultural issues, and that prior to deployment.

When the second detachment arrived in East Timor in September 1999, there was no law and order in the state. All but five PolRI officers had been withdrawn from East Timor, so from 9 September to 28 October (when UNTAET was established) the only law applicable was Indonesian law, enforced by the International Force in East Timor (INTERFET) military police. Civilian police advised the military police until 28 October, when they were given their own charter.

Drawing civilian police officers from such a range of countries gave rise to significant language – and therefore communication – problems. Some officers from non-English-speaking countries had great difficulty communicating with the rest of the civilian police detachment, and others – generally young officers – who did speak English did not have the necessary policing skills. There were some problems integrating the work of civilian police officers coming from a wide range of national criminal justice systems. Some civilian police officers could not drive, had only rudimentary policing skills, or were military police rather than civilian police officers. Australian civilian police officers were often regarded as brash, bold, and impatient – the "let's do it!" syndrome. Sometimes this did not go down well with the traditionalists and bureaucrats, but overall the Australians were well respected and liked, and they regarded their overseas deployments as a valuable personal and career development opportunity.

Overall in East Timor, civilian police performed very well, sometimes in exceptionally difficult and dangerous circumstances. They faced considerable personal risk and witnessed a great deal of violence and trauma. There was some criticism of the UN staff over the decision to evacuate the UN compound, but this criticism occurred in very emotional and difficult circumstances in which very delicate negotiations were being undertaken with PolRI, TNI, and the militia to secure the safe evacuation of the UN and locally engaged staff, and it was simply not possible to communicate with all the civilian police members on the background to the decision.[37] The problem here was not with decisions "on the ground", but with the wider structure of a mission in which there was no neutral UN security force to deter or confront the kind of violence which the militias unleashed. Nonetheless, some civilian police officers understandably became emotionally involved in the situation.

Concern was expressed on a number of occasions about the sustainability of the training of local police given by civilian police officers. It was considered that civilian police officers should remain in the country for training and advisory purposes until the local police force could stand on its own feet.

Most civilian police detachments are poorly selected, trained, and equipped, and deployed with very little knowledge of either the country to which they are going, the political situation behind the disruption in the country, or the UN doctrine to be implemented. This is not the case with the Australian detachments, which are generally very well briefed and prepared, although even in this case more priority should have been given to equipping the officers. There was no reconnaissance visit to East Timor prior to the deployment of the UNAMET detachment, and therefore most of the officers had no idea what equipment they needed.

Very little high-level intelligence is available to civilian police detachments in the field, and this made their role more difficult in critical times and added to the physical risks involved. Furthermore, in some deployments there was a lack of close coordination between the UN political and electoral officers, civilian police, the military, and aid workers. This resulted in too many agendas and a lack of a consistent aim, which sometimes resulted in confused civilian police tasking.

In East Timor there was no status of forces agreement and no memorandum of understanding between PolRI and the civilian police. It was not until 9 August 1999 – the month of the consultation – that a working agreement was entered into between the commissioner of the UNAMET civpol and Colonel Timbul Silaen for the regional police for East Timor. The fact that the civilian police relied on PolRI and TNI to provide their basic protection during the UNAMET period added to the tensions between the UN and Indonesian sides. In East Timor during the UNAMET period, some UN officers and many of the NGO representatives were seen as supportive of East Timorese independence. This added to the tensions with the Indonesians and made the civilian police role harder to perform.

Some AFP members have been disappointed with their reception since returning to Australia. The view is that although there was recognition of the role of civilian police during the UNAMET period, since the INTERFET[38] military deployment civilian police have been forgotten. Despite the best efforts of AFP Headquarters, the pace of events and the widespread deployment of civilian police officers in a fragmented state like East Timor meant that difficulties were sometimes experienced in keeping the families as informed as they wished as to where and how their loved ones were. This added to the trauma experienced by some of the families, particularly at the time of the evacuation from East Timor.

Comments on the United Nations

Many civilian police officers considered that the United Nations is too remote, too bureaucratic, and lacks vision and coordination. The lack of delegation of decision-making at the local level results in inertia. Even medical and disciplinary evacuations had to be referred to New York. There is too much reliance on decision-making in New York, where the relevant officers do not have detailed information on local circumstances. It appears that this restraint does not apply to military peacekeeping deployments, which for practical purposes remain under their own chain of command.

The United Nations needs to lift its game in this area, particularly in relation to the selection, training, and deployment of police in peace operations. What is often forgotten is that poor performance by police in peace operations can have a multiplier effect, with "good" officers having to shoulder an excessive workload in order to cover for the poor performance of some of their colleagues.

A frequently expressed criticism of the United Nations was that the best way to solve a problem (for example food or accommodation) was simply to "throw money at it", rather than address the longer-term issues. As far as the East Timor detachment was concerned, one problem was that they were allowed to buy virtually nothing locally, or in Darwin. If the required equipment was already in the UN store in Brindisi, Italy, it had to be ordered from there, even if this involved a delay of several weeks. In cases where essential equipment was required, such as generators, this delay had a very adverse effect on the members waiting for the equipment. Without electricity, fresh food could not be stored, and radios could not be used. It would be better if the United Nations could locate an Asian warehouse in Darwin, or somewhere more convenient than Italy. Also, in the absence of any morgue facilities in Dili, if the United Nations had allowed refrigerator trucks to be brought to East Timor on the ship HMAS *Jervis Bay*, deteriorating bodies awaiting forensic examination could have been kept refrigerated.

There was a marked disparity in living standards between many of the UN officials and the local people in the Dili area. Many UN and other staff (but not the civilian police officers) lived in a floating hotel in Dili harbour which was off-limits to the East Timorese, whereas many poor, hungry, and traumatized locals lived rough in Dili. This did nothing to endear the United Nations to the local people. Simple solutions, such as bringing up a large number of caravans from Darwin, could have alleviated this disparity somewhat.

It is now UN policy that all civilian police detachments will be multinational. No national detachments with designated sectors will be employed in future. Apparently this is an attempt to balance the quality of the available civilian police officers. Yet the United Nations apparently worked in East Timor on the understanding that where there were shortfalls in equipment, Australia would "chip in". This may have worked with the military, but it did not work with civilian police, who had very few resources.

Law and order

Public order is critical in a fragmented state. Civilian police can make a substantial contribution in operations under Chapter VI of the UN Charter by assisting in rebuilding the criminal justice system – the local police, local law, the courts, and the prison system. In East Timor, since 28 October 1999 the civilian police have had the sole responsibility for law enforcement, but they operate under Indonesian law until such time as a new legal system is authorized. The local citizens want law and order, and due process when they are offended against. The powers of entry and arrest must be clearly explained, courts re-established, and the confidence of the people in the criminal justice system obtained. These are tasks of great complexity.

After a honeymoon period in which the UNAMET civilian police detachment could do no wrong, having the prime responsibility for maintaining law and order the UNTAET civilian police detachment has come in for some criticism from some of the local people. The population is suffering from "crisis fatigue" and just wants life to return to normal. However, there is a disparity of living standards in East Timor between the UN staff, those East Timorese with jobs, and "really poor people". Against this background, many young men have become alienated from their families and villages, and are unemployed, homeless, hungry, and poor. Some of these people have formed street gangs, loosely connected with Falintil (Armed Forces for the National Liberation of East Timor), in order to survive and plunder.

Amongst these frustrated youths, and many other East Timorese, there is criticism of the slow pace of reconstruction and the re-establishment of services: expectations of a quick recovery have been dashed and disillusionment has set in. There is an angry reaction to the total destruction of East Timor, and suspect former members of the militias are targeted for retribution. There is a reaction against the culture of dependency – that is, frustration over the fact that they can do so little about the present situation. East Timor has missed a whole season of agriculture due to the security situation. There is a marked disparity between the living conditions of the people (including the East Timorese) in the towns and those in some of the rural areas where a UN presence and services have yet to been established. With very little to do, boredom has set in, and in such circumstances young men get into mischief.

Whilst not being responsible for this situation, the UNTAET civilian police detachment is seen by some as "an organ of repression" similar to PolRI in the previous regime. It is understandable that this feeling has had a demoralizing impact on some members of the civilian police.

Civilian police relations with the military

Overall, relations between the civilian police and the military, at least at the individual level, were good. The military were regarded as very professional and focused, but there were still problems, some of which are mentioned below.

In the initial stages of any peacekeeping operation, the military have the main carriage of the task, with responsibility being gradually handed over to the civil authority. In Cyprus, the role of civilian police is to keep the peace between the Greek and Turkish civilian communities, whereas the military role is to deal with opposing military forces and support civilian police should civil disturbances deteriorate into violence.[39] Although the components of a peacekeeping mission are supposed to be complementary, they are often placed within a hierarchy in which it is common for the military to take the lead role. The military tend to take this supremacy for granted, and therefore find it extremely difficult to relinquish control and accept civilian police primacy. Better understanding of the cultural differences between the police and the military, together with some standardization of equipment and procedures (such as communications), would reduce these difficulties. In comparison with the military, the police are individually empowered.

Military units are invariably far larger numerically than police units, with only the leadership of the military having the authority to decide on independence of action. On the other hand, with civilian police it is common for teams to be very small, to have junior leadership, and for national detachments to be dispersed. Civilian police members tend to be attuned to local cultural sensitivities because their role places them close to the community. This is a characteristic that military observers also develop, but it may be less highly developed in the ordinary military hierarchy.

There may be scope for fruitful cooperation between civpol and the military in this area.

Communication style is often a cause of friction between civilian police and the military. Military communications tend to be delivered in an authoritative manner, with little debate or clarification. As most military organizations work in this way, this communications system works well, even in a multinational force. However, when the military use this style of communication with civilians, including the police, problems can arise. Police communications tend to be less authoritative, with more negotiation and a greater two-way flow of information. This style appears to frustrate the military, as it can appear to be too indecisive and long-winded. However, as police operate in a more independent environment, they have more experience at dealing with members of the community – both victims and offenders – often in traumatic circumstances. The police may have highly developed negotiation skills which can be put to good use in reducing tension or resolving delicate situations. This characteristic is rarely recognized by the military component, which tends to be more demanding and aggressive.

Both the military and civilian components would benefit from a clearer demarcation of responsibilities, and from developing the flexibility to request the other component's help where appropriate. Training on how the other party works and appreciation of diversity, including the strengths and weaknesses of each approach, should lead to better relationships and true cooperation. There also needs to be more communication on the politics behind the role of each component: such knowledge would help adaptation to understanding and supporting each other's mandate within the mission.

In East Timor the ability of the military liaison officers (MLOs) to bring order and structure to a chaotic situation was greatly appreciated. On the other hand, dogmatic adherence to the military way of doing things created some difficulties. The two different communication styles contributed to tensions, but police negotiation approaches helped defuse these tensions.

Civilian police were sometimes equated with the military police, who are generally regarded as being at the lower end of the military hierarchy. In some developing countries the military police are feared as the most brutal instrument of the regime. Another problem in working with the military police is that the military police are usually attached to subordinate units, so there is little coordination of their activities and the information they obtain sometimes takes a long time to reach civilian police. Civpol are particularly alert to the importance of the proper collection of forensic evidence relating to human rights violations. It would have been better if civpol had been given the authority, from the start of the INTERFET period, to conduct investigations into these alleged violations, and had been properly equipped to do so.

At least in the early days of INTERFET, many of the civilian police felt that they were not treated with the respect they deserved. This caused some resentment and friction, although these diminished over time. The military tend to be more rank conscious than the police, more command conscious, and they are sometimes reluctant to accept advice from a more junior police officer. They generally do not understand the concept of "the office of constable" and what this means in police decision-making.[40] Some military members inappropriately regard the police as "dressed-up civilians". Civilian police members should *never* be given military ranks: it would be far better to have no ranks than to confuse the police role with that of the military.

The military can experience difficulty in crowd control. Some soldiers have difficulty with the use of minimum force, and this tended to be demonstrated on television in the form of very aggressive actions by Australian soldiers, particularly in the early days of INTERFET. This was sometimes characterized as the military's attempt to adopt a strongly anti-Indonesian posture, which, while understandable in the circumstances, may have compromised their neutrality.

Civilian police contact with the United Nations in New York is through the Australian military adviser. Whilst not criticizing the performance of the military adviser, there was strong preference expressed for locating a police officer as an additional adviser in New York, so that the operational and cultural problems could be better understood by all concerned.

Relations with the Indonesian national police (PolRI)

Normally, civilian police officers would not move without an escort from PolRI or the TNI. Even in the evacuation phase, although there were rogue PolRI members, generally the PolRI officers tried to do "the right thing". Most PolRI members never felt at ease with the role they were required to perform and there was a fair bit of "manoeuvring" about the way they performed their duties. Overall, relations between the civilian police and PolRI were very good, and on many occasions PolRI officers went out of their way to help or look after the civilian police members. PolRI was quite a professional organization, but during the UNAMET period PolRI officers were sandwiched between the TNI/militia and the United Nations – a difficult place to be.

Relations with the Indonesian police mobile brigade (Brigade Mobil, or BRIMOB) were also good, and on at least one occasion BRIMOB intervened to save civilian police officers from militia violence. In Maubissa, civilian police and BRIMOB played volleyball regularly together and a good spirit prevailed. Unlike the TNI, PolRI were not well equipped and, in particular, lacked transport, which severely limited their ability to protect civilian police. There were a number of East Timorese police in PolRI, both regulars and auxiliaries. Most of these people were supporters of the independence movement but could not show it. Some spoke very freely to civpol when other PolRI officers were not present. After the ballot on 30 August, most of the East Timorese police were disarmed and it is feared that a number were subsequently killed.

Human rights issues

During the UNAMET period, civilian police had to work in an environment in which there were no forensic scientists and no morgues, so conditions were very primitive and this made the investigation of human rights cases very difficult. When bodies were discovered (in all, there were probably some 3,000–4,000 people slaughtered) civilian police tended to leave them where they were (unless they were unburied or in a well), take statements, secure the evidence, arrange for the protection of the gravesite, and await the arrival of forensic experts.

Militia activities

The militias were a constant potential threat to civilian police. Usually, most of the militia members were well known to the local people, and many locals had been forced to join. The actual number of violent militia activists was very small, but they were extremely active. It was widely believed that the various militias were very closely linked with the TNI, and operated with their support. An example of their destructiveness is the frequent attacks on UNAMET vehicles. UNAMET was equipped with some 280 vehicles, but between the evacuation and the arrival of INTERFET about half were "trashed" or stolen. Of the remaining vehicles, many were badly vandalized with windows or lights broken. As a result, night mobile patrols had to be undertaken using torches to light up the road ahead. Oecussi was a very dangerous place because of its isolation and proximity to the Indonesian border.

Most Indonesians, including PolRI members, were genuinely surprised with the outcome of the ballot. They had believed the Indonesian propaganda, which stated that the outcome would be a resounding vote for autonomy within the Indonesian Republic. For this reason, in the immediate aftermath of announcing the results of the ballot the main targets for the militias were the locally engaged electoral officers, a number of whom were murdered. In most locations, it appeared that PolRI/BRIMOB and civilian police were able to work together to protect the locally engaged staff and the ballot boxes.

In one post, Maubissa, relations between the local militia (Mahidi) and the Council for the National Resistance of Timor (CNRT), the political wing of Falintil, were quite cordial prior to the ballot, thanks largely to excellent negotiations conducted by a Malaysian civilian police officer. The worst incident around the time of the ballot was the massacre of people in the church at Suai.[41] The UNAMET electoral officers and civilian police had encouraged the people to stay in the church for protection at the time of the vote, but many of these people were massacred when the civilian police were evacuated. The militia attempted to prevent the UNAMET evacuation from some areas, and a great deal of equipment and personal papers were left behind in the urgency of getting out safely.

Evacuation from the UN compound in Dili

Clearly, the whole scenario surrounding the evacuation of the UN and locally engaged staff from the compound in Dili from 6 to 14 September 1999 was very traumatic. A large number of East Timorese locally engaged staff and others were injured climbing into the UN compound when the TNI/militia opened fire on them, and many people appear to have been killed when they tried to escape up the hill behind the compound. The situation was an exceedingly dangerous and wrenching one, and no one who was there will be unaffected by the situation.

When the evacuation was finally ordered, there was resistance on the part of some of the civpol members, who thought that they were breaking a promise given to the local people that the United Nations would not abandon them. There was criticism of this decision, but those who felt this way were probably unaware of the delicate negotiations which were being undertaken to ensure safe passage of the UN and locally engaged staff. There really was no practical alternative, but many people were angry with the decision at the time. Apart from the question of physical safety in the face of TNI/militia violence, there were serious health and hygiene problems with so many people crowded into the compound.

Reconstructing a fragmented state

The local people may not understand the subtleties of fraud and white-collar crime, or the philosophy behind modern policing, but they have had direct experience of rape, theft, arson, and murder. Where no other law exists (as was the case in Cambodia) there is a need for a simple UN legal package which proscribes these crimes in a way which the local people can understand and view with confidence. It would not be appropriate simply to transpose Australian law and policing practices to a fragmented state like East Timor. The reconstitution of the criminal justice system must take into account local cultures and experiences.

Australian Federal Police members and other civpol officers are currently conducting training for East Timorese people seeking to join the indigenous police force. Vetting is undertaken with respect to former PolRI members who apply to join the East Timor police, using records that are still available and community consultation.

Civilian police can contribute in a significant way to changing the political environment in a state like East Timor, moving it away from a military towards a civilian political system, as in most democracies. This is one reason why peacekeeping should *not* be seen solely as a military operation. To do so misses the whole point of developing a sustainable democracy in a fragmented state like Cambodia or East Timor. Being a neutral, non-threatening entity, civilian police can move freely between all the parties involved in the political conflict and assist in building confidence and trust.

Traumas suffered by civilian police officers

For the UNAMET detachment, there was a feeling of absolute helplessness and powerlessness in the face of violence from which neither the PolRI nor TNI could or would protect them. There was a feeling of great insecurity in very unusual and dangerous circumstances, with only a police force of unknown reliability for back-up. This situation was totally alien to the normal assurance of support, even in the most difficult and dangerous situations, as a police officer in Australia. Basically, there was no fallback position from the circumstances in which they found themselves. Some officers who were Viet Nam veterans relived some of their old traumas, made worse by the fact that they did not have the bravado and mutual support of being in a cohesive military unit to see them through the crisis.[42] They witnessed some dreadful atrocities in which they were powerless to intervene – totally contrary to all their previous police training and experience. They also experienced very unpleasant, long-drawn-out traumas, like the exhumation of many bodies in a gravesite or from down a well.

There were many health problems, compounded by extreme fatigue. Most officers worked very long hours and there was no "down time" to recover. In the initial phases boredom was also a problem. With no electricity, there were no reading lights, no radio, no television, and no refrigeration, so the officers tended to go to sleep with the sunset and return to work at dawn. It was very difficult to live in a community where so many of the population were also terrified and traumatized. As there was no defined beginning or end to the commitment (very much like the Viet Nam syndrome), some officers feel that their task has not been completed. This may result in some loss of objectivity, introversion, and some difficulty in re-establishing relationships within their families.

There was great loss of professional pride in having to be evacuated from the UN compound in Dili, particularly when the United Nations gave undertakings to the locally engaged staff that they would not be deserted. Some officers felt as if they were "traitors" and suffered from "survivor guilt". Some have become obsessed with Timor and will take a long time to get over the experience.

For the UNTAET detachment, there was a huge disparity between the working and living conditions for civilian police and the military. Not only did this materialize in terms of mutual support, equipment, communications, and transport, but the public relations image of the military dwarfed that of the civilian police. There was a very distinct "first 11 versus second 11" feeling amongst the civilian police members.

Some members of the UNTAET detachment were very upset with their loss of popularity and confidence with the local population, for the reasons given above – it made them question whether the commitment was really worth it.

Policing in context

Tables 11.2 and 11.3, developed by Hills,[43] help to identify some of the key functions and roles associated with civil policing in different socio-political contexts.

Table 11.2 The policing of fragmenting states: a spectrum of levels of function and role

Phase	Function	Role
Strong central government	• Enforcement and maintenance of civil order • Regime representation • Regulatory activities	• National public police performing conventional duties
Fragmentation	• Functions limited by absence of single civil order • Authority and power devolve to regions	• Formal police force replaced by informal localized policing provided by other suppliers (e.g. militia, mosques, security companies)
Collapse	• Formal police system either ceases to exist or its existing functions are shaped by military goals	• Localized policing provided by various (armed) groups

Table 11.3 Spectrum of levels of formal policing functions and roles in relation to the state

Phase	Police system (police organization)	Police system (policing activity)	Function	Role
Post-colonial	• National force derived from colonial models	• Localization • Rural/urban split • Recruitment ethnicized	• Law and order enforcement • Paramilitary support • Regime representation	• Regulatory (e.g. border and traffic control)
Fragile	• Visible coercive agent	• Rural/urban split • Recruitment ethnicized	• Order enforcement • Paramilitary support • Regime representation	• Inconsistent patterns of activity
Fragmenting	• Loss of central control and formal infrastructure	• Selfish • Survival activities only	• Repression	• Roles may be maintained by smaller units
Fragmented	• System fragmented	• Security privatized	• No formal functions	• Security maintained by a range of armed groups
Conflict	• State policing suspended	• Remaining activities suspended		
Collapsed	• Power vacuum			• Regulation and security provided by private suppliers (e.g. militias or vigilantes)
Reconstruction	• New civilian national force	• Bureaucratic practices (e.g. criminal records) • Training provided by overseas aid	• Law and order enforcement • Paramilitary operations • Regime representation	• Regulatory activities

Conclusions

With the strong possibility that there will be further requirements for Australia to respond with peacekeeping commitments in the Asia Pacific region, it is essential that the difference between military peacekeeping and police peace operations be clearly understood both at the UN and national levels. It is clear that at this stage it is not, with the result that police peace operations are often neglected in comparison with the military peacekeeping role. This applies particularly in relation to doctrine, UN administration, equipment, and personnel issues, including public recognition of the role civilian police members perform. The authors hope that discussion of the Brahimi Report will help overcome this neglect.

However, in rebuilding a fragmented state, the reconstitution of the rule of law and the criminal justice sector is probably the single most critical issue in re-establishing and sustaining the state. This will probably require a civilian police policing, training, advisory, or human rights investigative presence long after the military peacekeepers have been withdrawn. The effective integration of these efforts with UN and other international initiatives, aid projects, and the work of NGOs will determine, to a large extent, whether the progress made in reconstituting a fractured state will be sustainable, and whether that state will adopt a democratic system supported by a transparent and accountable criminal justice system, or whether it will rely on military and other coercive measures to maintain itself in power. It is in this area that civilian police have a truly vital role to perform.

Acknowledgement

A previous version of this chapter, with the same title, was published by the Australian Defence Studies Centre as Working Paper No. 64, April 2001.

Notes

1. For more extensive discussion of these themes, see Abdul Razak Baginda and Anthony Bergin (eds), *Asia-Pacific's Security Dilemma: Multilateral Relations Amidst Political, Social and Economic Changes*, London: ASEAN Academic Press, 1998; William T. Tow, Ramesh Thakur, and In-taek Hyun (eds), *Asia's Emerging Regional Order: Reconciling Traditional and Human Security*, Tokyo: United Nations University Press, 2000.
2. See Wendy Way (ed.), *Australia and the Indonesian Incorporation of Portuguese Timor 1974–1976*, Melbourne: Melbourne University Press, 2000; Desmond Ball and Hamish McDonald, *Death in Balibo, Lies in Canberra*, Sydney: Allen & Unwin, 2000; Damien

Kingsbury (ed.), *Guns and Ballot Boxes: East Timor's Vote for Independence*, Melbourne: Monash Asia Institute, 2000; William Maley, "Australia and the East Timor crisis: Some critical comments", *Australian Journal of International Affairs*, Vol. 54, No. 2, July 2000, pp. 151–161.

3. See Jarat Chopra, "The UN's kingdom of East Timor", *Survival*, Vol. 42, No. 3, Autumn 2000, pp. 27–39.

4. The population of West Papua is about 2.5 million, of whom approximately one million are "transmigrants" from the rest of the Indonesian archipelago, especially Java and Suluwesi. See Ben Bohane, "The next East Timor", *The Australian Magazine*, 19–20 February 2000, pp. 24–27.

5. UNAMET was the UN Assistance Mission in East Timor. UNAMET was established on 11 June 1999 and was terminated in East Timor on 25 October 1999.

6. *Report of the Panel on United Nations Peace Operations*, New York: UN General Assembly/Security Council, A/55/305-S/2000/809, 21 August 2000, paragraph 126.

7. For other comparative perspectives, see Duncan Chappell and John Evans, "The role, preparation and performance of civilian police in United Nations peacekeeping operations", *Criminal Law Forum*, Vol. 10, 1999, pp. 171–271; Chuck Call and Michael Barnett, "Looking for a few good cops: Peacekeeping, peacebuilding, and civpol", *International Peacekeeping*, Vol. 6, No. 4, Winter 1999, pp. 43–68.

8. See I. William Zartman (ed.), *Collapsed States: The Disintegration and Restoration of Legitimate Authority*, Boulder: Lynne Rienner, 1995. On sovereignty, see Robert H. Jackson, *Quasi-states: Sovereignty, International Relations and the Third World*, Cambridge: Cambridge University Press, 1990; Joseph A. Camilleri and Jim Falk, *The End of Sovereignty? The Politics of a Shrinking and Fragmenting World*, Aldershot: Edward Elgar, 1992; Daniel Philpott, "Sovereignty: An introduction and brief history", *Journal of International Affairs*, Vol. 48, No. 2, Winter 1995, pp. 353–368; Michael Barnett, "The new United Nations politics of peace: From juridical sovereignty to empirical sovereignty", *Global Governance*, Vol. 1, No. 1, Winter 1995, pp. 79–97; Michael Ross Fowler and Julie Marie Bunck, "What constitutes the sovereign state?", *Review of International Studies*, Vol. 22, No. 4, October 1996, pp. 381–404; Öyvind Österud, "The narrow gate: Entry to the club of sovereign states", *Review of International Studies*, Vol. 23, No. 2, April 1997, pp. 167–184; Samuel M. Makinda, "Sovereignty and global security", *Security Dialogue*, Vol. 29, No. 3, September 1998, pp. 281–292; Stephen D. Krasner, *Sovereignty: Organized Hypocrisy*, Princeton: Princeton University Press, 1999; Martin van Creveld, *The Rise and Decline of the State*, Cambridge: Cambridge University Press, 1999.

9. See Max Weber, *Economy and Society: An Outline of Interpretive Sociology*, Berkeley and Los Angeles: University of California Press, 1978, Vol. I, p. 56.

10. A. E. Hills, "The policing of fragmenting states", *Low Intensity Conflict and Law Enforcement*, Vol. 5, No. 3, Winter 1996, pp. 334–354 at pp. 334–335. For some historical background, see L. J. Hume, *Bentham and Bureaucracy*, Cambridge: Cambridge University Press, 1981, pp. 33–34.

11. Hills, *ibid.*, p. 339.

12. *Ibid.*

13. Thomas G. Weiss, *Military-Civilian Interactions: Intervening in Humanitarian Crises*, Lanham: Rowman & Littlefield, 1999.

14. Chapter VI of the UN Charter allows the Security Council to call on members to settle a dispute by peaceful means. Under this Chapter, peacekeepers can only be introduced into a member state's territory with the concurrence of that member (as was the case in East Timor). Chapter VII provides the Security Council with extensive powers to authorize the use of armed force against a member state for the purpose of maintaining international peace and security. Member states are compelled to comply with decisions

of the Security Council, and action can be taken in violation of their sovereignty if they do not. Such was the case following the 1991 invasion of Kuwait by Iraq.

15. Unfortunately, at the UN Secretariat in New York there is a division of responsibility for the control of UN-sanctioned military peacekeeping and police peace operations. Military peacekeeping is administered by the Department of Peacekeeping Operations (DPKO), whereas police peace operations are generally administered by the Department of Political Affairs (DPA), each headed by an Under-Secretary-General. It appears that there is a lack of coordination and sometimes conflict between these two departments that detracts from the efficiency and cohesion of the UN's efforts in fragmented states.

16. John McFarlane, "Enforcing laws: Is there a growing role for the military?", in *Australian Security in a New Era: Reform or Revolution?*, Canberra: Australian Defence Studies Centre, Special Report No. 5, 1998. The valuable contribution of Associate Professor Hugh Smith of the School of Politics, University College, University of New South Wales, Australian Defence Force Academy, in developing this table is gratefully acknowledged. This table relates primarily to "Western-style" policing: in many developing countries or countries in transition, the demarcation between the military and police roles is much less clearly defined.

17. Hills, note 10.

18. As at November 1999, the United Nations did not have the specific authority to investigate atrocities in *West* Timor, where a gravesite containing 26 bodies was discovered.

19. See Robert L. Caslen, Jr, "Sustaining democracy in Haiti: Challenges for the United States and international community", *Low Intensity Conflict and Law Enforcement*, Vol. 5, No. 2, Autumn 1996, pp. 149–164.

20. *Ibid.*, p. 153.

21. *Ibid.*, p. 154.

22. On the complexity of democratization processes, see Guillermo O'Donnell and Philippe C. Schmitter, *Transitions from Authoritarian Rule: Tentative Conclusions about Uncertain Democracies*, Baltimore: Johns Hopkins University Press, 1986; Giuseppe DiPalma, *To Craft Democracies: An Essay on Democratic Transitions*, Berkeley and Los Angeles: University of California Press, 1990; Samuel P. Huntington, *The Third Wave: Democratization in the Late Twentieth Century*, Norman: University of Oklahoma Press, 1991; Juan J. Linz and Alfred Stepan, *Problems of Democratic Transition and Consolidation: Southern Europe, South America, and Post-Communist Europe*, Baltimore: Johns Hopkins University Press, 1996; Gretchen Casper and Michelle M. Taylor, *Negotiating Democracy: Transitions from Authoritarian Rule*, Pittsburgh: University of Pittsburgh Press, 1996; Larry Diamond, *Developing Democracy: Toward Consolidation*, Baltimore: Johns Hopkins University Press, 1999; Jack Snyder, *From Voting to Violence: Democratization and Nationalist Conflict*, New York: W. W. Norton & Co., 2000.

23. See, for example, Sir Robert Mark, *In the Office of Constable*, London: Collins, 1978.

24. In Somalia, the military continued offensive operations against any armed entity. This policy made it more difficult for civilian police to achieve their objectives.

25. The information contained in this section of the chapter is based on voluntary, personal, and semi-structured interviews with 20 AFP officers in February and March 2000. In addition, one of the authors attended a collective debrief of members of the first detachment to East Timor. These officers – male and female – included commissioned officers, non-commissioned officers, and constables. The officers interviewed had served in one or more of the following overseas commitments: Cyprus, Thailand, Cambodia, Somalia, Mozambique, Haiti, Bougainville, and East Timor. Some of the AFP Headquarters staff responsible for their deployment, training, welfare, and administration were also interviewed.

26. For a detailed discussion of the 5 May 1999 agreements, see William Maley, "The UN and East Timor", *Pacifica Review*, Vol. 12, No. 1, February 2000, pp. 63–76 at pp. 70–72.

27. The UN Transitional Administration in East Timor (UNTAET) was established in response to UN Security Council Resolution 1272 of 25 October 1999.

28. For discussion of the lessons of some of these commitments, see Peter McAuley, "Civilian police and peacekeeping: Challenges in the 1990s", in Hugh Smith (ed.), *Peacekeeping: Challenges for the Future*, Canberra: Australian Defence Studies Centre, 1993, pp. 33–40; Joint Standing Committee on Foreign Affairs, Defence and Trade, *Australia's Participation in Peacekeeping*, Canberra: Australian Government Publishing Service, 1994, pp. 89–102.

29. David R. Calhoun (ed.) *Britannica Book of the Year 1999*, London: Encyclopaedia Britannica, 1999, p. 387.

30. In East Timor, prior to the act of self-determination the responsibility for security, law, and order rested firmly with the Indonesian national police, and the foreign civilian police were effectively in East Timor by invitation. After the popular ballot and the Indonesian withdrawal, the civilian police were allowed to be armed where the assessment of risk to their safety was high. Generally, however, the presence of armed police tends to escalate a potentially violent situation.

31. For an interesting account of the civilian police role in East Timor, refer to the AFP publication *Australian Federal Police in East Timor*, Canberra: AFP Media and Public Relations.

32. Senator the Hon. Amanda Vanstone, Minister for Justice and Customs, referring to the AFP UNAMET detachment, 1999.

33. Where good ideas are put up to the United Nations in relation to police peace operations they will generally be accepted, if only because the UN doctrine in this area is so poorly developed.

34. One of the authors (William Maley) visited Thmar Puok during the 1993 Cambodian election in the company of the UNTAC chief electoral officer, Reginald Austin. While the security situation in the wider area was far from satisfactory, it was striking that in Thmar Puok families of diverse political affiliations had queued to exercise their right to vote. This remarkable outcome certainly owed a great deal to the atmosphere created by the Australians' philosophy of policing.

35. This simple legal code was subsequently published by the United Nations and used in training other civpol detachments.

36. Senator the Hon. Amanda Vanstone, Minister for Justice and Customs, referring to civilian police operations in East Timor.

37. Civpol Commissioner Alan Mills was the last civilian police officer to leave Dili in the UNAMET evacuation.

38. The International Force in East Timor (INTERFET), under Australian command, was deployed in East Timor from 20 September 1999 to 23 February 2000.

39. On the UN Force in Cyprus (UNFICYP) mission, see David Morris, "Keeping but not making peace: The UN peacekeeping force in Cyprus", in Kevin Clements and Robin Ward (eds), *Building International Community: Cooperating for Peace Case Studies*, Sydney: Allen & Unwin, 1994, pp. 273–279.

40. The term "office of constable" goes back to the Norman invasion of the British Isles in 1066. In current terms, the "office of constable" requires an individual police officer not only to maintain fairly and impartially the "king's (or queen's) peace", but also to accept individual responsibility for the way in which he/she carries out that function.

41. As the local priests played a critical role in the ballot exercise, some of them became prime targets for the militias.

42. On the importance of such ties of solidarity, see M. W. Jackson, "All against all", *Journal of Political and Military Sociology*, Vol. 13, No. 1, 1985, pp. 125–132.

43. Hills, note 10, pp. 353–354.

Part IV

A new beginning? The road to Brahimi and beyond

12

Peacekeeping and the changing role of the United Nations: Four dilemmas

Margaret P. Karns and Karen A. Mingst

Ten years after the dramatic events of the Cold War's end, the turbulence in world politics has hardly subsided. The seismic changes associated with those events are compounded by the powerful processes of economic globalization, technological change, environmental degradation, and evolving norms of human rights and humanitarianism as well as the presence of new actors. Like the countries of the old Soviet bloc, the world is still very much in a transitional period, with the outlines of the emerging system still unclear.

As Secretary-General Kofi Annan noted in his 1999 address and annual report to the General Assembly:

State sovereignty, in its most basic sense, is being redefined by the forces of globalization and international cooperation. The State is now widely understood to be the servant of its people, and not vice versa ... [with] renewed consciousness of the right of every individual to control his or her own destiny. These parallel developments ... demand of us a willingness to think anew – about how the United Nations responds to the political, human rights and humanitarian crises affecting so much of the world; about the means employed by the international community in situations of need; and about our willingness to act in some areas of conflict, while limiting ourselves to humanitarian palliatives in many other crises whose daily toll of death and suffering ought to shame us into action.[1]

A key question for the new millennium is whether there will be the necessary political will and organizational effectiveness to respond to the types of conflicts likely to threaten international peace. Will complex internal conflicts and humanitarian disasters in Africa and elsewhere be ignored, for example, because of the UN's difficulties in such early post-Cold War conflicts as Somalia, Bosnia, and Rwanda? Or will media and public pressures to "do something" about massive violations of human rights, dislocation of local populations, ethnic cleansing, or genocide, lead to the authorization of more peacekeeping missions with vague mandates and inadequate resources to ensure reasonable chances of success?

Meeting these challenges will require strengthening preventive diplomacy as well as the UN's capacity to support increased numbers of peacekeeping operations performing complex tasks in collaboration with member states and NGOs. It will also require member states to reconcile the dilemmas of the post-Cold War world in making choices about where and how to utilize UN capabilities for peacekeeping, peacemaking, and peacebuilding. The United Nations recognizes the problem. The Secretary-General's decision to appoint an international expert panel on UN peace operations clearly emphasizes this recognition.

With sharply increased demand for UN peacekeeping in different forms and experiences of both success and failure, developments in the decade since the Cold War's end have foreshadowed four dilemmas that will face UN peacekeeping in the new millennium. The first dilemma is linked to changes in the types of conflicts that demand the organization's attention, specifically to the shift from interstate to more intrastate or internal conflicts, to Article 2(7) of the UN Charter, and to the norm of non-intervention in a state's internal affairs. Two questions arise from this dilemma. When and how is UN intervention justified? On what basis should choices be made as to where to direct scarce resources? The second dilemma has emerged from changing international expectations about the responsibilities of states and of the international community for halting gross and systematic violations of human rights with grave humanitarian consequences. How should the goals or objectives of humanitarian intervention be delimited? Should the UN's priority be peace or justice, if by serving justice through humanitarian aid it may jeopardize the peace objective? Thirdly, there has been a major change in the number and types of players involved in complex peacekeeping operations, raising issues of coordination and legitimacy. Regional and non-governmental organizations have distinct roles and identities, and varying organizational capacities. Subcontracting some interventions to ad hoc multilateral coalitions of states raises concerns about bias and selectivity. How can the United Nations enhance coordination in the absence of institutional mechanisms for involving multiple actors? How can legitimacy of the actions be assured when the legitimacy of the Security Council itself is increasingly questioned and other actors' impartiality may also be suspect?

The fourth dilemma concerns the need for leadership in the next phase of the post-Cold War era and the diffusion of both power and willingness of states, and especially the USA as sole superpower, to commit. What will be the role of the United Nations in forging and sustaining support for future peacekeeping operations? How can the United Nations reduce its dependence upon the USA, yet ensure the necessary leadership and resources to meet rising demand and expectations?

This chapter is organized around discussion of each of these dilemmas and the developments in the international system which are likely to sharpen them in the new millennium. It argues that the United Nations needs to strengthen its ability to learn from both successes and failures and that, along with member states and NGOs, it needs to focus its future peacekeeping efforts where they can be most effective in serving the purpose of peace, first and foremost. In this new millennium, the UN's new role will be more constrained; the challenge will be to make it both more effective and legitimate.

The changing nature of conflict and the dilemma of when to intervene

In the first decade of the post-Cold War era, the United Nations has been confronted with a significant change in the types of conflicts that demand the organization's attention. The twentieth century has succeeded in delegitimizing interstate wars of territorial conquest, as confirmed by the Gulf War, Indonesia's policy reversal on East Timor, and the condemnation of the Ethiopian-Eritrean war. Interstate wars have become more the exception than the rule. Post-Cold War conflicts have been predominantly intrastate conflict or civil war, ethnic conflict, and terrorism. In several situations, such as Somalia, Liberia, Haiti, Sierra Leone, and Congo/Zaire, conflicts have entailed civil chaos resulting from the post-Cold War phenomenon of failed states. According to Zartman, this is:

... a deeper phenomenon than mere rebellion, coup, or riot. It refers to a situation where the structure, authority (legitimate power), law, and political order have fallen apart and must be reconstituted in some form, old or new ... It is not necessarily anarchy. Nor is it simply a byproduct of the rise of ethnic nationalism: it is the collapse of old orders, notably the state.[2]

As one scholar notes: "State failure is a complex, multifaceted phenomenon that defies conventional methods of peacekeeping, peacemaking, and peace-building, and challenges the standard conceptual and operational frameworks within which international relations theorists and practitioners function."[3] Because no two situations are alike, it can be difficult to determine "when state failure has occurred and when intervention is justified".[4] The key question for the international community is what are the responsibilities of states, the United Nations (or regional IGOs), and other actors when states fail?

Furthermore, an increasing number of actors add to the complexity of post-Cold War conflicts. In many intrastate and ethnic conflicts there is not just a single rebel group fighting against government forces. Within collapsing states there are rival warlords, thugs, factional leaders, paramilitary forces, and even criminal groups, none of whom is bound by the UN Charter, let alone international humanitarian laws. They do not care about either, nor do they have any reason to respect them. The principle of reciprocity that has historically given states an incentive to cooperate with each other and to respect international norms and rules is inoperative in most such situations. So is the principle of state sovereignty that has defined whose consent was traditionally sought before undertaking a peacekeeping operation. Post-Cold War conflicts have thus blurred what lines existed between national and international, military and civilian, organized crime and legitimate political groups, and civil war and interstate war.[5] The key problem in many situations is controlling anarchic violence within countries, not the use of organized military force between them.

The bases of future UN interventions

Changes in the nature of conflicts clearly create problems with the established bases for intervention in international law and political theory. In particular, the likelihood that the new millennium will see more intrastate and ethnic conflicts, terrorism, and failed states poses a challenge to the Charter provision that the United Nations shall not interfere in the domestic affairs of member states.

The first issue to be resolved in considering the bases of future UN interventions is the question of their legal basis. While the United Nations was established to deal with interstate conflict, it has in fact intervened in a substantial number of internal conflicts since 1960. Studies of international and civil wars show that of 29 civil wars that ended between 1960 and 1998, the United Nations intervened in 12. Of 35 civil wars under way in 1999, the United Nations had peacekeeping operations in 10.[6] These data have led one analyst to conclude, "[h]istorically, the UN has attempted to bring about alternative, more peaceful endings to more civil conflicts than any other multilateral organization or state".[7] The Congo operation of the 1960s might now be viewed as the precursor of post-Cold War peacekeeping challenges, although Zartman argues that the nature of that earlier rescue of the Congo provided "the elements in its gradual collapse again two or three decades later".[8] In the last decade, the United Nations has been an agent in the successful transitions from civil wars to peace in Central America (Nicaragua and El Salvador), southern Africa (Namibia and Mozambique), and Cambodia. These operations are a source of lessons for some of the future conflict situations the United Nations may face as well as for techniques for successful second-generation peacekeeping.

Consent of parties to UN peacekeeping has been a cardinal rule of traditional first-generation peacekeeping. Yet post-Cold War crises have shown the difficulties of reconciling this rule with demands for action, the realities of civil violence, state collapse, multiple actors, genocide, and other humanitarian disasters. The UN's inaction in the early months of the Somali famine because of the absence of any Somali governmental consent was later deemed a mistake. In Somalia and elsewhere in the post-Cold War era, the UN's responses have blurred the line between enforcement and peacekeeping. The international community is far more ready to use Chapter VII enforcement today than it was prior to the Cold War's end. Among the UN's lessons of the last decade, however, must be a more careful distinction between the use of specially constituted military forces to end violence or to provide a credible deterrent to attacks on refugees, food convoys etc., and the use of peacekeeping forces to maintain cease-fires, monitor disengagement, arms control, or human rights, distribute food and medicine, supervise elections, and perform other peace-building tasks. Enforcement actions do not expect parties' consent; while peacekeepers can only be effective when consent is present.

Even without changing the Charter, the reality, then, is that the United Nations is now operating under a *de facto* norm of intervention in civil conflicts, using limited force to stop anarchy and humanitarian disaster. Civil violence in many situations has come to be seen as an international security problem. The coupling of such violence with unprecedented humanitarian disasters in many situations has provoked media attention, major power interest, and regional states' support for the United Nations to act in some, but not all, civil conflicts and state failures, even without a clear legal basis for such actions. To date, as the American historian Marc Trachtenberg has noted, "no firm legal principle separating 'legitimate' from 'illegitimate' intervention has yet emerged in the post-Cold War period".[9]

The second issue to be resolved in determining the bases of future UN interventions relates to the realities of finite resources and the necessity for making choices in where, when, and how the organization should intervene in the future. Can the United Nations reasonably be expected to manage large, complex peacekeeping operations in East Timor simultaneously with ones in Kosovo, Sierra Leone, and Central Africa? Can the organization serve both peace and justice purposes in dealing with the variety of post-Cold War conflicts, or should members be prepared to choose peace over justice as some would suggest?[10] What are the international community's responsibilities when states fail? How should choices be made as to where to direct scarce resources?

Boutros Boutros-Ghali chided the Security Council members in 1993 for paying more attention to the former Yugoslavia than to Somalia. Why was quick action forthcoming in summer 1999 as East Timor slipped into chaos when civil war in the Sudan has been ignored for years and the Great Lakes region of Africa is widely described as experiencing the most serious conflict of the post-Cold War period? Africa constitutes the region of particular concern because of its marginalization in the post-Cold War era and the extent of state collapse. It leads the world in refugee populations, especially those internally displaced by armed conflicts, communal violence, and gross violations of human rights. As Nigeria's representative to the United Nations noted in a 1999 speech before the Security Council: "For Kosovo, the international community spent some $1.50 a day per refugee, while African refugees in Rwanda and Sierra Leone received an equivalent of 11 cents ... It was morally repugnant that the West was prepared to spend $40bn to fight a war in the Balkans, and less than 1 per cent of that to save the lives of tens of millions in Africa." To retain their legitimacy, he argued, the United Nations and the Security Council need "to match words with deeds and apply a single standard when responding to conflicts".[11]

Because the new millennium will see more intrastate and ethnic conflict and terrorist activities as well as state collapse, learning from successes and failures has become more important than ever as a basis for future choices. The DPKO's Lessons Learned Unit was a step in the right direction, but has now been disbanded and its functions absorbed by others. Nevertheless, lessons learned from single missions provide few reliable outcomes. This kind of systematic study can seldom be accomplished satisfactorily from within an organization, especially one that is severely understaffed.

A great deal of attention has been given to the "disaster" cases of Somalia, Rwanda, Bosnia, and Angola. Yet as Howard notes, the United Nations "has experienced quite a lot of success".[12] Determining why the United Nations failed in some instances but succeeded in others is crucial to addressing policy-makers' and practitioners' concerns about when and how the United Nations can most successfully intervene in the future, especially in civil conflict situations. For example, recent findings in the literature on civil war termination indicate that situational factors in the wars themselves are less important to the durability of peace than the content of peace agreements and outside assistance in constructing and maintaining those agreements.[13] At what point in time lessons are drawn from UN experience can also be significant. What is thought a success at one moment could well be considered less positively several years later, as is the case with developments in Cambodia since UNTAC's conclusion (see John Sanderson's chapter in this volume). Such policy analyses may be routine in management textbooks and even for some national governments; they are not yet so for the United Nations.

A final aspect of making choices in directing scarce resources concerns the question of member states' contributions to peacekeeping. If a sharper distinction is drawn in the future between enforcement actions and peacekeeping, the United Nations should be able to return to the practice common in first-generation operations of utilizing contingents and personnel predominantly from small and middle powers and from countries without direct interests in conflict situations. This will help restore the perceived legitimacy and impartiality of peacekeeping itself. This chapter considers the issue of resources for enforcement when discussing the growing trend of subcontracting interventions to multinational coalitions of states. Suffice it to note here, however, that the United Nations has shown in Bosnia, Somalia, and Rwanda that it is not well suited to enforcement actions. Because states have rarely made available the necessary resources for enforcement to the United Nations itself, conflicts requiring more forceful actions are clearly best delegated to "coalitions of the willing".

The third issue to be considered in determining the bases of future UN interventions is the strength of political support. Although the post-Cold War era began with unprecedented unity among the five permanent members of the Security Council, future decisions over UN intervention are likely to be much more divisive. The Kosovo situation demonstrated the sharper P5 divisions over intervention issues. China, Russia, and other states, particularly developing countries, are jealous of their sovereignty and wary of precedents for international interventions, even under UN auspices, that may look like American or Western neo-imperialism. The debates over East Timor illustrate this problem. The problem of P5 division, however, might only be solved by a return to a narrow interpretation of when the United Nations can or should intervene – only in interstate wars. The Cold War's experience, let alone a realist interpretation of international relations, should quickly dispel any premature optimism on that score. Nonetheless, UN or Security Council support for future interventions in post-Cold War conflicts is essential; should the Security Council be blocked from action by one or more vetoes, the precedent of a "uniting for peace resolution" should be considered in preference to actions such as that by NATO against Serbia in 1999. This chapter will address the question of the Security Council's own legitimacy shortly, but note here that the problem of division among permanent members of the Council would only be magnified were their number enlarged and veto power granted to other states in the future as part of an effort to recognize power realities in the new millennium.

Reasonable people will differ in debates over when and where the United Nations should intervene in the future. The international community is not likely to revise the Charter or concur on a fundamental change in the traditional international norm of non-intervention any time soon. The authors suggest some feasible ways of addressing the dilemma of choice posed by the changing nature of conflicts demanding the UN's attention and intervention. That dilemma is compounded by changing expectations about the international community and the UN's roles in ensuring the welfare and safety of the world's peoples based on evolving human rights and humanitarian norms. Disputes over the implications of these norms have sharpened with post-Cold War crises demanding action.

Changing expectations affecting UN peacekeeping: The dilemma of disputed norms

The post-Cold War era has been marked by significant changes in expectations about what responsibilities should be assumed by the international community for individual and group welfare. Both the content of these expectations and the application of them have changed with the spread of technology and widespread acceptance of human rights and humanitarian norms.[14] These changing expectations have been a major factor in the increased demands for UN peacekeeping in the 1990s, particularly in situations involving ethnic conflict, state failure, and humanitarian disaster.

What has been distinctive about the post-Cold War conflicts of all types is the number and scope of humanitarian disasters they have produced: displaced populations, starvation, deliberate targeting of civilians, ethnic cleansing, and genocide. UNHCR, along with a plethora of humanitarian NGOs, has been challenged as never before to cope with human tragedy on a massive scale. A recent report by the US National Intelligence Council estimates that 35 million people – a number nearly equal to the population of Argentina – have faced humanitarian crises in the last decade of the twentieth century. "Civilians have increasingly become the key targets for combatants in many conflicts", the report notes. "War has become as much about displacing people as moving borders."[15] Kofi

Annan put the problem even more bluntly in a statement to the Security Council in September 1999, saying: "We are at the end of a century that has seen the creation and refinement of much of the corpus of international law ... Yet civilians have rarely been so vulnerable."[16]

Through the successful achievement of the International Bill of Rights and various human rights covenants, as well as the increased promotion and monitoring of human rights by the UN system and the networks of human rights NGOs, the following have emerged as fundamental expectations of people worldwide in this post-Cold War era.

- Individuals have a right to be protected from undue suffering.
- Individuals have a right to live in a relatively stable political system.
- Individuals have a right to live in a representative democracy.
- Individuals have a right to development and a clean environment.

These changing expectations have placed more demands on the United Nations and other international actors to act to curb abuses and meet positive expectations. Coupled with the effects of media attention and globalization in dramatizing disasters – the so-called "CNN effect" – they have promoted the norm of humanitarian intervention. They also lead to a conflict between the norms of state responsibility for alleviating human suffering and those of state sovereignty, as legitimizing humanitarian intervention constitutes a fundamental change in international law.

Thinking about the meaning of state sovereignty is also evolving in ways that affect these expectations. UN Secretary-General Kofi Annan has noted that sovereignty is now "a matter of responsibility, not just power", with a rapid shift occurring from indifference to its misuse to a willingness to uphold basic humanitarian and human values.[17] His predecessor, Boutros Boutros-Ghali, in *An Agenda for Peace* wrote: "The time of absolute sovereignty ... has passed; its theory was never matched by reality."[18] Legitimizing humanitarian intervention, then, constitutes a fundamental change in international law. It also requires returning to the question of what moral purposes call states to use force, particularly in the difficult case of using force because of the domestic character of another state's conduct and policy.[19] It has revived discussions of just war doctrine.

These expectations pose their own problems of legitimacy, priority, scope, and scarce resources. Can the United Nations successfully intervene in situations of ethnic conflict, genocide, civil war, and state collapse in such a way that it truly does serve the humanitarian needs in the short term and improve the human rights of peoples in the long term? Certainly, it has proved capable of doing just this in several post-Cold War situations. It also failed to do so in the so-called "safe areas" of Bosnia and in the Rwandan genocide. Kofi Annan has had the courage to call for an independent inquiry of the Rwandan situation in particular, and to note in December 1999 when he accepted the report of the independent inquiry: "the whole international community ... failed to honour that obligation [to prevent genocide] ... All of us must bitterly regret that we did not do more to prevent it ... On behalf of the United Nations, I acknowledge this failure and express my deep remorse."[20]

Should the United Nations intervene to serve justice purposes? Are states willing to put peacekeepers' lives at risk to stop inhumane violence when there is not a direct threat to international peace? Is it the UN's responsibility to go beyond stopping massacres, famine, displacement of peoples, restoring a minimum of security and stability to rehabilitation, and peace-building?[21] And, in future situations such as Kosovo where P5 division blocks Security Council action, do gross and systematic violations of human rights justify international interventions without prior UN or Security Council approval? Do human rights and humanitarian norms, in short, now take precedence over not only national sovereignty but also UN authority?

The American Cold War historian John Lewis Gaddis has noted that "We are at one of those rare points of leverage in history when familiar constraints have dropped away; what we do now could establish the framework within which events will play themselves out for decades to come."[22]

If changing norms have now created an expectation that the international community will respond to future humanitarian disasters, then there is all the more need for preventive actions where such crises can be anticipated. As much as preventive diplomacy is a key part of the UN's repertoire for dealing with threats to international peace and security, intelligence data-gathering and analysis on situations that might pose future humanitarian disasters could lead to timely, well-planned interventions that avert them. The United Nations is likely always to face the problem of responding to crises, yet that truism should not be a substitute for efforts to act before they fully develop.

Multiple players and the dilemmas of coordination and legitimacy

The challenges posed by different types of conflicts, changing normative expectations, and uncertain bases of intervention must be considered in the context of a more complex, diverse cast of players on the international stage. The increased involvement of these various players constitutes a trend that will continue in the new millennium and pose dilemmas of both coordination and legitimacy.

The cast of players

By the late 1980s, regional organizations acquired new momentum and responsibilities, participating increasingly in actions both independent of and in cooperation with the United Nations as the normative expectations of the international community expanded and superpower interventions in regional conflicts ended. The Organization for Security and Cooperation in Europe (OSCE), with its High Commissioner on National Minorities and its Conflict Prevention Centre, the Organization of American States (OAS) with its work promoting democracy and human rights, and the Economic Community of West African States (ECOWAS) are prominent examples. Beginning in the late 1980s, several regional organizations teamed up with the United Nations in joint peacekeeping: for example, in Nicaragua, the United Nations joined with the OAS in monitoring elections, and in Western Sahara, the United Nations and the OAU cooperated on a peace plan that has not yet been implemented.

During the 1990s the Western European Union (WEU) was revived as a defence component of the European Union and the European pillar of NATO. Acting under the 1992 Petersberg Declaration, WEU ministers have proposed preventive missions that include peacekeeping and peace enforcement operations, as well as refugee and humanitarian assistance. WEU-sponsored police participated in the Bosnian operation. Both WEU and NATO members sent naval forces to monitor Yugoslavia's compliance with economic sanctions authorized by the Security Council. In addition, both the OAS and ECOWAS expanded their respective activities. Members of the OAS agreed to act when democratic norms were violated, even if it meant intervention in another state's internal affairs, and ECOWAS undertook new responsibilities for preventing and settling regional conflicts.

Most importantly, NATO has transformed itself from a Cold War defensive alliance to a new entity of like-minded democratic states seeking both stability in the region and renewed relevance in the post-Cold War era. That transformation began during the Bosnian conflict with involvement in enforcing sanctions and conducting limited air strikes under UN authorization in support of UNPROFOR. Following the Dayton Peace Accord of November 1995, the UN's peacekeeping role in Bosnia was then replaced by the NATO-sponsored Implementation Force (IFOR), comprising units from almost 20 non-NATO countries, including Russia. IFOR represented NATO's first effort do what UN peacekeepers have done in the past: separate forces, supervise withdrawals, interpose itself between the parties, and provide a safe environment in which peace may take root. NATO's second major undertaking – enforcement action against Yugoslavia/Serbia in Kosovo from March to June 1999 – was undertaken without clear Security Council authorization. Participation by NATO in such traditionally "out-of-area" activities has been a dramatic step. NATO, both with and without UN authorization, has become a major actor in European peace and security generally, and in enforcement more specifically.[23]

The revival of regional activity in conflict prevention, peacekeeping, peace-building, and peace enforcement activities has both positive and negative repercussions. On the positive ledger, the expansion of activity by regional organizations means that those states and/or organizations closest to a conflict situation can respond. Those in geographic proximity may be better acquainted with the issues and the terrain. They could potentially mobilize faster for acute emergencies. They may also have more direct interests at stake.[24] These are the arguments put forth by the USA and France in support of an African crisis response team composed of contingents from African countries. Such regional arrangements can provide alternatives to always employing the United Nations.

On the negative side, however, regional organizations may be dominated by a regional hegemon which is capable of capturing organizational interests and resources, leading to a situation where there is little effective counterweight to the hegemon's exercise of power. In addition, regional organizations with the exception of NATO have typically suffered from a lack of both financial resources and organizational capacity. Unless members provide new financial resources and enhanced organizational capability, regional organizations may not be able to carry out the complex challenges of the new millennium.

To meet the increasing demands by the international community for enforcement as well as peacekeeping in dealing with the variety of post-Cold War conflicts, ad hoc multilateral coalitions of states and international organizations (including the United Nations) have filled key diplomatic gaps. Such an approach will continue to be useful under certain conditions: when available international organizations are unacceptable as mediators or conciliators; when no one country has a dominant interest or influence over the parties; when several countries, each important to the disputing parties, share a similar attitude about how the conflict might be resolved; or when a team of individuals are able to sustain an effective coordination effort over lengthy negotiating periods.

In the 1990s, NGOs have joined in such ad hoc multilateral initiatives. As international expectations about peacekeeping have expanded to include support for individuals to be protected from suffering, to enjoy a stable political system, to participate in democratic institutions, and to enjoy a right to development, non-governmental actors and groups from civil society have played key roles, both independently and in collaboration with the United Nations – a trend which the authors believe will continue. Of the thousands of NGOs active in the world today, it is estimated that some 400–500 international NGOs are involved in humanitarian activities, spending US$9–10bn annually.[25]

In peacekeeping operations, particularly complex ones, there has been increased delegation of responsibilities from states and IGOs to NGOs. They deliver humanitarian aid, including medicine, food, and housing, to victims of famine and war. They mobilize mass publics. They are critical to monitoring the implementation of human rights norms and warning of violations. They are active in all the world's troublespots, in part because of some of their comparative strengths – "flexibility, speed of reaction, comparative lack of bureaucracy, operational and implementation capacity, commitment and dedication of the usually young staff".[26] Yet ensuring the coordination of their activities with those of UN agencies responsible for humanitarian relief and other aspects of complex peacekeeping operations has proven to be a difficult task.

Of greater importance for UN peacekeeping and enforcement, however, has been the emergence in the 1990s of ad hoc coalitions of states undertaking what amounts to subcontracted roles: the USA in Somalia and Haiti, France in Rwanda, and Australia in East Timor. This pattern has coincided with the increased involvement of major powers generally in providing military forces for peacekeeping, and with the development of third-generation peacekeeping itself. Participation by major powers entails risks either because they have a history of past involvement (for example, the USA in Haiti and France in Rwanda) or because the national interests of the major powers and international interests may not coincide.[27] The practice of "subcontracting" raises a number of difficult issues. In particular, the leading power is unlikely to place its troops under UN command, which compromises the UN's control over the force's actions.

There are costs and benefits to the trend of having more parties involved in international interventions. On the benefits ledger, if the Security Council is more able to delegate – subcontract – some of the demand for peacekeeping and enforcement operations to specific states and other organizations, more operations can be conducted, assuming the continued willingness of states to lead such operations and others to accept such subcontracting. Those states and organizations closest to the geographic area can be called upon to participate, and may more willingly participate because of particular interests of geography or history. More operations, if successfully conducted in the eyes of a majority of the international community, may lead to lessened charges of selectivity and racism, assuming that African conflicts in particular receive a reasonable share of attention. Burden-sharing through subcontracting also lessens the added burden on the UN's already strained financial resources, and can result in the more rapid interjection of forces into a conflict situation.

The liabilities of burden-sharing and ad hocism are real. Motivations to participate vary widely among states and many are not in the interests of the international community, leading to potential charges of racism and selectivity. Why intervene in Kosovo and not in Liberia? Why East Timor and not Central Africa? For the USA, unwillingness to take on additional financial commitments, reluctance to commit its own military personnel in potentially dangerous undertakings, and increased scepticism about UN capabilities have led it to welcome alternatives to UN operations, most notably in situations requiring the use of military force. For the UK and Russia, participation in ad hoc operations may be to affirm great power status, and, for Russia, to ensure its interests are protected (especially in its so-called "near abroad"). French initiatives likewise affirm its great power status, but may also be intended to counter the role of the USA or, as in the case of Operation Turquoise in Rwanda, to act on behalf of a long-time client. States other than the P5 also have particular interests which are used to justify burden-sharing. For Nigeria, it may have been to exercise regional hegemonic leadership, a motivation similar to Russia's willingness to join a CIS peacekeeping force alongside UNOMIG in Georgia. Australia volunteered to lead INTERFET, the multilateral force in East Timor, because of its strong national interest in regional stability and desire to see East Timor achieve a peaceful transition to independence following the UN-monitored vote in August 1999. Thus, the practice of burden-sharing on the part of the UN Security Council enables a few states to satisfy national interests while serving the international community's interest in restoring peace to a region in conflict.

The United Nations cannot "do it alone", but dilemmas of coordination and legitimacy need to be resolved. To make this burden-sharing both effective and legitimate, "the UN needs to develop safeguards and oversight mechanisms to monitor these measures. It cannot simply leave member states and regional organizations to their own devices and expect them to do its bidding."[28]

Coordinating the action

With new players, problems of coordination have multiplied. At times, different players have intervened at different stages of an operation, each playing particular roles in turn. In East Timor, the UN-authorized multinational coalition, INTERFET, led by Australia, was replaced by a UN peacekeeping force. UN peacekeepers followed NATO forces into Kosovo, once the bombing was halted and agreement secured. These are sequencing approaches to the problem of coordination.

More often, various organizations are working side by side, making a clear division of labour the coordination issue. For example, in the aftermath of NATO intervention in Kosovo, the UN Interim Administration Mission in Kosovo (UNMIK) worked to prevent the chaos that pervaded the relief effort in Albania with 200 disparate groups, yet coordination was not all effective. UNHCR reportedly was ill-prepared to handle the flood of refugees back into Kosovo. The speed and size of the exodus required services only the military could provide, such as air and port facilities, logistics, transport of refugees, camp construction, and road repair.

The more complex the conflict itself and the requirements for securing, maintaining, and building conditions of stability and peace, the more difficult the dilemmas of coordination among the variety of new players. Individual international organizations, including the United Nations, will have insufficient resources and capacity, as well as prestige, to "go it alone". Interorganizational cooperation and coordination will be increasingly necessary, but more difficult due to competition for scarce resources, divergence in mandates and constituencies, and the complexity of tasks to be performed. This problem will be particularly acute for conflicts in Africa and other areas outside the greater European/Middle Eastern areas.

When NGOs are added to the interorganizational mix, the coordination problems become all the more difficult. NGOs may possess the needed information, but there is no systematic way to get that information conveyed to the proper authorities. NGOs often themselves operate under severe economic restraints and are frequently competing for the same scarce donor dollars, making them less of an independent resource. Furthermore, with the proliferation of NGOs themselves there has been an increasing problem in high-profile conflicts and humanitarian disasters of "crowded spaces". "Being there" and being seen as directly dealing with refugees have become almost necessities for many actors, in large part to demonstrate their relevance to their supporters. The result is a further deepening of the coordination dilemma. The problem is clear; the challenge daunting:

The mix of actors involved in these conflicts creates a situation where responsibility for delivering security is at best blurred, but too often delegated to others – by states to organizations, by organizations to NGOs, by NGOs to their volunteers, and by the volunteers to the victims à la self-help. The challenge is to develop a series of interlocking legal and logistical safeguards – shored up by the political will of countries to enforce them, and operationalized through a coherent UN system that functions in tandem with regional, national, and local institutions.[29]

Coordination problems among the United Nations and its specialized agencies, the regional organizations, ad hoc coalitions, and NGOs are likely to grow in the new millennium given the types of conflict situations predicted and the changing expectations regarding international intervention. There will need to be agreements on division of labour. The United Nations has the comparative advantage of being the only global organization, with the most extensive experience with complex peacekeeping operations and coordination. Yet post-Cold War experience with third-generation peacekeeping has demonstrated that the United Nations does not have a comparative advantage in using military force itself. Its most effective role, especially in civil wars, comes once a cease-fire is in place and in the form of traditional peacekeeping, combined if appropriate with peacemaking and peace-building activities.[30] Likewise, an ineffective and inefficient United Nations, caused in part by the failure to address its own long-standing coordination problems, has jeopardized the legitimacy of the organization. Despite changes in practices (Secretariat directorates identifying lead agencies), the dilemma of coordinating a larger set of players in complex and often confusing conflict situations remains real. Similarly, the involvement of other players raises a set of thorny legitimacy issues.

Challenges of legitimacy

As vexing as the coordination problem is, the more difficult problem may well be the need to ensure legitimacy of the actions undertaken by the myriad groups. Legitimacy is being challenged at several different levels and in various ways. First is the questionable legitimacy of a regional organization or ad hoc coalition acting without UN or Security Council authorization, as NATO did in Kosovo. While several states have defended the action on the basis of a pressing and urgent humanitarian emergency and the emerging norm of humanitarian intervention, others are clearly dissatisfied with resort to ad hoc procedures that undermine recognized legal practices.

Second, as discussed earlier, is the challenge of legitimacy posed by regional organizations, ad hoc coalitions, or NGOs that are not viewed as impartial by parties in a conflict and outsiders. Regional organizations may be dominated by a regional hegemon; ad hoc coalitions almost by definition are led at least by a state with strong national interests at stake in a conflict situation. UN authorization helps but does not entirely dispel the problem. NGOs, despite assertions that their legitimacy is derived from their neutrality, pose other dilemmas. What are NGOs? Are they nothing more than another, albeit a different, élite? Are they actually neutral and impartial actors? Can they really be apolitical? How are

NGOs held accountable to the constituencies they serve – the victims? Some anecdotal evidence suggests that NGOs in Bosnia are not only failing to represent local constituencies, but are also pressing their own position on the population rather than responding to local needs.[31] Clearly, just as there are increased demands for accountability and transparency in UN operations, there are also needs for accountability and transparency of NGOs, particularly to victims, an unrepresented group, and other local constituencies, as well as to the international community. Thus, multiple players complicate the problem of establishing the legitimacy and impartiality of UN-led interventions.

To make UN-authorized ad hoc multilateral coalitions composed of states alone or a mix of states and IGOs and NGOs more legitimate requires, first, that those states and international organizations selected to participate must be wisely chosen to assure neutrality and legitimacy. Such a coalition cannot always be the G8, any more than it can always include the USA. There is a need to include other states and organizations. Second, the coalition must be given a clear mandate – the trade-off between peace and justice needs to be clearly elucidated. To have such a mandate, there needs to be a range of action alternatives. The choice cannot be just between traditional peacekeeping and enforcement, but needs to include alternatives in between. Third, the coalition must have the needed capabilities at its disposal, something it has not had in Sierra Leone. Increasing capabilities includes improving indigenous and regional capabilities such as proposed for the African continent. Fourth, multilateral coalitions must be monitored. The United Nations has to seize the task of critical oversight and disseminate frequent and thorough reports widely to ensure the legitimacy of the ad hoc initiative.

The third challenge is the threat to the legitimacy of the UN's own humanitarian agencies posed by governments and military organizations bypassing them in crisis situations. The UNHCR head, Sadako Ogata, noted the danger in reference to Kosovo. She argued that direct involvement by NATO forces in providing humanitarian aid not only "undermined coordination and deprived civilian humanitarian agencies of effectiveness and clout", but could jeopardize their legitimacy. "The military can support but should not substitute for agencies with humanitarian mandates", she said. "The experience and expertise to deal with the human dimension of crises – the suffering of civilians, their traumas, the terror of flight, the pain and uncertainty of exile – are with us, the civilian humanitarian agencies."[32]

Fourth is the declining legitimacy of the Security Council itself. As more Security Council resolutions are taken either authorizing a state or multinational coalition to act on behalf of the international community or authorizing a direct UN operation, those unrepresented on the Security

Council, including those who may be asked to provide troops and/or funds, question the legitimacy of the organ, specifically its limited membership and the P5's veto. The P5 veto power and the practice of informal consultations between the Secretary-General and the P5, without open and transparent consultation with other states, have led to objections even from some of the UN's more staunch supporters such as Canada and Norway. The same practices have given potential members of the Security Council, including Germany, Japan, and India, renewed interest in pursuing Charter reform. Unless and until the issue of Security Council reform is squarely addressed and a diplomatic formula found to retain the efficiency of the Council's small size while expanding its membership, the Council's legitimacy will continue to erode.

These legitimacy questions must be addressed as the United Nations grapples with the variety of conflicts and changing expectations for interventions in the next millennium. Legitimacy must be maintained, and indeed enhanced, if the United Nations itself, regional organizations, ad hoc multilateral coalitions, and NGOs are to be successful in responding to these challenges.

Leadership and the dilemma of commitment

Similarly crucial as the first three dilemmas is this fourth: where will the leadership and commitment come from in the future? There may be a single superpower in this post-Cold War era, but that superpower is an increasingly reluctant leader and contributor to the United Nations and to multilateralism more generally.[33]

The role of the USA

American ambivalence toward multilateralism is legendary, making it an unpredictable leader and coalition partner. Optimism about the possibilities of UN action specifically and assertive multilateralism more generally was highest during the Gulf War. Confronted by the crisis posed by the Iraqi invasion of Kuwait and the threat to the world's oil supplies, and galvanized by the changes in the Soviet Union, the USA assumed a leadership role. There was no doubt that the interests of the USA and UN principles overlapped. In response to *An Agenda for Peace* in 1992, the Bush administration pledged to train American troops for multilateral peacekeeping and humanitarian operations. In the first Clinton administration, with the realization that the USA could no longer be the world's policeman, support was given to more equal sharing with other countries and the United Nations was deemed the appropriate vehicle.

The optimism proved short-lived. Galvanized by the loss of American soldiers in Somalia, the president issued the 1994 Presidential Decision Directive (PDD-25) outlining a more circumspect view of UN peacekeeping and US participation. PDD-25 suggested that to support future UN peacekeeping operations, the USA must be satisfied that "there is a genuine threat to international peace and security, a major humanitarian disaster requiring urgent action, a legitimate democratic government ... in danger, or ... a gross violation of human rights".[34] With PDD-25, the USA went from a position of broadly supporting and even strengthening UN peacekeeping to one of reduced commitment.

Since 1994 Congress has refused to pay US dues and arrears to the United Nations. It has disputed the amount owed, called for reimbursement of peacekeeping support, and proposed unilaterally to reduce the US assessment to 20 per cent. In November 1999 a breakthrough on the arrears issue was reached by Congress in the Helms-Biden agreement. Although the compromise safeguards the US vote in the General Assembly through the year 2000, discussions will continue on several issues and the outcome is not assured.[35] Meanwhile, Security Council reform is largely on hold, putting the United Nations further from the possibility of real reform. These actions have also made it clear that the USA has adopted a unilateralist policy, reversing the multilateralism of the early 1990s.

This has led to a lively debate in American foreign policy circles about the shift from the assertive multilateralism of the early 1990s to the more unilateral policies of the late 1990s. While multilateralism had seemed to become a "dirty word",[36] this change was accompanied by a major bureaucratic debate within the US government.[37] Bruce Jentleson articulates the broader American dilemma as follows:

We make the claim of being the sole surviving superpower, we contend that we don't want to renounce the unilateralist option, and we excoriate "multilateralism" when it appears to impose restrictions on our freedom of action – but we also want there to be enough multilateralism so that others carry their share of the global peace burden.[38]

American foreign policy will continue to be shaped by the domestic debate over the USA's proper and legitimate role in the world. Viet Nam shattered the dominant Cold War consensus, and a new one has yet to emerge. Post-Cold War crises and changes in both administration and Congress sustain that debate, and will continue to do so in the foreseeable future.

In addition, the USA's articulated policy on responding to humanitarian crises is ambivalent and potentially contradictory. On the one hand, the Clinton administration identified responding to humanitarian crises as a key responsibility of democratic countries, saying that "[t]he failure to deal adequately with such strife, to do something about mass murder and genocide, corrodes the essence of a democratic society".[39] On the other hand, such a response is only possible if it is inexpensive and there is little probability of loss of American life. As Edward Luttwak so bluntly notes with respect to how NATO fought in Kosovo, "[t]he immediate possibility of saving thousands of Albanians from massacre and hundreds of thousands from deportation was obviously not worth the lives of a few pilots".[40] And in Sierra Leone, the USA made it clear that it would not put American officials on the ground, leaving countries ill-equipped to carry out the mission. This ambivalence and contradiction in American policy will make the task of forging future multilateral coalitions with US participation all the more difficult. There is, however, no possibility of excluding the USA in the new millennium. The USA is an almost indispensable member of every multilateral coalition, as the only military superpower with the logistical and technological capacity to engage in complex peacekeeping operations and enforcement activities.

Yet from a political and financial standpoint, the UN's dependence upon US leadership makes it highly vulnerable to perceptions of being a captive to American interests or disinterest. And, as the world's only global body, leadership in the United Nations has to include not just the USA and other major industrialized countries, but followership (and occasionally leadership) of other countries. It is clear that many other democratic states, like the USA, are unwilling to make commitments to multilateral activities when the lives of their nationals are jeopardized. It is also clear that most UN members are no longer willing to accept leadership by a superpower which continually threatens to thwart reforms that would make the organization more representative, legitimate, effective, and transparent. The United Nations is not a revolutionary organization, nor do its dominant members desire fundamental change that would undermine their own power. Of more serious concern perhaps is the danger of the United Nations becoming marginalized in world politics, with a more unilateralist sole superpower, economic decision-making centred outside the UN system, and an enlarged NATO taking on more security threats.

The UN role in peacekeeping in the next millennium

The United Nations faces serious challenges and dilemmas in the next millennium. First, it will be constrained by the tension between the desire for respect for state sovereignty and the demand for humanitarian intervention. National sovereignty has eroded and there are demands for justice, for humanitarian interventions as well as for promoting human rights. Until the old norm of non-intervention is soundly rejected and a new norm of humanitarian intervention articulated, the United Nations will be constrained by the contest between old and new norms and play a diminished role.

The United Nations will also be constrained by the increasing roles of regional organizations, ad hoc multilateral coalitions, and NGOs, many with divergent interests. Until coordinating policy-making among these entities is institutionalized, the United Nations will be challenged by un-authorized actions and unprecedented challenges for sequencing actions of different players or coordinating complex divisions of labour. It cannot act alone; it needs the cooperation of others.

Finally, the United Nations will continue to be constrained by the di-visions and vagaries of American domestic politics and the continued re-luctance of the USA to commit resources to undertake these new peace-keeping operations and enforcement actions, except those that it decides to lead unilaterally or through NATO. And there is always the danger of complete US disengagement.

The United Nations also has opportunities in the coming millennium, and it needs to capitalize on these. It can provide the forum for forging a consensus on the intervention dilemma and on whether, where, and how the United Nations should involve itself in the future. Secretary-General Kofi Annan is himself articulating the *de facto* changes in state sover-eignty and international norms of intervention. In a context of contested norms, its members will make choices about when and how to act. The UN Secretariat will be the primary international body able to distil and articulate the lessons of when and how the United Nations (and other actors) can be most effective on behalf of the international community – of people and of states. The United Nations can play a leadership role in forming and managing coalitions of the willing and in providing the nec-essary oversight so essential to their legitimacy.

The United Nations can improve its own implementation procedures, building on the lessons learned from systematic and comparative exami-nation of success and failures. Such lessons provide a basis for judging when and how the United Nations can best serve international interests.

The United Nations can strive to reinvigorate its own legitimacy, and that clearly means Charter reform and managerial reforms, as difficult and controversial as these tasks may be. Secretary-General Annan has taken substantial steps towards the latter; the former can only be accom-plished by the member states. It is only through Charter reform, however – most notably revamping the Security Council and its procedures and permitting increased meaningful participation by NGOs and regional organizations – that the United Nations will be able to claim its place as the hub of global governance in the new millennium.

Notes

1. Address of Secretary-General Kofi Annan to the UN General Assembly, 20 September 1999 (GA/9596).
2. William Zartman, "Introduction: Posing the problem of state collapse", in I. William Zartman (ed.), *Collapsed States: The Disintegration and Restoration of Legitimate Authority*, Boulder, CO: Lynne Rienner, 1995, p. 1.
3. Tonya Langford, "Things fall apart: State failure and the politics of intervention", *International Studies Review*, Vol. 1, No. 1, Spring 1999, p. 59.
4. *Ibid.*, p. 61.
5. Pierre Hassner, "From war and peace to violence and intervention: Permanent moral dilemmas under changing political and technological conditions", in Jonathan Moore (ed.), *Hard Choices: Moral Dilemmas in Humanitarian Intervention*, Lanham, MD: Rowman & Littlefield, 1998, p. 11.
6. These figures are cited in Lise Morje Howard, "The United Nations and civil war termination: Success, failure, and organizational learning", draft introductory chapter presented at the 1999 ACUNS/ASIL Summer Workshop, Yale University, p. 1. See also UN Department of Public Information, *Current and Completed Peacekeeping Operations*, www.un.org/depts/DPKO.
7. Howard, *ibid.*
8. Zartman, note 2, p. 2. For further discussion of peacekeeping in civil conflict situations, see Paul F. Diehl, "Peacekeeping in civil wars", in Ramesh Thakur and Carlyle A. Thayer (eds), *A Crisis of Expectations: UN Peacekeeping in the 1990s*, Boulder, CO: Westview Press, 1995, pp. 223–236. This volume represents an earlier multi-authored review of some of the same issues discussed in this chapter.
9. Marc Trachtenberg, "Intervention in historical perspective", in Laura W. Reed and Carl Kaysen (eds), *Emerging Norms of Justified Intervention*, Cambridge, MA: American Academy of Arts and Sciences, 1993, p. 31. For further discussion of the issues of intervention from a variety of disciplinary perspectives, see other chapters in this volume and also Michael J. Glennon, "The new interventionism: The search for a just international law", *Foreign Affairs*, Vol. 78, No. 3, May/June 1999, pp. 2–7.
10. Hassner, note 5, p. 16; for more on this debate, see Duane Bratt, "Peace over justice: Developing a framework for UN peacekeeping operations in internal conflicts", *Global Governance*, Vol. 5, No. 1, January–March 1999, pp. 63–83.
11. Statement by the Permanent Representative of Nigeria, Ibrahim Gambari, to the Security Council, 30 September 1999 (SC/6736).
12. Howard, note 6, p. 4.
13. See, for example, Stephen John Stedman, *Peace-making in Civil War. International Mediation in Zimbabwe, 1974–1980*, Boulder, CO: Lynne Rienner, 1991.
14. Among others, see Martha Finnemore and Kathryn Sikkink, "International norm dynamics and political change", *International Organization*, Vol. 52, No. 4, Autumn 1998, pp. 887–918; Thomas G. Weiss and Cindy Collins, *Humanitarian Challenges and Intervention*, Boulder, CO: Westview Press, 1996; and Langford, note 3.
15. US National Intelligence Council report, quoted in *Dayton Daily News*, 19 September 1999, p. 25A.
16. Statement by Secretary-General Kofi Annan to the Security Council, 16 September 1999 (SC/6729).
17. Kofi Annan, "Peacekeeping, military intervention and national sovereignty in internal armed conflict", in Moore, note 5.
18. Boutros Boutros-Ghali, *An Agenda for Peace: Preventive Diplomacy, Peacemaking and Peacekeeping*, New York: UN Department of Public Information, 1992, p. 44.

19. J. Bryan Hehir, "Military intervention and national sovereignty: Recasting the relationship", in Moore, note 5, p. 33.
20. Kofi Annan, "Statement on Receiving the Report of the Independent Inquiry into the Actions of the United Nations During the 1994 Genocide in Rwanda," 16 December 1999, www.un.org/news/ossg/sgsm-rwanda.htm.
21. Trachtenberg, note 9, p. 31.
22. John L. Gaddis, "Coping with victory", *Atlantic Monthly*, May 1990, p. 49.
23. For coverage of these regional organizations, see Carnegie Commission on Preventing Deadly Conflict, *Preventing Deadly Conflict*, Final Report with Executive Summary, Washington, DC, 1997, see especially pp. 147–148, 169–173.
24. For an instructive case study of regional peacekeeping, see Neil MacFarlane's contribution to this volume.
25. Francis Kofi Abiew and Tom Keating, "NGOs and UN peacekeeping operations: Strange bedfellows", *International Peacekeeping*, Vol. 6, No. 2, Summer 1999, p. 90.
26. Martin Griffiths, Iain Levine, and Mark Weller, "Sovereignty and suffering", in John Harriss (ed.), *The Politics of Humanitarian Intervention*, London: Pinter, 1995, p. 72.
27. See, for example, Robert C. Johansen, "Reconciling national and international interests in UN peacekeeping", in Thakur and Thayer, note 8, pp. 281–302.
28. Eric G. Berman, "The Security Council's increasing reliance on burden-sharing: Collaboration or abrogation?", *International Peacekeeping*, Vol. 4, No. 1, Spring 1998, p. 3.
29. Ambassador Juan Somavia, Permanent Representative of Chile to the United Nations, quoted in Abiew and Keating, note 25, pp. 101–102.
30. Diehl, note 8, pp. 234–235.
31. David Chandler, "The limits of peace-building and international regulation and civil society development in Bosnia", *International Peacekeeping*, Vol. 6, No. 1, Spring 1999, pp. 109–125.
32. Ogata, quoted in "UNHCR's Ogata warns against attempts by governments, military to bypass aid agencies in crises", 4 October 1999, http://www.unhcr.ch/refworld/unhcr/hcspeech/991004.htm.
33. Karen Mingst and Margaret P. Karns, *The United Nations in the Post-Cold War Era*, 2nd edn., Boulder, CO: Westview, 2000, see especially Chapter 7.
34. Paul Lewis, "US plans peacekeeping guidelines", *New York Times*, 18 November 1993, p. A10.
35. On the role of the US Congress, see Margaret P. Karns and Karen A. Mingst, "The past as prologue: The United States and the future of the UN system", in Chadwick F. Alger, Gene M. Lyons, and John E. Trent (eds), *The United Nations System: The Policies of Member States*, Tokyo: United Nations University Press, 1995, pp. 424–435. For an update on the financing issue, see Steven Dimoff, "UN arrears: The deal is done! But US plan for payment faces tough battle in world today", *The Interdependent*, Vol. 25, No. 4, Winter 2000, p. 5.
36. Bruce W. Jentleson, "Who, why, what, and how: Debates over post-Cold War military intervention", in Robert J. Lieber (ed.), *Eagle Adrift: American Foreign Policy at the End of the Century*, New York: Longman, 1997, pp. 39–70.
37. Michael G. Mackinnon, "Rival or partners? Bureaucratic politics and the evolution of US peacekeeping policy", *International Peacekeeping*, Vol. 6, No. 1, Spring 1999, pp. 32–54.
38. Jentleson, note 36, p. 40.
39. Leslie H. Gelb, "Quelling the teacup wars: The new world's constant challenge", *Foreign Affairs*, Vol. 73, No. 6, November/December 1994, pp. 5–6.
40. Edward Lutwak, "Give war a chance", *Foreign Affairs*, Vol. 78, No. 4, July/August 1999, pp. 36–44.

13

From *An Agenda for Peace* to the Brahimi Report: Towards a new era of UN peace operations?

Albrecht Schnabel and Ramesh Thakur[1]

The UN's expanded peacekeeping role during the past 10 years has overall been a disappointing experience. The hopes for a truly global security role for the United Nations, in part through principled application of traditional peacekeeping and not-so-traditional peace enforcing, were shattered in Somalia, Bosnia, Rwanda, and, recently, Sierra Leone. There are numerous political, financial, organizational, and operational reasons for the UN's inability to put effective peacekeeping troops on the ground whenever and wherever needed. Those have been examined throughout this volume from a number of perspectives – of the scholar, the police and military officer, the force commander, the special representative, and the UN Secretariat. At the end of the Cold War the United Nations showed great willingness and some promise to assume a greater global security role, as expressed in Secretary-General Boutros Boutros-Ghali's *An Agenda for Peace*.[2] An expanded role for the United Nations did not unfold over the years that followed: in part because of a lack of support from the most powerful of its members; in part because of the UN Charter's own principles on the virtual inviolability of state borders; and in part due to the UN's underestimation of the complexity and danger of post-Cold War crisis situations and an overestimation of the international community's willingness to match broad mandates with necessary resources.

Surely, the UN's "failure" to solve ongoing conflicts does not mean a failure of UN peacekeeping *per se*. But the United Nations (and the international community) failed when it introduced military conflict management as a core component of broadly defined peacekeeping strategies without backing up these expanded peacekeeping mandates with the necessary political support and military resources.

This concluding chapter focuses on three main issues. First, it briefly reviews the failure of post-Cold War peacekeeping from the 1992 *Agenda for Peace* to the 2000 Brahimi Report on UN peace operations. It then examines the lessons learned in the Brahimi Report from post-Cold War peacekeeping practices, and its recommendations for future peacekeeping operations. Many of these suggestions are congruent with and support the reflections offered by the preceding chapters in this volume. Finally, the chapter examines what may be the most sensible responses to today's peacekeeping crisis: effective conflict prevention and, if necessary, humanitarian enforcement operations in failing and failed states to protect the basic rights and security needs of individuals.

Hopes belied: Boutros-Ghali's *An Agenda for Peace* and an empowered United Nations

When the United Nations was created in 1945, the mutual acceptance by all member states of the principles of non-intervention and the inviolability of state sovereignty was held to be a crucial guarantor of international order and stability. The Article 2(7) proscription on intervening in a state's internal affairs could be lifted under Chapter VII of the UN Charter for collective enforcement of international peace. This had to be accomplished by unanimous agreement of the five permanent members of the Security Council (China, the USSR, the USA, France, and Britain) that international peace and security were threatened by a particular conflict. The general antagonism of the Security Council members during the emerging East–West conflict rendered the Charter's collective security system virtually dysfunctional. Nevertheless, the practice of impartial peacekeeping evolved as an alternative instrument in preventing low-level, often internal, conflicts from escalating to superpower confrontations.

Although Chapter VI allowed for involvement of the United Nations in the pacific settlement of internal and interstate disputes, conflicts increasingly required more vigorous approaches. Peacekeeping during the Cold War era was only possible to a very limited degree and within very limited mandates.[3] As a result of the intense and extended application of UN peacekeeping activities in the initial euphoria following the end of the Cold War, peacekeeping became a major source of hope for a new era of international cooperation in defence of human and global security matters. Not only did peacekeeping gain the moral support of much of the world community; it also gained significant financial and political support from many major peacekeepers, big and small powers alike.

In 1992, Secretary-General Boutros-Ghali published *An Agenda for Peace*, a much-discussed report "on ways of strengthening and making more efficient within the framework and provisions of the Charter the capacity of the United Nations for preventive diplomacy, for peacemaking and for peacekeeping".[4] Boutros-Ghali had great hopes for a fundamental restructuring of the tasks of, and approaches to, post-Cold War UN peacekeeping. These changes were to take place as soon as possible in order for the United Nations to keep up with the rapid pace of changing international politics:

Reform is a continuing process, and improvement can have no limit. Yet there is an expectation, which I wish to see fulfilled, that the present phase in the renewal of this Organization should be complete by 1995, its fiftieth anniversary. The pace set must therefore be increased if the United Nations is to keep ahead of the acceleration of history that characterizes this age. We must be guided not by precedents alone, however wise these may be, but by the needs of the future and by the shape and content that we wish to give it.[5]

Unfortunately, those changes did not materialize. The United Nations has entered the twenty-first century virtually unchanged and unreformed, and the enthusiasm and momentum for UN reform has largely dissipated. The Millennium Report by Secretary-General Kofi Annan attempts to regain the momentum of change in the face of continued state-centrism by many of the UN's member states. It addresses the many challenges to human security not by threatening states' authority and sovereignty, but by strengthening their ability to serve the interests of their citizens and the international community.[6]

In *An Agenda for Peace*, Boutros-Ghali had called for a new role for the United Nations in managing global security. He identified the Security Council as the catalyst for such reform:

[The UN's] security arm, once disabled by circumstances it was not created or equipped to control, has emerged as a central instrument for the prevention and resolution of conflicts and for the preservation of peace. Our aims must be:
- To seek to identify at the earliest possible stage situations that could produce conflict, and to try through diplomacy to remove the sources of danger before violence results;
- Where conflict erupts, to engage in peacemaking aimed at resolving the issues that have led to conflict;
- Through peacekeeping, to work to preserve peace, however fragile, where fighting has been halted and to assist in implementing agreements achieved by the peacemakers;

- To stand ready to assist in peace-building in its differing contexts: rebuilding the institutions and infrastructures of nations torn by civil war and strife; and building bonds of peaceful mutual benefit among nations formerly at war;
- And, in the largest sense, to address the deepest causes of conflict: economic despair, social injustice and political oppression. It is possible to discern an increasingly common moral perception that spans the world's nations and peoples, and which is finding expression in international laws, many owing their genesis to the work of this Organization.[7]

Boutros-Ghali's *An Agenda for Peace* was a bold attempt to expand traditional peacekeeping to include various new forms of peacekeeping – from preventive diplomacy to such tasks as election monitoring and peace enforcement. It called for a new and comprehensive way of thinking about global peacekeeping responsibilities. It envisioned peacekeeping as an institutionalized instrument for global security patterns and structures which serve two primary purposes: to enhance the political and military position of the UN system,[8] and to promote the political and legal status of individuals and subnational groups governed by states that could or would not fulfil their basic responsibility to provide for their citizens' security.[9]

When there is no peace to keep: The shift towards peace enforcement

The introductory chapter, along with several contributions to this volume, traced and assessed the multi-generational evolution of peacekeeping. As has been mentioned a number of times throughout the volume, peacekeeping reached an impasse when it turned into peace enforcement. Peace enforcement operations attempt to address the weaknesses of the expanded, yet non-enforceable, tasks in the often hostile environments of post-Cold War peacekeeping operations. Military force is used to compel all or individual belligerents into compliance with Security Council resolutions and to enable peacekeepers to fulfil their extensive mandates. Also called "robust peacekeeping" or "muscular peacekeeping", the use of the term "peacekeeping" seems utterly inappropriate in this context. "Peace enforcement" is an oxymoron, given the inherent contradiction of peacekeeping and the use of military force. These missions have been the greatest challenge for the United Nations in its quest for a greater role in global security politics. The core elements of traditional peacekeeping missions have been abandoned in the context of peace enforcement: the peacekeepers' neutral role in the conflict, non-use of force, and consent of the belligerent parties to outside involvement. As a result, UN-sponsored peacekeeping (performed by the United Nations itself, or regional or state actors) has assumed the role of an active participant in internal conflicts.

Peace enforcement operations apply and/or threaten military force to enforce and support expanded peacekeeping tasks. This is done to prevent the return of fighting, protect humanitarian aid deliveries and corridors, and secure airports and other logistical locations. They guard so-called "safe areas" to protect endangered populations and UN personnel and facilities. They use force to disarm warring parties. In the cases of Yugoslavia and Somalia, these mandates were developed and promoted by the Secretary-General and then presented to the Security Council for modification and ratification. Boutros-Ghali proved much more aggressive in pushing peace enforcing measures than the members of the Security Council: realizing that the United Nations would not have the necessary means to send a mission to Somalia, he welcomed the American offer to conduct a multilateral intervention under US command (Unified Task Force, or UNITAF).[10]

Peace enforcement operations become deeply involved in the internal affairs of their target states, and the lack of consent of the conflicting parties is considered as no more than a hindrance to the missions' expanded mandate. In addition to fulfilling typical traditional and expanded peacekeeping functions, heavily armed combat and élite troops are deployed to confront and resist opposition from local troops (ranging from massive onslaughts to guerrilla fighting). If applied successfully, continuously, and in a principled fashion, peace enforcement would have a strong humanitarian character. When peacekeepers are willing to put their lives on the line to guard safe havens and humanitarian aid deliveries, or retaliate when belligerents violate the human rights of minority groups, they are part of a humanitarian operation. Nevertheless, the selective application and frequent failure of many peace enforcement missions in triggering lasting peace questions the assumption that peace and justice can indeed be achieved through war.

The Brahimi Report on UN peace operations

In March 2000, Secretary-General Kofi Annan convened, "a high-level Panel to undertake a thorough review of the United Nations peace and security activities, and to present a clear set of specific, concrete and practical recommendations to assist the United Nations in conducting such activities better in the future".[11] The Panel on United Nations Peace Operations was chaired by Lakhdar Brahimi, the former foreign minister of Algeria and since 1997 Under-Secretary-General for Special Assignments in Support of the Secretary-General's Preventive and Peacemaking Efforts. The members of the panel included nine distinguished military and non-military peacekeeping experts from various countries around the world. The panel produced a comprehensive report that, according to Kofi Annan, is "frank yet fair; [while] its recommendations are far-reaching yet sensible and practical".[12] Annan encouraged all member states to consider, approve, and support the implementation of the report's recommendations, which is, in his words, "essential to make the United Nations truly credible as a force for peace".[13]

The Brahimi Report is unusual in the candour of its analysis and recommendations. It pulls no punches, using forceful language to describe the sad state of the UN's recent peacekeeping record. Operational failure in the field often flows from the diffusion of responsibility at the United Nations. Analysis of the structural flaws of UN peacekeeping is accompanied in the Brahimi Report by efforts to point the way forward to improve the quality and results of UN missions. In order to reoccupy its niche as a major actor in international security, the United Nations requires consistency of purpose, the resources to give it substance, and a convincing attention span. Of course, it remains to be seen if member states will add the necessary substance to the report's findings and recommendations.

The report makes 20 main recommendations, ranging from general peacekeeping strategy to logistical and administrative issues in the field and at UN Headquarters. It comes to the overall sound conclusion that "when the United Nations does send its forces to uphold the peace, they must be prepared to confront the lingering forces of war and violence with the ability and determination to defeat them". For, in the final analysis, "no amount of good intentions can substitute for the fundamental ability to project credible force if complex peacekeeping, in particular, is to succeed".[14] Mandates, and the resources to match them, have to be guided by pragmatic, realistic analysis and thinking. The UN Secretariat "must not apply best-case planning assumptions to situations where the local actors have historically exhibited worst-case behaviour".[15]

Moreover, it is very important for the United Nations to learn to say "no". The Secretary-General must have the authority and courage of conviction to reject missions that have been approved because of confused, unclear, or severely under-resourced mandates. This can only begin to take place if the United Nations develops the professional civil service culture of providing advice that is sound, based on a thorough assessment of options, independent of what might be politically popular or fit the preconceptions of the decision-makers, and free of fear of consequences for politically neutral officials. The Brahimi Report recommends that the Secretariat should tell the Security Council what it needs to hear, not what it wants to hear.

In general, the recommendations make perfect sense and are testimony to the years of neglect on the international community's part to endow the United Nations with the minimum requirements necessary for successful peace operations. Most of what the report asks for should have been part and parcel of peacekeeping missions all along. The fact that there is a need to ask for those issues to be addressed today is an embarrassing comment on the institutional inertia and reform-proof lethargy of the United Nations. The Brahimi panel and its report are part of a series of courageous steps taken by Kofi Annan to force the United Nations, through internal and external panels, to evaluate its own record and present the findings and recommendations to its member states for consideration. The report offers a solid package of recommendations that would undoubtedly improve peace operations if implemented. However, *implementation* is the key word, greatest challenge, and main obstacle. Should the Brahimi Report's recommendations be successfully implemented, UN peace operations would look as follows.

- The international community would be deeply committed to effective conflict prevention and peace-building. The United Nations, governments, regional organizations, and civil society actors would be working closely together in fact-finding, conflict management, and post-conflict reconstruction.[16] The emphasis on peace-building would be on the protection of human rights, demobilization, and reintegration of the displaced. "Quick-impact projects", specially funded, would address particularly crucial challenges to peace and stability.[17]

- Peacekeeping operations would be much more effective. Peacekeepers would be well trained and have the mandate and resources to defend themselves and the mission's mandates forcefully against local violence and renewed conflict escalation.[18] Peace operations would enjoy broader mandates, and have the permission to use force and to give priority to mission and mandate success rather than the political sensitivities of the permanent five Security Council members (P5) or major troop contributors' domestic and other constraints. Mission resources would be provided as required, and commitment of contributors would be sustained. Although broad, mandates would be achievable. Basic conditions for the deployment of military and civilian personnel would be met. These include agreement on tasks, timelines, troops, and equipment, the full support of troop-contributing states, and a clear chain of command and unity of effort.[19]

- A mission's work would be supported and enhanced by an information and strategic analysis secretariat and an expert team that advises and assists in the tasks of a transitional civil administration.[20] Peacekeeping operations would be deployed promptly – within 30 days in the case of a traditional mission, and within 90 days for complex operations. Mission leaders, including the special representatives and force commanders, would be drawn from previously established lists of potential candidates, be intimately involved in the planning of the mission from

the very start, and be able to rely on UN Headquarters for routine strategic guidance.[21]

- Military personnel would be equally well prepared and readily available
for potential deployment. Member states would maintain multilateral
forces within the UN standby arrangements system. The Secretary-
General would initiate plans for the deployment of peace operations
before the actual signing of a cease-fire agreement. The UN Secretariat
would refuse to deploy troops from contributors who did not meet basic
training and equipment requirements.[22] The same high standards would
apply to civilian police and other specialists: they would be carefully
pre-selected, trained, and ready for deployment.[23]

- More attention would be given to funding for public information, logistic support, and expenditure management. The UN Secretariat would
have start-up funds to begin planning for peace operations prior to approval of deployment by the Security Council, and field missions would
have greater control over the management of their budgets.[24] In addition to greater financial stability, the Department of Peacekeeping Operations would be well staffed, and the Lessons Learned Unit would
provide precise and useful information for mission planning.[25] Public
information in peace operations would be greatly enhanced, and a
Peace-building Unit within the Department of Political Affairs would
permit more effective planning and implementation of post-war peace-
building activities.[26] Personnel would be recruited on merit, and only
the most competent staff members would be entrusted with responsibilities that are crucial to regional, international, and human security
needs. Member states would fulfil their obligations and commitments
to the sustained provision of financial assistance and political support.

In many ways, the Brahimi Report represents a more comprehensive,
detailed, and thorough examination of the requirements for peace operations in the twenty-first century than Boutros-Ghali's *An Agenda for
Peace* eight years earlier. Nevertheless, both are products of a commitment to help the United Nations to live up to its mandate. Its success will
depend on the commitment of member states to permit true reform – it is
now up to them to breathe new life into UN peacekeeping.

Assessing the Brahimi Report: Regional perspectives and the way forward

Six months after the release of the Brahimi Report, its findings, recommendations, and potential impact were discussed in four regional meetings in Africa, Asia, Latin America, and Europe.[27] Since the Brahimi
panel did fail to engage in a regional consultative process prior to issuing

the report, the meetings in Johannesburg, Singapore, Buenos Aires, and London of representatives of states, intergovernmental and regional organizations, and NGOs and academic circles were long overdue, yet critically important to build regional and local constituencies for UN peace operations. The perspectives of the regional meetings offer an important supplement to the findings and suggestions of the report itself.[28]

Most participants across all regions found the report to be a necessary and useful assessment of the UN's record in peacekeeping. In the words of the report itself, its recommendations describe only the "minimum threshold of change"[29] that is required to render UN peace operations truly effective in the future. The participants emphasized that the report dealt with "technical and operational solutions to essentially political problems".[30] In an environment where the political will of member states largely determines what the United Nations and regional organizations can accomplish, technical and operational issues are important, but only secondary. In addition, political will is very selective – most participants did not fail to notice the huge discrepancy between political support and financial and military resources committed to conflicts in Europe as compared to Africa. All the more important did it seem to many participants from developing countries that the United Nations improve on its partnership with regional and subregional organizations, international financial institutions, NGOs, and local actors. Since the United Nations must recognize that it is only one of many actors whose successful interplay is fundamental to success in peace operations, it has to seek cooperation and consultation with regional and local actors.

The same applies to preventive measures. While the regional meetings reflected a sense of frustration over the barely symbolic attention given to conflict prevention, fact-finding and information-gathering represent only one of many long- and short-term approaches to successful prevention. In particular, there needs to be commitment to address the root causes of conflict, not simply its symptoms – while preventive diplomacy usually takes place when conflicts are well advanced, structural prevention must begin much earlier. Although the office of the Secretary-General was generally seen to be very important in conflict prevention, regional and subregional organizations and individual heads of state were seen to be more crucial than other UN agencies and departments. The various regional organizations in all parts of the world were seen as the main sources of long-term conflict prevention, and stronger operational links are necessary between them and relevant UN bodies. While some regional organizations already possess enhanced capacities in early-warning and preventive measures (such as the OSCE and OAS), others still have a long way to go (the OAU and ASEAN). Moreover, the United Nations itself must enhance its own analytical capacity, improve interagency information-sharing and strategic planning, and strengthen the Secretary-General's office in its capacity to be more effective in early-warning and early preventive action.[31] Much of this will inevitably require further resource commitments in the form of additional personnel and training, while "[z]ero-growth budgetary restrictions impede and undermine the current efforts to reform United Nations peace operations".[32]

Across all regions, the core principles of peacekeeping – consent of local parties, impartiality, and the use of force only in self-defence – are considered to remain important components of peacekeeping missions. However, "impartiality should be seen in terms of the fair application of a mandate, not as an excuse for moral equivocation".[33] Two main points of caution were raised. First, African contributors in particular argued for more forceful approaches to deal with "spoilers". Second, there should be more emphasis on training regional staff and regional peacekeeping forces in places where major powers are reluctant to commit their own troops.[34] In order to prevent regional hegemons from dictating regional security operations, close cooperation with and monitoring by the United Nations is particularly important for strengthening regional capacities in peacekeeping and peace enforcement.

The need for training and empowering regional and local staff was even more pronounced when discussed in the context of post-conflict peace-building. This process must focus more on local ownership, and the United Nations must draw on the knowledge and experience of local and regional actors. Only local ownership will result in sustainable peace-building efforts. Training is again an important component – training of local civil society actors as well as government staff. "Emphasis should be on building the capacity for local governance ... rather than on employing a vast number of international staff of highly uneven quality."[35] While European organizations have proved that the main tasks of peace-building can be accomplished by regional organizations, this would not hold true outside of Europe. There, the United Nations should be expected to carry the main responsibility, as well as the financial and personnel burden of peace-building missions. To give peace-building greater weight in overall UN missions and uncouple it from the fragility of voluntary contribution, funds should be included in peacekeeping assessments. As the regional meetings argued, peace-building requires a reasonable time frame, and "quick-impact projects [recommended by the Brahimi Report] should not be temporary-impact projects". Further, "[t]he essential elements for a sustainable peace – including rule of law institutions – need to be identified and adequately financed, and there should be a 'seamless transition' from peacekeeping to peace-building".[36]

Most importantly, the report's recommendations should unite, and not further divide, the international community's sense of responsibility and commitment to conflicts around the globe:

There is a perception in many parts of the world that the first world is partial in its selection of countries in which to become involved. Many developing countries argue that the richer countries apply double standards. There should therefore be consistency. When Africans argue that the US and Europe take human rights violations more seriously in some parts of the world than in Africa, they have a point. The definition of human rights should be that of the UN – not that of the US – it should incorporate not only civil and political rights, but also social, economic, and cultural rights, with an emphasis on the right to development.[37]

If the international community could come together to maintain and strengthen peace, stability, and democratic and participatory governance, peace could actually be kept before the outbreak of violence. In a way, conflict prevention is just another word for "peacekeeping". Should prevention fail, intervention should be swift, fair, just, and applied wherever and whenever universally agreed-on thresholds of human decency have been transgressed. It is these thoughts to which the authors turn for the remainder of this chapter.

The new challenges: Principled intervention and effective prevention

The Brahimi Report has been a response to the dramatically changing nature of peacekeeping operations – increasingly more intrusive activities in the unstable and violent affairs of sovereign states. Since the end of the Cold War, UN peacekeeping has been seriously affected by two sets of developments. On the one hand, the nature of armed conflict has changed considerably, moving from interstate to intrastate conflict. This has reinforced the trend of civilians being on the front line of organized armed violence, from around 10 per cent at the start of the twentieth century to close to 90 per cent by the close. As the assumptions departed increasingly from the requirements of the post-Cold War conflicts, so traditional peacekeeping fell into increasing desuetude.

On the other hand, so too have our notions changed of state sovereignty, international community, and national and international responsibility for the protection and welfare of peoples without discrimination on grounds of race, religion, gender, or territoriality. Indeed, the Brahimi Report notes that even so-called intrastate wars are typically transnational in character, involving the dark side of globalization or elements of uncivil society (arms flows, refugees, illicit commodity flows like drugs and diamonds, etc.).[38] Consequently, even though the major tenets of traditional peacekeeping were increasingly abandoned in the 1990s, there was no corresponding disengagement of the international community from the rising and falling tide of violent conflicts in the closing decade of the twentieth century.

The United Nations is an organization dedicated to the territorial integrity of its member states, and the maintenance of international peace and security on that basis. This has presented the organization with great difficulty in the past decade: how to reconcile its foundational principle of member states' sovereignty with the primary mandate to maintain international peace and security.

If the recommendations of the Brahimi Report are accepted and implemented, the international community will be in a better position to conduct peace operations. But the implementation of the recommendations will be neither easy nor cheap. It will cost much money and political compromise. In some cases it will be worth it to the P5 and the wider international community: a new consensus seems to be emerging in support of a more intrusive approach to human rights protection, one that punishes aggressors when heinous crimes against humanity are committed. "Humanitarian" intervention has surfaced as a concept that raises expectations for greater justice: when citizens' rights are violated on a mass scale, simple reference to state sovereignty no longer protects abusive regimes from outside interference. However, in the absence of internationally recognized standards on armed intervention for humanitarian purposes, only those populations with strategic importance for regional organizations or for the United Nations are likely ever to see assistance from these organizations.

On the other hand, many countries fear the negative impact of looser interpretations of state sovereignty and international intervention. They have doubts and suspicions about intrusive and sometimes self-righteous attempts by some countries to impose their values on others. It is the strong and wealthy regional organizations that can afford to throw their political, economic, and military weight around – and it is the strong powers that dominate the main decision-making organ of the United Nations, the Security Council.

Without proper guidelines that permit intervention when necessary and in response to agreed-upon thresholds, and without the proper mechanisms, resources, and equipment to handle such interventions effectively and successfully, any such operations will probably be based on ad hoc decisions, actions, and commitment. This cannot and should not be the basis for the international community's response to human suffering. All citizens of this world have a right to satisfy their basic human needs. If societies cannot provide for these needs themselves (though responsible governments), the international community at large has an obligation to fill the gap.

The obligation of the international community extends to pre-crisis foundational peace-building and post-crisis reconstruction and repair. The responsibility to protect, under whose cloak the international community intervenes in defence of human rights, is conceptually inseparable from the correlative responsibility to assist in the tasks of development and state-building. Not only is armed intervention fiercely contested as an emerging new international norm; its legitimacy is also undermined by normative incoherence when official development assistance flows have declined and post-intervention assistance is not forthcoming.[39]

Moreover, a consensus needs to be forged on the definition of a failed state and, closely related, on appropriate legal responses by the United Nations and other actors to assume the normal functions of a failed (or a failing) state. There needs to be a consensus on when and how protectorates should be established, and how long they need to stay in place.

Above all, however, we have to overcome and avoid arbitrary interpretations of international legal principles, the UN Charter, and the supposed authority of regional organizations or ad hoc alliances that claim to "represent" world opinion and action. Addressing the human catastrophes caused by failing states must not lead to further instability, loss of trust in international organizations, and new tensions or conflict.

Intervention must not become an alibi for individual states or groups of states to enhance their relative power in regional and world politics. Intervention must be focused on the alleviation of human suffering – in the short and the long run. No other interests should guide the interveners as the primary motivating force for intervention. Alternatively, they should not intervene at all, unless monitored and/or supervised by the United Nations to ensure compliance with international legal and moral principles and to avoid abuse.

Instead, the focus of international intervention should in the first instance be on proactive conflict prevention. Unfortunately, it is much easier to secure political support and the necessary means for intervention once blood has been spilled, civilians are massively threatened and displaced, and conflict spillover is likely to destabilize the wider region. In those instances it is also easier to justify overstepping international legal norms of non-intervention and sovereignty. Either with or without UN Charter compliance or Security Council approval, in cases of massive violations of human rights the ends tend to justify the means, even if the latter violate standing procedures and rules. When blood is spilled, reference to morality and values replaces commitment to legal norms – at least for those who are motivated to act. This is virtually unthinkable at the pre-conflict stage.

Mainstreaming conflict prevention

Guaranteed provision of human security needs – by governments in the first instance, by outside actors if governments fail – is the best prerequisite for the prevention of violent conflict. If disputes are solved without resort to oppression and arms, if governments are held accountable to their people and the international community for their actions, and if basic development and environmental needs are met, few societies would disintegrate into chaos and violence – and thus require peace operations and more intrusive interventions. Human security has been a recurring theme at the highest levels in the United Nations. The Secretary-General's recent Millennium Report is organized around the themes of the quest for freedom from fear (through conflict management and resolution), freedom from want (through economic development and growth), and sustaining the future (through careful protection of the earth's resources and ecosystem). A recurring theme in the Millennium Report was also the need for the transition from a culture of reaction to one of prevention. Long-term human security needs can be monitored and, if necessary, addressed by long-term preventive measures. If a society disintegrates, short-term, emergency, preventive measures (such as preventive diplomacy) can facilitate negotiation and mediation between conflict parties and settle a conflict before it breaks out in self-perpetuating violence and societal breakdown. Both long-term prevention and emergency prevention require the active involvement of trustworthy external actors, including regional and intergovernmental organizations and their representatives.[40] Long-term prevention must be part and parcel of those organizations' daily activities, must be the guiding principle of their programmes' and agencies' work, and needs to define their success and failure. Short-term preventive measures need to be provided by the most visible members and representatives of these organizations – including in particular the good offices of the Secretary-General and his/her regional counterparts. In short, the prevention of conflict ranges from long-term peace stabilization to short-term conflict reduction. The roots for potential conflict need to be eradicated, while their offshoots need to be cut.[41]

However, the prevention of conflict is a difficult task – so difficult that its frequent failure leads to levels of violence that require the type of outside military intervention whose difficulties and inadequacies have been discussed throughout this volume.

Long-term prevention of violent conflict takes place in an environment that lacks a sense of urgency. It thus always depends on the willingness of government authorities to allow external assistance and interference. It is much more difficult to override rules of law and order in the absence of visible urgency. Success of long-term prevention is very difficult to measure. Stabilizing the *status quo* in anticipation of a potential breakdown of rule, peace, and order is a noble task, but difficult to quantify in terms of cost and definite benefit. Long-term prevention requires foresight, vision, and the belief that investing in a potentially unstable society may benefit the region and oneself. Few leaders and societies are that prudent. Moreover, collective intervention needs to secure the cooperation of affected states. Failing states need to be identified and their governments convinced, by governments, regional organizations, and influential individuals that are politically, geographically, ideologically, or otherwise close to them, to agree to humanitarian preventive assistance by outside parties – preferably regional organizations and/or the United Nations.

If conflict prevention is to be successful, a number of basic issues need to be addressed. First, working relationships on shared conflict-prevention strategies need to be dramatically improved between regional organizations and the United Nations, among regional organizations, and between organs, departments, and institutions of the United Nations. Second, conflict prevention needs to focus more closely on the local level: local conflict-prevention initiatives need to be supported, and national and international efforts have to be well tuned to local needs and invest in local capacity-building. Third, conflict-prevention activities have to be sustainable and sustained to assure meaningful results. Fourth, regional organizations and the United Nations should have at their disposal readily available expert groups with theoretical, practical, and regional expertise on conflict prevention for urgent advice on early-warning and preventive measures. Fifth, academics and policy-makers alike need to develop successful approaches to sell conflict prevention to decision-makers and opinion-formers. Sixth, lessons-learned exercises undertaken by regional organizations and UN institutions need to be thoroughly evaluated by all actors involved in conflict-prevention activities. Seventh, although difficult to measure, efforts need to be undertaken to determine, evaluate, and explain successful preventive action. Finally, beyond the rhetoric about cooperation between the United Nations, regional organizations, and civil society actors, the relationships between them need to be understood, pragmatically assessed, and translated into honest long-term steps towards the prevention of breakdown of political, economic, and social relations of societies at risk.[42]

If the international community truly wants to address conflicts seriously, globally, and principally, it has to learn how to prevent conflicts if possible, intervene to terminate conflict when prevention fails, and rebuild society, judiciary, economy, and government through effective and sustained commitment to international protectorates after conflict has been terminated. Finally, it must incorporate post-war societies into larger regional and international communities to stabilize peace, order, and development and thus prevent future conflict. Wherever along this line the international community becomes involved, prevention is key to peace, stability, and human dignity and security.

Unfortunately, much evidence shows that, instead of principled action, ad hoc coalitions and reactions drive international relations. However, too many of today's problems are too urgent, complex, and comprehensive to rely on ad hocery. The war over Kosovo in 1999 has once more shown that urgent crises require urgent responses. Urgent responses are only possible if plans, strategies, and means are on standby, ready to be used immediately when necessary and authorized to do so. The Security Council members, most importantly the P5, need to take the first step in that direction. Without their guidance, ad hocery will continue to harm the United Nations, justice, security, and order. Ad hocery made possible Srebrenica and Rwanda – and should the world again face similar situations, it must act decisively, effectively, and with good intentions. If it fails again, much of what has been promised during the Millennium Summit, in the Brahimi Report, and in other soul-searching exercises throughout the year 2000 will be little more than meaningless rhetoric. That must not happen.

A new beginning for UN peace operations needs to be firmly anchored in international commitment to effective prevention and, if prevention fails, to effective intervention to enforce peace, secure peace, and reinstate and solidify justice, security, and order. If prevention fails, peace enforcement, peacekeeping, and peace-building missions must follow. If the Brahimi Report (including the various regional responses and suggestions) is implemented in full as a "minimum threshold of change",[43] both the capacity and the political will would obviously be present to make the best of an otherwise disastrous situation. If prevention fails and the reform of UN peace operations generated by the Brahimi Report does not materialize, the international community will have little to be proud of. Peace operations would continue to take place haphazardly, selectively, dominated by one or more major powers, and with little attention to sustained efforts of prevention, resolution, and rebuilding.

Notes

1. The views expressed in this chapter are the personal opinion of the authors. They do not necessarily reflect the views of the United Nations University.

2. Boutros Boutros-Ghali, *An Agenda for Peace*, New York: United Nations, 1992.
3. During this period, Security Council action was paralysed by 279 vetoes in all. See Boutros-Ghali, *ibid.*, paragraph 14.
4. *Ibid.*, paragraph 1.
5. *Ibid.*, paragraph 85.
6. Kofi A. Annan, *We the Peoples: The Role of the United Nations in the Twenty-first Century*, Report of the Secretary-General, New York: UN General Assembly, Doc. A/54/2000, 27 March 2000.
7. Boutros-Ghali, note 2, paragraph 15.
8. See also Boutros Boutros-Ghali, "Empowering the United Nations", *Foreign Affairs*, Vol. 71, Winter 1992/1993, pp. 89–102; "UN peacekeeping in a new era: A new chance for peace", *The World Today*, Vol. 49, April 1993, pp. 66–69; and "*An Agenda for Peace*: One year later", *Orbis*, Vol. 37, Summer 1993, pp. 323–332.
9. See Steven E. Goldman, "A right of intervention based upon impaired sovereignty", *World Affairs*, Vol. 156, No. 2, Winter 1994, pp. 124–129.
10. UNITAF was authorized by the Security Council with Chapter VII Resolution 794.
11. *Report of the Panel on United Nations Peace Operations*, A/55/305-S/2000/809, New York: UN General Assembly/Security Council, 21 August 2000, p. i.
12. *Ibid.*
13. *Ibid.*
14. *Ibid.*, p. viii.
15. *Ibid.*, paragraph 50.
16. *Ibid.*, paragraph 34.
17. *Ibid.*, paragraph 47.
18. *Ibid.*, paragraph 55.
19. *Ibid.*, paragraph 64.
20. *Ibid.*, paragraphs 75 and 83.
21. *Ibid.*, paragraphs 91 and 101.
22. *Ibid.*, paragraph 117.
23. *Ibid.*, paragraphs 126 and 145.
24. *Ibid.*, paragraph 169.
25. *Ibid.*, paragraph 233.
26. *Ibid.*, paragraphs 238, 243, 245, 251, 258, and 263.
27. Ramesh Thakur participated in the Asia regional meeting in Singapore on 26–27 February 2001. See Ramesh Thakur, "Cambodia, East Timor and the Brahimi Report", *International Peacekeeping* (2001, forthcoming).
28. For a detailed summary of these meetings, see Center on International Cooperation (New York University) and the International Peace Academy, *Refashioning the Dialogue: Regional Perspectives on the Brahimi Report on UN Peace Operations*, forthcoming in 2001; available at www.ipacademy.org.
29. *Report of the Panel on United Nations Peace Operations*, note 11, paragraph 7.
30. *Refashioning the Dialogue*, note 28, p. 7.
31. See also David Carment and Albrecht Schnabel, *Building Conflict Prevention Capacity: From Rhetoric to Policy*, IDRC Working Paper, Ottawa: International Development Research Institute, forthcoming in 2001.
32. *Refashioning the Dialogue*, note 28, p. 24.
33. *Ibid.*, p. 8.
34. On this point, see also the chapters by O'Connor, Malan, Hayes, and McFarlane and Maley in this volume.
35. *Refashioning the Dialogue*, note 28, p. 8.
36. *Ibid.*, p. 9.

37. *Ibid.*, p. 37.
38. *Report of the Panel on United Nations Peace Operations*, note 11, paragraph 7.
39. See, for example, many of the essays in Albrecht Schnabel and Ramesh Thakur (eds), *Kosovo and the Challenge of Humanitarian Intervention: Selective Indignation, Collective Action, and International Citizenship*, Tokyo: United Nations University Press, 2000.
40. See Albrecht Schnabel, "Human security – the key to effective conflict prevention?", in David Carment and Albrecht Schnabel (eds), *Conflict Prevention: Path to Peace or Grand Illusion?*, Tokyo: United Nations University Press, 2001.
41. *Ibid.*
42. Abdul-Rasheed Draman, David Carment, and Albrecht Schnabel, *From Rhetoric to Policy: Towards Workable Conflict Prevention at the Regional and Global Levels*, Occasional Paper No. 23, Ottawa: Centre for Security and Defense Studies, Carleton University, 2000, pp. 37–38.
43. *Report of the Panel on United Nations Peace Operations*, note 11, paragraph 7.

Contributors

Yasushi Akashi is chairman of the Japan Centre for Preventive Diplomacy in Tokyo. A former ambassador at the Permanent Mission of Japan to the United Nations, Mr Akashi joined the UN Secretariat in 1957. He served as Under-Secretary-General for Disarmament Affairs and Under-Secretary-General for Humanitarian Affairs. He was special representative of the Secretary-General for Cambodia (from January 1992 to September 1993) and the former Yugoslavia (from January 1994 to October 1995). From 1998 to 1999 he was president of the Hiroshima Peace Institute. A graduate of the University of Tokyo, he studied as a Fulbright Scholar at the University of Virginia and the Fletcher School of Law and Diplomacy.

Vere Hayes is a retired brigadier in the British armed forces. He most recently served as the commander of the British Military Advisory and Training Team for Southern Africa, which is based in Harare, Zimbabwe. He was commissioned into the Royal Green Jackets in December 1964, and served with his regiment in Borneo, Malaysia, Germany, Canada, and Northern Ireland. He commanded the Second Battalion, Royal Green Jackets, from 1985 to 1988 in their mechanized role in Germany and on operations in Belfast in Northern Ireland. He has been the chief of staff of an armoured brigade and an armoured division. His recent appointments have been as commander of British forces in northern Iraq in 1991; chief of staff of UN forces in Bosnia-Herzegovina in 1993; commander of the Second (South East) Brigade from 1993 to 1995; and ACOS Operations at Headquarters Land Command from 1996 to 1998. He attended the Army

Staff College in 1978, the Higher Command and Staff Course in 1988, and the Royal College of Defence Studies in 1992.

Margaret Karns is a professor of political science at the University of Dayton. She received her PhD from the University of Michigan. From 1983 to 1995 she was the first director of the university's Center for International Programs. A specialist in international politics and organizations, she co-authored *The United Nations in the Post-Cold War Era* (with Karen Mingst, 1995 and 2000) and has published numerous articles on UN peace-keeping, the UN system, and global governance. In 1995–1996 she was visiting professor of international relations at the Johns Hopkins University-Nanjing University Center for Chinese and American Studies. She is currently working on a project on Asia Pacific institution-building and cooperation.

S. Neil MacFarlane is Lester B. Pearson professor of international relations and director of the Centre for International Studies at St Anne's College, University of Oxford. He is also an adjunct professor of political science at Dalhousie University. He was educated at Dartmouth College, USA, and the University of Oxford. He held post-doctoral appointments at the International Institute for Strategic Studies (IISS) in London, Harvard University, and the University of British Columbia. Before coming to Oxford, he held professorships at the University of Virginia, USA, and Queen's University, Canada, where he was

also director of the Centre for International Relations (QCIR). He has written extensively on Soviet and post-Soviet politics, Russian foreign policy, and the southern Caucasus in general and Georgia in particular.

Roger Mac Ginty is a lecturer in the Department of Politics and the Post-War Reconstruction and Development Unit at the University of York, UK. He received his PhD from Queen's University of Belfast. He has published widely on ethnic conflict issues, including, with John Darby, the co-edited book *The Management of Peace Processes* (2000).

John McFarlane is the executive director of the Australian Committee of the Council for Security Cooperation in the Asia Pacific (CSCAP) at the Strategic and Defence Studies Centre, Australian National University, Canberra. He is also a visiting fellow at the Australian Defence Studies Centre, Australian Defence Force Academy, Canberra. He is pursuing a PhD in political science through the University of New South Wales. John McFarlane retired from the Australian Federal Police on 31 December 1999, having most recently served as a special adviser in the Office of the Commissioner, and previously as the AFP's director of intelligence. He has written extensively on transnational crime and corruption and their impact on Asia Pacific security and stability, as well as on issues such as military support for law enforcement and police peace operations in disrupted states. He is co-editor (with Beno Boeha) of *Australia and Papua New Guinea: Crime and the Bilateral Relationship*.

Mark Malan is a senior researcher and head of the Peace Missions Programme at the Institute for Security Studies in Pretoria, South Africa. For the past five years he has headed the Training for Peace in Southern Africa project at the ISS, which has facilitated specialized training in support of ongoing efforts to establish indigenous southern African capacities for participation in contemporary multilateral peace missions. He has published extensively on issues relating to regional security and peacekeeping in Africa. Mark Malan joined the ISS in January 1996 after some 20 years of service in the South African Army. He held the rank of lieutenant-colonel before resigning from the military. Prior to joining the ISS, he was a senior lecturer in political science at the Faculty of Military Science of the University of Stellenbosch.

William Maley is associate professor of politics, University College, University of New South Wales, and a research associate of the Centre for Arab and Islamic Studies at the Australian National University. He has served as a visiting professor at the Russian Diplomatic Academy, a visiting fellow at the Centre for the Study of Public Policy at the University of Strathclyde, and a visiting research fellow in the Refugee Studies Programme at the University of Oxford. He is also a barrister of the High Court of Australia, chair of the Refugee Council of Australia, and a member

of the Australian Committee of the Council for Security Cooperation in the Asia Pacific (CSCAP) and of the Foreign Affairs Council. His recent publications include his edited and co-edited volumes *Shelters from the Storm: Developments in International Humanitarian Law* (Australian Defence Studies Centre, 1995), *Fundamentalism Reborn? Afghanistan and the Taliban* (New York University Press, 1998), and *Russia in Search of its Future* (Cambridge University Press, 1995). He has recently produced a paper on *The Foreign Policy of the Taliban* (Council on Foreign Relations, 2000).

Karen Mingst is a professor of political science and chair of the Department of Political Science at the University of Kentucky. She received her PhD from the University of Wisconsin. Professor Mingst has published extensively on international organization and law, international political economy, international environmental politics, and African politics. With support from the Carnegie Endowment, Ford Foundation, Fulbright Program, and others, she has done research in several countries in West Africa. She has co-edited three books and co-authored *The United Nations in the Post-Cold War Era* (with Margaret Karns, 1995 and 2000). She is currently working on two books on *State Participation in Multilateral Peacekeeping* and *Elements of International Relations Theory*.

Satish Nambiar is a retired lieutenant-general of the Indian Army and currently director of the United

Service Institution of India. He saw active service in Jammu and Kashmir, and participated in counter-insurgency operations in the north-east of India and in the 1965 and 1971 operations in the subcontinent. A graduate of the Australian Staff College, he served with an Indian Army training team in Iraq and as the military adviser at the Indian High Commission in London. He was the director-general of military operations at Army Headquarters in New Delhi, in which post he led two defence delegations for talks with Pakistan. Deputed as the first force commander and head of mission of the UN Protection Forces in the former Yugoslavia, he set up the mission and ran it from March 1992 until March 1993. He declined an offer of extension, returned to India, and retired as the deputy chief of the army staff in 1994. He continues to take a keen interest in matters of national and international security, peacekeeping operations, and international relations.

Michael O'Connor is executive director of the Australia Defence Association (since 1981). He was educated at the Australian School of Pacific Administration and the Royal Australian Air Force Staff College. From 1957 to 1966 he was a patrol officer and assistant district officer of the Papua New Guinea administration, and from 1966 to 1974 he served as assistant director, counter-intelligence, at the Naval Intelligence Division of the Royal Australian Navy. From 1974 to 1989 he was State Secretary of the Nation Civil Council in Melbourne. In 1993 he was a visiting fellow at the

Australian Defence Studies Centre, Australian Defence Force Academy. Mr O'Connor has authored numerous reports for the government, parliamentary committees, and the military on various aspects of national security policy. He is the author of *To Live in Peace: Australia's Defence Policy* (1985) and the co-editor of *Safely by Sea* (with Malcolm J. Kennedy, 1990).

Gillian Robinson is a senior lecturer at the University of Ulster. She is director of the Northern Ireland Social and Political Archive (ARK). Previously, she was research director of INCORE, the Initiative on Conflict Resolution and Ethnicity. Her research interests focus on social attitudes and social policy, and she is a co-editor of the *Social Attitudes in Northern Ireland* series. Within INCORE her interests concentrate on social policy in divided and transitional societies. She is currently working on a project on the development and implementation of public policy (community policing and victims policy) in Northern Ireland and South Africa.

John Sanderson, currently Governor of the State of West Australia, is a retired lieutenant-general of the Australian Army. In 1991 he was appointed military adviser on Cambodia to the Secretary-General of the United Nations, and from 1992 to 1993 he served as force commander of the United Nations Transition Authority in Cambodia (UNTAC). Thereafter, he served as commander, Joint Forces Australia, and chief of the general staff before retiring in 1998 as chief of the

Australian Army. General Sanderson has taught at military colleges in Australia and the UK, and has published numerous papers on peace operations and military training.

Albrecht Schnabel is an academic programme officer in the Peace and Governance Programme of the United Nations University, Tokyo, Japan. He was educated at the University of Munich, the University of Nevada, and Queen's University, Canada, where he received his PhD in political studies in 1995. He has taught at Queen's University (1994), the American University in Bulgaria (1995–1996), and the Central European University (1996–1998). He served on OSCE election monitoring missions in Bosnia-Herzegovina, was a visiting fellow at the Institute for Peace Research and Security Policy at the University of Hamburg, and is currently a trainer in early-warning and preventive measures for the UN Staff College in Turin and president of the International Association of Peacekeeping Training Centres. His publications focus on international organizations, ethnic conflict, refugee policy, peacekeeping, conflict prevention and management, and humanitarian intervention. He has contributed articles on these topics to numerous journals and edited volumes. Recent books include *The South-east European Challenge: Ethnic Conflict and the International Response* (with Hans-Georg Ehrhart, 1999), *Kosovo and the Challenge of Humanitarian Intervention: Selective Indignation, Collective Action, and International Citizenship* (with Ramesh Thakur, 2000), and *South-east European Security: Threats, Responses, Challenges* (2001).

Hisako Shimura is president of and a professor at Tsuda College, Tokyo. She was educated at Tsuda College, pursued graduate studies in international affairs in the USA, and taught in the Department of Political Science at the University of Nevada, Reno, before joining the UN Secretariat in 1970. In her 24 years at the United Nations she worked primarily in the field of peacekeeping, dealing with operations in the Middle East, Cambodia, Haiti, and the former Yugoslavia (among others). When she left the United Nations in 1995, Professor Shimura was appointed director of the Europe/Latin America Division of the UN Department of Peacekeeping Operations (DPKO). She recently served as a member on a high-level international panel on UN Peace Operations, appointed by Kofi Annan and led by Lakhdar Brahimi.

Ramesh Thakur is vice rector and head of the Peace and Governance Programme, United Nations University. After completing his undergraduate degree at the University of Calcutta, he earned his PhD in political studies at Queen's University, Canada. Dr Thakur taught at the University of Otago (New Zealand) from 1980 to 1995. In 1995 he was appointed professor and head of the Peace Research Centre at the Australian National University in Canberra. In September 2000 he was appointed as a member of the International Commission on Intervention and State Sovereignty (ICISS). Professor Thakur's books include 14 volumes in print. Among his latest edited books are *Past Imperfect, Future UNcertain: The United Nations at Fifty* (1998), *Nuclear Weapons-Free Zones* (1998), and *Kosovo and the Challenge of Humanitarian Intervention: Selective Indignation, Collective Action, and International Citizenship* (with Albrecht Schnabel, 2000). He is a regular contributor to such newspapers as the *Asahi Shimbun*, the *Asahi Evening News*, the *Asian Wall Street Journal, The Australian*, the *Australian Financial Review*, the *International Herald Tribune*, and the *Japan Times*.

Index

Catalogue Request

Name: _____

Address: _____

_____

Tel: _____

Fax: _____

E-mail: _____

To receive a catalogue of UNU Press publications kindly photocopy this form and send or fax it back to us with your details. You can also e-mail us this information. Please put "Mailing List" in the subject line.

United Nations University Press

53-70, Jingumae 5-chome
Shibuya-ku, Tokyo 150-8925, Japan
Tel: +81-3-3499-2811 Fax: +81-3-3406-7345
E-mail: sales@hq.unu.edu http://www.unu.edu